'At the Royal Botanic Garden Edinburgh a growing belief in the power of storytelling to communicate on environmental matters has led to us scouring the world for sources of inspiration. This book has come along as an answer to our prayers and makes us feel part of something big and profoundly important to life.'

Ian Edwards, Head of Exhibitions & Events, Royal Botanic Garden Edinburgh

'I believe this resource will demonstrate the importance of storytelling to the unconverted, and provide resources and sustenance to those who are already using storytelling in their work. I commend the project unreservedly.'

Dr Tom Shakespeare, Professor of Disability Research,
London School of Hygiene & Tropical Medicine, and broadcaster

'The human and environmental crisis of our times is not one of reason or technology. On those fronts everything is with us. Our burning need is to recover a sense of meaning, to call back the soul, to recover love in all its meanings. This book is a guide to such reconnection with the imagination and these writers are the alchemists of our times.'

Alastair McIntosh, author of Soil and Soul *and* Poacher's Pilgrimage

'... this book brings much excitement. We swim in an ocean of stories and once we recognise this, we see they are all exerting influences – direct and indirect upon our behaviour as individuals and as members of societies. *Storytelling for Nature Connection* is a much needed exploration of how stories and the intentional work of storytellers can effect change.'

Ben Haggarty, Honorary Professor of Storytelling, Berlin University of the Arts

'I have worked with hundreds of post-graduate adult students using story and narrative leadership for sustainability. I know from experience just how important narrative approaches are for them in their ongoing work as organizational change agents ... I hope to be able to use the book with my students as soon as possible.'

Dr Chris Seeley, Co-Director, Ashridge MA in Sustainability and Responsibility

'In these times of difficult transition this book is a source of light in the hands of those who wish to inspire the imagination of our living futures.'

Mary-Jayne Rust, author, Jungian analyst, and ecopsychologist

'There is a great and previously unfilled need for a book of this kind, which will be of interest and usefulness to many people engaged, in different ways, in conservation, environmental education, business training, sustainability and social and economic change.'

Jean-Paul Jeanrenaud, Senior Adviser, WWF International, and President of OPEN

'Story has an extraordinary power to bring people together, to build common bonds across ages and cultures and to connect people with their roots. A book like this that supports us, adults and children alike, will be a massive benefit to help us all prepare for an uncertain future.'

Professor Perry Else, Course Leader, BA (Hons) Children and Play Work, Sheffield Hallam University

'Worldwide, the renaissance of traditional storytelling is moving our hearts, spirits and bodies back into closer connection with the natural world. I cannot imagine a more important, distinctive and appropriate purpose than *Storytelling for Nature Connection*.'

Donald Smith, Director, Scottish Storytelling Centre, and Chief Executive, TRACS

'I have worked from as far east as Japan and as far west as California, as far north as the Arctic circle and south to Cape Town, and the one thing that joins all these places is the hunger for story. Sustainability is the key to the survival of this planet. Mak

Jer

'This book will act as a much needed tool ... for people in the teach

Rose James, Property Administrator, Bod

'This book is a great example of a joined-up approach to change.'
Malcolm Learmonth, Arts and Environments Development Lead, Devon Partnership NHS Trust

'Science is important, but only the stories we weave together will create the common purpose and energy to meet the environmental challenges of the 21st century. For that reason this book is more than just a valuable contribution. It describes an essential framework of the Ark that we need to build.'
Angus Jenkinson, The Centre for Integrated Marketing and Stepping Stones Consultancy

'Given the excitement of the debate about the environment and ecology today, this book opens up new areas of interest and brings new people into the conversation about our global future. The important aspect of storytelling makes the book of interest to a very wide readership, including students ... As a professor of psychiatry and a leader in the creative arts therapies field internationally, I know that ... it will be on my bookshelf!'
Dr David Johnson, Co-Director, Post Traumatic Stress Center, Yale University Medical School, USA

'Anyone interested in combating the world-wide destruction of our environment should read Storytelling for Nature Connection. Not only does it contain effective stories, essays, and activities for young and old to address problems of pollution, climate change, and endangered bio-diversity, it also promotes sustainable attitudes and behavior that will enable readers to be pro-active in making our world more humane. Above all this book combines theory with practice that will inspire readers to create their own pro-environmental programs.'
Jack Zipes, Professor Emeritus, University of Minnesota, founder of Neighborhood Bridges, and founder of Little Mole and Honey Bear Press

'Storytelling for Nature Connection will be a powerful tool for change when placed in the hands of those who are at the front line of environmental education and campaigning.'
Rebecca Laughton, author of Surviving and Thriving on the Land, organic market gardener, and lead researcher, the Landworkers' Alliance

'Climate change is arguably the greatest threat facing society in the immediate future and storytellers, like other artists, are increasingly turning their attention to the issue of promoting more sustainable ways of living. This book is important, not least because it brings together scholars and practitioners in the field to reflect on their work at this critical juncture. It will be a welcome and significant addition to the literature on the role of storytelling in an increasingly fragile world. Perhaps more importantly, it is an articulate and collective call to action.'
Mike Wilson, Professor of Drama, Head of Creative Arts, Loughborough University

'A book such as this is extremely useful to environmental professionals and educationalists who often struggle to find relevant resources.'
Liz Carding, Senior Parks and Countryside Officer, Ty Mawr Country Park

'Stories are a powerful way in which we can connect with the people and places around us. Storytelling for Nature Connection will be a great resource for those working to encourage that connection.'
Paul Hibberd, Visitor Services Manager, Forestry and Land Scotland

'If we are to be able to move to a more sustainable, more resilient future, we first have to be able to imagine it. We need to be able to tell its stories, weave its magic, bring it alive so we can see, smell, hear, taste and touch it. Storytelling for Nature Connection does just that, showing the powerful role storytelling can play, and the rich insights the storytellers bring with them. It is rich, powerful and of immense importance.'
Rob Hopkins, Co-Founder, Transition Network, and author of From What Is to What If

Storytelling Series

Storytelling for Nature Connection

*Environment, Community and
Story-Based Learning*

Edited by
Alida Gersie, Anthony Nanson *and* **Edward Schieffelin**
with **Charlene Collison** *and* **Jon Cree**

Foreword by **Jonathon Porritt**

Hawthorn Press

Hawthorn Press
Published by Hawthorn Press, Hawthorn House,
1 Lansdown Lane, Stroud, Gloucestershire, GL5 1BJ, UK
Tel: (01453) 757040
Email: info@hawthornpress.com
Website: www.hawthornpress.com

Cover photo © Terrance Emerson
Design by Lucy Guenot
Printed by Severn, Gloucestershire
Printed on environmentally friendly paper from renewable forest stock.

British Library Cataloguing in Publication Data applied for

ISBN 978-1-912480-59-3

Preface

Fraser McKechnie, a ranger who used this book in his work for National Trust for Scotland says, 'We are all playing a part in the story of our beautiful world. In too many places the beauty now lies sleeping ... This book brings fuel for the imagination, techniques for telling tales and hope for a happy ending.' In 2014 the book was titled *Storytelling for a Greener World*. We have now changed this to *Storytelling for Nature Connection* in order to emphasise that the book discusses creative activities that aim to generate a deep experience of nature connection in children and adults who may think that nature is 'not for them'. Each chapter describes in detail how certain stories, creative techniques, and group processes can be used to achieve this outcome with people who feel nature shy.

Nature connection matters. It benefits people's well-being in countless physical, mental, and social ways. But there is more to it than that. Nature connectedness inspires the desire to act in pro-environmental ways. Urgent action is needed now at personal, economic, and political levels in order to overcome the climate crisis and environmental degradation that surround us. Nature has tremendous powers of regeneration, but the speed at which it can do so is presently overwhelmed by the damage that we inflict upon it. A deep sense of nature connectedness can guide people's actions in a sustainable direction.

Our contributors, world leaders in this field, tell about their work with groups of people, young and old, indoors and outdoors, in cities and the countryside. They explore how and why their approach elicits in people a sense of joy, pride, constructive hope, and empathy with all that lives. It feels good to discover your own way of relating to nature. To actually *do something* in service to the environment feels even better. That could mean taking part in the greening of an inner-city area, the rewilding of kerbsides or a park, active recycling, or campaigning for pro-environmental policies. Conservation ecologist and storyteller Lisa Schneidau says, 'This is a treasure trove of a book that I return to time and time again. It's full of inspiration and ideas that are grounded in the real world and in real practice.' We hope the book will serve you in kindred ways, and thank you for what you do to nurture a vibrant connection between people and nature.

Alida Gersie, Anthony Nanson, Edward Schieffelin. June 2021

Contents

Foreword

I used to tell a lot of stories. Then I stopped telling stories, for more than twenty years. Now I'm on the point of becoming a storyteller all over again.

When I was Head of English and Drama in a big West London comprehensive, back in the 1970s, storytelling was part of the deal. With encouragement, nearly all of our kids could 'do stories', and, with the usual rich mix of cultures and ethnicities in that part of London, their lives came alive through storytelling in a way that would otherwise have been difficult to achieve.

We even did some 'storytelling for a greener world', though as I was an active member of the Green Party (then the Ecology Party) it had to be somewhat camouflaged! Our school backed on to Wormwood Scrubs, where almost all wildlife was managed, mown, and sprayed into near total oblivion. It was, in effect, a green desert. But we made good stories out of what was left, and created an entire phantasmagoria of imaginary creatures that brought the Scrubs to life in a way that even Nature had had to give up on.

Then I went to work at Friends of the Earth in 1984. We didn't 'do' stories at FoE. We stuck to the science, to the facts, to the rational advocacy. If we told stories at all, we only told them to help raise money, or to provide tragic case studies to underpin our campaigns. And that's pretty much how it was for me until recently.

But no longer. In 2013, I brought out a new book, published by Phaidon, with the title *The World We Made* and the subtitle 'Alex McKay's Story from 2050'. It's written through the words of a teacher in 2050, looking back over the last 35 years to tell the story of how we get to be living in a brilliant, fair, and genuinely sustainable world in 2050!

All of which is a rather long-winded way of explaining why I feel part of the community of people who tell stories to which *Storytelling for Nature Connection* is primarily aimed. And I just loved these personal stories from the front line, teasing out what it is that constitutes good practice both in the design and in the delivery of storytelling, without in any way being prescriptive or judgemental. In essence, it's an inspiring toolkit that will enrich the work of people who already use storytelling, and will inspire others to get stuck in.

In one sense, it's about storytelling *in general*. Contributors speak eloquently of the power of storytelling to make connections, to enable people to see things afresh, to galvanise them into actions that might otherwise seem beyond them, to make whole those things that are split apart, to conjure visions out of the everyday, and, above all, for me at least, to fashion the context in which real empathy can flourish.

Beyond that, however, there's still 'the green bit'. And that goes to the heart of today's environmental crises. Right now we need storytelling more than ever before, in all its different guises, to help people reimagine their own personal relationship with the natural world.

The truth is that our current stories (as captured in our day-to-day discourse about what people mean by progress, purpose, and meaning) are constantly reinforcing an inherently unsustainable way of creating wealth.

So what will make that change? Scientifically, we already know just how differently we need to do things, on a stressed-out, warming planet, with a population set to exceed nine billion by 2050. And we know how urgently those things need to get done. But the political will simply isn't there – and part of the reason is that science alone just doesn't cut it. As the wonderful Thomas Berry demonstrated throughout his life, there are currently no adequate stories to give meaning to our lives, and to place us properly in the physical world. And one of the consequences of that is that our politicians just don't seem able to cope with the scale of this existential challenge.

I live with that reality, day in, day out. My twenty-plus years focusing on the science and on strictly rational forms of advocacy may well have made a bit of a difference along the way. In 2012, however, 20 years on from the hugely significant Earth Summit in Rio de Janeiro, which was a bit of a turning point for me personally, I had to confront just how small a difference that was. Listening to the vapid generalisations of a generation of politicians who seemed to understand less than their predecessors in 1992 was a sobering experience.

So it's back to storytelling for me – in this case, a personal story communicated through the words of Alex McKay, a 50-year-old history teacher looking back from 2050. It's an unapologetically upbeat and positive story, showing how it was that we weathered some horrendous shocks to our erstwhile political and economic orthodoxies (today's grim reality!) to fashion a fair, resilient, and more or less sustainable world by 2050, very much against the odds.

There are countless ways of thinking about what our world will look like in 2050. This is just one of them. But what I know is that we have so little time to help make people feel good (let alone excited!) about a sustainable world, rather than grudgingly accepting its inevitability. Only stories can do that. Only stories can get people to stop turning away from the reality of today's 'unprecedented planetary emergency', and start recognising the true significance of their own contribution, without endlessly defaulting to the excuses of 'too little' and 'too late'.

As the Introduction to this collection points out, it's something of a Trojan horse that is being deployed here – 'storytellers can sneak their message into the fortified citadel of the human mind'. And there's a particular challenge here for storytellers seeking a greener world: to ensure that they open the human spirit as much to the wonders of a genuinely sustainable world as to the horrors of an increasingly unsustainable world. The great Thomas More described his own *Utopia* as 'a fiction whereby the truth, as if smeared with honey, might a little more pleasantly slide into men's minds'.

In a funny kind of way, that means we all need to become storytellers if we are to seize hold of this amazing window of opportunity that we still have to bring sustainability to life – for majorities of people, not just for the already persuaded minority. As David Orr is quoted as saying in this book's introduction:

> The plain fact is that the planet does not need more successful people. But it does desperately need more peacemakers, healers, restorers, storytellers and lovers of every kind. It needs people who live well in their places. It needs people of moral courage willing to join the fight to make the world habitable and humane.

Indeed it does. And this collection of storytelling experiences, enriched by more than forty actual stories studded throughout the book, will undoubtedly help to inspire and inform the many thousands of people involved in telling stories. It will help all of us to use our own 'untrammelled' imagination and creativity to make some small contribution to the 'Great Turning' that is going on all around us.

Jonathon Porritt
October 2013

Introduction

Word of mouth is still the most powerful form of
communication; it is 'the wind of change'.

Ben Haggarty[1]

This book is about the uses of story and storytelling to promote meaningful change in people's pro-environmental and pro-social attitudes and behaviour: at home, at work, and at play. Such change is both individual and social. It may, for example, include: spending more time outdoors; volunteering to clear paths in a nature reserve; rewilding a local area; adopting sustainable business practices; creating a forest garden in school grounds; using green transport; or organising green-inspired community events. The chapters contain many tried and tested stories and creative activities that our contributors, all cutting-edge professionals in this field, have used to nurture people's joy in pro-environmental ways of living. Our contributors discuss how they achieved this with children and adults who come from wide-ranging social backgrounds and have diverse attitudes to sustainability. The work takes place in both urban and country environments.

This Introduction explains the core ideas behind this story-based work, which is guided by four principles:

- both nature and culture are our teachers;
- sustainable behaviour is an individual, social, and community practice;
- the real world is our optimum learning environment;
- sustainable living in all its facets and manifestations is rooted in a deep knowledge of place and an intimate relationship with it.

These ideas broadly resonate with those formulated by Fritjof Capra and Michael Stone.[2]

Let us see what all of this means.

Four stories and their consequences

Over the years, we have asked many people who consciously try to live with the environment in mind what inspired their resolve to do so.We have been struck by the importance many attribute to the role of a story told by a sympathetic person in bringing about this resolve.

Louise, for example, recounted how, during a coffee break at a large accountancy firm where she worked, her colleague Odo shared his joy at having seen a skein of geese in the sky at the weekend. The image his story evoked in her 'heart's eye' would not leave her alone.

Nisha recalled a time when her family lived next door to an elderly woman called Marianne. One day Marianne casually told Nisha, who was then sixteen, about picking blackberries with her granddaughter and making blackberry pies. The feelings this conversation aroused in Nisha stayed with her.

Simon, the manager of an insurance business, said that some years previously he'd been at a dinner where one of his friends talked enthusiastically about a story he'd heard on the radio, in which a bird created the earth. Everyone there had chipped in with memories of things they loved about the living earth. Simon remembered feeling deeply touched by the realisation that nature mattered so very much to him and his friends.

Hong, a medical doctor, recalled a lecture he attended in which a much-respected professor recounted a traditional tale about a girl who killed a dragon that lived in a mountain cave, in order to illustrate the important role of a patient's relationship with the outdoors in their recovery from physical and mental illness.

Within several years of these encounters each of these four 'story-givers' made important changes in their lives. Louise left her accountancy job to retrain as a wildlife ranger. Nisha initiated a project in her neighbourhood to collect and process unused garden fruit and vegetables. Simon joined Friends of the Earth and changed many aspects of his business to make it more ecologically sustainable. Hong said that, since that lecture, he had prescribed weekly 'nature experiences' to his patients. All four unhesitatingly situated the beginning of their long-term commitment to sustainable living in these specific stories and events. It was not the burden of more bad news, or increasingly dire warnings that catalysed their change of direction towards more sustainable living. 'I just felt overwhelmed', Simon said, 'by this sudden realisation that nature meant so much to all of us. We laughed a lot that night. And we weren't drunk. It was as if I could suddenly bear to feel this intense sense of belonging. That's the best I can say. But the hope I felt that night has never left me.'

We share these stories for several reasons. Firstly, they illustrate some of the effects that people who use stories in the sustainability and pro-environmental field aim to achieve among the people they work with: such as finding a deep sense of belonging in the natural world, living more sustainably at home and at work, spending more time outdoors, developing ideas for community re-skilling projects, or giving greater support to organisations that promote environmental policies or causes.[3] Secondly, these anecdotes raise important themes about the uses of story and storytelling, including: the 'ripple effect' of a told story (see below), the relationship between informal and intentional storytelling, and the extent to which a remembered story can serve as a mnemonic anchor for the gradual integration of a story's lessons in the teller's and/or the listener's later behaviour.[4] Though the person may not recall the subtleties of that integration process, they often remember as a kind of headline the composite of the story together with the circumstances in which it was told. The third reason involves the unique ways in which a storyteller or facilitator can tell or use stories to elicit the kinds of change that our four story-givers bear witness to.[5]

From hearing a story towards more sustainable behaviour

In the context of this book the notion of learning to live 'with the environment in mind' refers to people becoming committed to leaving as light an ecological footprint on the environment as possible, in both their private life and their work.[6] Humanity's current ecological footprint is already well beyond the earth's carrying capacity, and must be reduced.[7] This is especially important for every human being and company in developed parts of the world and for rich individuals and organisations in less developed nations.[8] Another way of expressing the attempt to live 'with the environment in mind' is to say that men and women who do this carry out 'sustainable' policies, practices, and behaviour. These include all actions that are pro-environmental, financially and materially frugal, warm-hearted, and equitable.[9] Building on ideas first formulated by Forum for the Future, the leading environmental NGO that helps organisations to adopt sustainable practices, Arran Stibbe argues that the capacity to live sustainably includes 'skills, attitudes, competencies, dispositions and values that are necessary for surviving and thriving in the declining conditions of the world in ways which slow down that decline as far as possible'.[10] Our contributors use the terms 'sustainability' and 'pro-environmental' or 'sustainable behaviour' to refer to similar ideas and practices.

The concept of 'sustainability literacy' can be unpacked by using the ideas of the eminent Brazilian educator Paulo Freire, who points out that the process of becoming literate in any field involves empowerment, social transformation, and liberation.[11] Our contributors, being aware of this, structure creative learning experiences that explore aspects of sustainability and sustainable development, increase reflection on the complexities of green thinking, and support participants in making pro-environmental decisions. John Blewitt notes that the concept of interrelatedness familiar to sustainability-literate people needs to 'incorporate a practical understanding of two things, namely that human agency is necessarily both individual and collective, and that human conduct occurs within an environment as well as by means of an environment'.[12] Ecopsychologists have many terms to describe this process of coming home to an interrelated sense of self and otherness.[13] We simply acknowledge that facilitating this process is extremely important and is intrinsic to pro-environmental storywork, because interrelatedness is deeply entailed in the very dynamics of storymaking and oral storytelling.[14]

Living sustainably is, we believe, fundamental to human and ecological well-being and resilience. We define 'resilience', following Rob Hopkins, as 'the ability of a system, from individual people to whole economies, to hold together and maintain their ability to function in the face of change and shocks' from both within and without.[15] Our title's metaphor 'for a greener world' encapsulates the complex process of stimulating new and continuing sustainable behaviour through individual and group action. Underpinning our contributors' writing is a shared belief that it is in the interest of the common good – of humankind and the earth – for people to live in fair, transparent, and sustainable ways.

'Environmental storytelling': the wider context

In this section we want to clarify the relationship between the practices discussed in this book and those generally known as 'environmental storytelling'. In recent years this term has acquired somewhat different meanings among people in two divergent fields: those who work in the pro-environmental domain and those who create computer games. This divergence is important to our discussion.

The games and theme-park designer Don Carson says that 'environmental storytelling' is about creating environments that draw the player or audience into the designer's imagined world and make them want to stay. The trick, he says, is to play on people's memories and expectations, since this heightens the thrill of venturing into the invented universe of game or theme park.[16] In a paper about 'environmental storytelling' the media scholar Henry Jenkins outlined four preconditions to bring about a game-player's immersion in the digital realm: The space in which the story is set needs to evoke pre-existing narrative associations. It must provide a staging ground where narrative events are enacted. And it has to embed further narrative information and provide resources for emergent narratives.[17]

Matthias Worch and Harvey Smith, also game designers, add that meeting these four preconditions integrates the player's perception of the game world with their active problem-solving capacity.[18] They too view players as active participants in the game's environment, who choose between a number of offered goals and find their own story route through the game. These ideas resonate with some approaches to oral storytelling presented in this book.

Before we go further, let's return to the meaning of 'environmental storytelling' as normally understood in the pro-environmental field. Here the term primarily refers to oral storytelling used to engage people directly with the intricacy of the physical world and to address the real-life complexities of how to protect it. Some botanical gardens, for example, have created special areas, or 'storytelling hubs', where visitors can hear and tell stories.[19] Many museums offer story-based workshops for children and adults to explore natural history in a fun and engaging way. Ecological scientists create stories to communicate scientific discoveries, processes, history, or current activities. Heritage and conservation organisations – such as the National Trust, Sierra Club, Forestry Commission, nature reserves, and national parks – arrange events where storytellers tell environmental tales about animals, plants, the seasons, or related topics like the history of the pelt trade. In countless cities and villages, there are nature-based story-walks. People can hear stories on city farms, or in meetings, and no visit to a zoo or aquarium is complete without a tale about a spider, a panda, a shark.[20]

In such environmental storytelling, Fran Stallings says, the stories that are told facilitate learning about the natural world and people's relationship to it.[21] Kevin Strauss, who has published widely on 'environmental storytelling', defines 'environmental stories' as narratives that teach the listener something about the animals, plants, and natural wonders of our world, or communicate an ecological concept like diversity, sustainability, food chains, or adaptation.[22] The Scottish Storytelling Centre similarly sees the function of storytelling in environmental interpretation as being 'to inspire people to look again, with new perspectives, at their local built and natural environments and the plants and animals in them'.[23]

What these two different notions of 'environmental storytelling' share – and is relevant to this book – is an understanding of the importance of narrative as well as an awareness that people need help to connect with a new environment when they first encounter it, whether this be an unfamiliar milieu in the real world or a virtual environment in a game. Game designers create a virtual world on a screen and 'sculpt spaces' using tools such as scripted events, texturing, lighting, scene composition, and props.[24] The oral storytelling discussed in this book has its own array of tools, but instead of presenting images on a screen it evokes imaginary worlds that come to life in the listener's mind's eye.[25] In addition, oral storytelling generates intimate connections between all involved: teller, listener, and the place of telling. This, as we'll see below, makes oral storytelling well suited to the aim of developing relationships between people and the real physical environment where they can touch and smell a living plant, sense the humidity in the air, dig their hands into rain-wet soil, hear the calls of birds that are actually there – and look directly into another's eye (Hall; Shaw, this volume).[26]

The digital world permeates many parts of our lives. It is available nearly everywhere we go. The average 8–18-year-old in the developed world now spends seven hours a day with screen-based media: watching TV, surfing the web, using social networking sites, playing computer games, and doing schoolwork.[27] Their level of absorption in screen-based media, combined with parental fears about the safety of the outdoors and restricted access to natural areas, led Richard Louv to coin the term 'nature deficit disorder'.[28]

Many ordinary people today, upon first encountering the natural world with all their senses – the darkness of night, stormy weather, or being with horses in a field – feel some degree of alienation, even fright. When they enter a natural environment they know they are in the real world but find it difficult to deal with it or to understand their own responses (see East, this volume). They can't make sense of what they feel and may say things like:

'It doesn't do anything for me.'

'It's so not cool.'

'I just feel lost here.'

'It's pretty, but that's all.'

One young woman protested, 'I know where I'm at with buildings or a zebra crossing; I don't know where I'm at with a cow.'

Given the ubiquity of screen-based lifestyles, many pro-environmental organisations combine face-to-face oral storytelling sessions with the use of digital resources. People who want to find out which storybooks are best for children of different ages can get help on the websites of the Royal Society for the Protection of Birds (RSPB), Conservation International, or the Woodland Trust.[29] Friends of the Earth Europe has launched a Climate Justice Toolkit, an online resource that enables people everywhere to give personal testimony about the effects of climate change and climate injustice on their life.[30] Acting as a WWF ambassador, Dutch astronaut André Kuipers launched WWF's *Earth Book* at the International Space Centre in 2012. This online storybook similarly invites young and old alike to share their experiences of the natural world online.[31] In an ongoing development of this trend, Mike Wilson, an expert in storytelling and principal investigator at Project Aspect, initiated an exciting investigation into the use of new communication tools to engage the wider public with 'important but inaccessible issues such as the complex issue of climate change'. By means of digital storytelling and related processes, individuals and groups will be encouraged to express their story about climate change using words, images, and sounds and, most importantly, to share these with others.[32] In a video on the Greenpeace website the singer Regina Lund says, 'This earth is not a resource; it's a relationship. It's a love story. That's what the earth is.'[33] It was his sudden awareness of the existence of this loving relationship that so deeply touched Simon, one of our four story-givers, that evening on the restaurant terrace sharing nature stories with his friends.

Let's keep in mind John Blewitt's observation that the concept of in-terrelatedness used by sustainability-literate people must 'incorporate a practical understanding of two things, namely that human agency is necessarily both individual and collective, and that human conduct oc-curs within an environment as well as by means of an environment'.[34] This book's contributors consistently aim to increase people's ability to discover and to integrate a deeply felt sense of such interrelatedness as themselves active agents within and by means of their physical surround-ings – their school playground, local park, or nearby river valley.[35]

Modes of oral storytelling

In this book 'storytelling' means oral storytelling, that is, storytelling that happens face to face, eye to eye, gesture to gesture, voice to ear, heart to heart, and mind to mind in one location by one person to one or more others.[36] The chapters address two main modes of oral storytelling: per-formance-oriented storytelling and various forms of applied storytelling.[37] In a performance-oriented storytelling situation, one or more storytellers do most of the telling, usually as a solo voice, to an audience of listeners (for example, Hall; Manwaring).[38] In an applied storytelling event, such as a workshop, the participants do most of the telling and the facilitator focuses more on listening (for example, Cree & Gersie; Gersie; Holland). Though the facilitator usually recounts a story or two during a workshop, these stories are chiefly used to inspire the participants' creative activi-ties and associated storytelling. In the work described in some chapters the facilitator does not tell a story; they simply enable the participants to make and share their own tales (Collison; Hurley & Gersie).

Between these two modes is a continuum of intermediate situations, where, for example, a storyteller may tell stories that elicit discussion among the listeners (East; Nanson, this volume), or in a way that invites them to contribute to the telling (Medlicott; Salisbury, this volume); or a compère may facilitate other people's performance of stories to the rest of the group (Metcalfe, this volume). To work effectively with stories in the service of a greener world, both storytellers and facilitators need knowl-edge and skills in three areas: the ability to tell a story well; the skills to engage people with stories in ways that promote sustainable behaviour; and knowledge about the natural world and sustainability.

Preparing to tell stories

During oral storytelling, people recount their tales 'in the absence of picture books or PowerPoints', as Michael Harvey puts it.[39] In order to do this well, most storytellers cultivate their ability to remember and shape a story. This is especially important in situations where a storyteller or facilitator needs to shift back and forth between everyday or professional language and focused storytelling. It is much easier to manage such shifts when you:

- can distinguish how orally told stories relate to other forms of verbal interaction;
- have explored beforehand the story's background, its personal meaning to you, and potential relevance to your listeners;
- have participated in story-based workshops run by colleagues;
- invite feedback from colleagues;
- have built up a repertoire of oral stories well suited to the people you normally work with.[40]

Whether you lead a workshop-based programme in a nature reserve, tell a story at a staff meeting or conference, or use a story to engage local residents with green issues during a community festival, some of the same factors will help to bring about successful outcomes. These include the ability:

- to choose an appropriate time and context for the telling;
- to elicit the listeners' interest and focus their attention on the story;
- to maintain congruence between your behaviour and what the story conveys;
- to pick up on the listeners' mood and adapt or abandon a story on this basis;
- to show that you enjoy the intimacy of the storytelling situation.

It is the quality of the relationship between teller, listener, and the time and place of telling that largely determines whether or not the teller will succeed in transferring his or her concern about something in their story to the listener. Our four story-givers demonstrate that such transfer is the central driver of change in the listener's attitudes, ideas, or intentions.[41] Remember the skein of geese, the blackberry-pies, the friends who talked about why nature mattered, and the girl who killed a dragon on the mountain? Because of this successful transfer the tales told by Odo, Marianne, Simon's friends, and Hong's professor became potent mnemonic anchors for change. Their listeners did not doubt these tellers' authenticity or the congruence between their words and actions. The person Louise knew Odo to be was reflected in the story he told her. To reiterate: though the specific stories do matter, the long-term potency of a story's pro-environmental effect on the listener depends in large measure on the quality of relationship between teller, listener, story, time, and place before, during, and after the telling. In order for this kind of 'I–Thou' relationship to emerge, the teller and the listener need to draw on their individual capacity to recognise, initiate, and collaborate in maintaining their affectional bonds with others, including the more-than-human world.[42] This is crucial because the capacity for affective attachment critically underpins our ability to engage in meaningful relationships with other people and with our environment.[43]

Performing a story or sharing it?

What part, then, does the quality of the telling – in terms of skills of language, voice, and body – play in establishing and sustaining the teller–listener relationship and in the process of instigating elective behavioural change? Does it make a difference whether a story is wonderfully told or only told in a 'good enough' way? It depends on what you hope to achieve. If the goal is to engage workshop participants in exploring the story's meanings, associations, and personal relevance, then the answer is: yes, the quality of the telling matters, but not necessarily that much. Although a facilitator needs to be able to tell the story well enough to hold their listeners' attention, chances are that what comes across is their relationship with the story: whether they love it, know it, carry it in their heart, and are willing to share their engagement with it. In this situation the changes that the storytelling aims to inspire are generated less by the quality of the telling and more by the process of enabling people to develop an informed, passionate relationship with the story that you tell.

In performance-oriented storytelling, on the other hand, the story's impact on the listeners depends much more on the quality of the storytelling. The storyteller and storytelling coach Dough Lipman says that performance storytelling is about bringing life and power to stories.[44] The skills for this may build on a natural gift for oratory, but the gift should be honed. This involves learning about the uses of oral language; the transfer of imagery; different cultural traditions and styles of storytelling; how to engage the senses; pauses, timing, and pacing; gaze maintenance; the use of asides; body language; breath and voice; creating fluid relationships with listeners; and a good deal more (see Manwaring, this volume).

In medieval times, the training of a 'bard' or 'troubadour' took ten or more years. There were many stages they had to go through before they could claim such a title. Ashley Ramsden and Sue Hollingsworth, directors of the International School for Storytelling, affirm that this length of development still rings true. Becoming a good storyteller can happen in an instant, but becoming a great storyteller is a lifelong learning process.[45] A scene in a medieval romance by Chrétien de Troyes illustrates the point:

> At the court of King Arthur a knighted troubadour is about to start his telling. The King lies aslumber in a bedchamber that adjoins the castle's great hall. Queen Guinevere, however, is there to listen to his tale. It is late in the evening and the knights, ladies and maidens attending the court's celebration of the Feast of Pentecost are telling each other stories. They talk of love. So Chrétien recounts. Let's for a moment imagine the great hall's soundscape, never mind its smells: men and women were drinking, eating, walking across the hall to catch up with someone else, fires crackled, the dogs yawned or whined and maybe the wind howled through draughty corridors. Then a troubadour, Chrétien tells us, a man named Calogrenant, spoke up and said: 'Give me your hearts and ears, for words are lost unless they are heard with the heart.' Hardly had he uttered these words when Calogrenant continued in true oral storytelling style: 'It happened some years go that I wandered ...'[46]

If you've ever tried to gather the attention of a sizeable group of people who were deeply engaged in conversation, you know that something is left out of this scene. Calogrenant didn't just utter his opening words in an everyday kind of way. As a true master of attention he would have moved into a riveting performance mode and drawn his listeners' attention towards himself (see Manwaring, this volume). With 17 carefully chosen words he changed an animated social occasion into one where his own storytelling performance could and would happen.

That varied group of people transformed into an audience before whom and with whom Calogrenant now could tell his story. A child who returns from school, barges into the living room, and declares with a dramatic gesture to his or her preoccupied parents, 'Listen to me ... I ...' is trying to achieve a similar transformation in them and likewise hopes to gather their full attention to what he or she is about to say. The skills that the child and the professional storyteller employ are intimately related, and yet years of training apart. They are separated not by the three percent inspiration that underpins their shared ability to tell a story, but by the 97 per cent perspiration that enables them to do so expertly.

Getting to know a Trojan Horse

It is tempting to focus on the fact that oral storytelling can create an intimate, binding connection between teller and listener and to ignore the fact the opposite can also happen. Although this sense of connection may include most listeners in a group, it rarely involves everyone present. Some people may not like the story, the teller, or the occasion, and may even feel quite alienated by the assumption of agreement that binds the others. A thoughtful facilitator or storyteller will be mindful of this: they'll invite the expression of a range of feelings or opinions in response to a story, and thereby normalise the predictable diversity of people's reactions and show how important it is to resist the temptation to appear to agree with a dominant position while actually disagreeing with it. In a group the sharing of minority views increases the opportunities for prosocial learning and the resolution of otherwise hidden tensions.

The 'binding' quality of storytelling has attracted the attention of professionals in diverse fields who wish to use stories in the pursuit of widely different agendas. Politicians, marketing executives, journalists, thought leaders, parents, and teachers all use oral and written stories to convey their messages and try to bind others to them. As image-management consultants might say, 'everyone wants to hear a good story, and great storytellers can bring an entire room to a standstill', so why not make use of these skills?[47] Sometimes the story's messages are authentic and transparent. But sometimes also they are deceptive and hidden. There is no such thing as morally neutral participation in storytelling for either teller or listener; but a special responsibility lies with the teller.

Melanie Green, Jeffrey Strange, and Timothy Brock draw attention to the fact that entering a spoken, storied world radically alters the listener's capacity to process the information the story contains.[48] The more absorbed we are in a told story, the more its message can potentially affect us without our being fully aware of it.[49] When stories are enchantingly told, the listener's ability to detect false notes, inaccuracies, or special agendas is lowered. Jonathan Gotschall, noting that some modes of storytelling exercise a moulding and persuasive power, suggests that storytelling can be seen as a kind of 'Trojan Horse' delivery system for a teller's purpose. Tellers can sneak their message into the fortified citadel of the human mind. Viewed in this light, Gotschall continues, storytelling is a uniquely powerful form of persuasive jujitsu and, given that the world is filled with black-belt storytellers, we'd all better start to train our defences.[50] Alert defensiveness, however, is a self-limiting position. Joanna Macy argues to the contrary that in order to fall in love again with time we need to open ourselves up to narrative.[51] Our contributors propose that storytellers and facilitators, in whatever situation they tell their stories, must responsibly embrace the fact that oral storytelling has the potential to generate a wondrous sense of awe, as well as reflective thinking, along with the potential to foreclose or constrict these. The chapters show how the contributors consciously balance their ideas and practice somewhere between the promotion of alert defensiveness and mindful openheartedness.

Thinking about stories as stories

So far we have used the word 'story' to denote any narrative that recounts an event or series of events.[52] Louise and Nisha, for example, listened to a personal story and recounted a personal story. Simon's friend recounted a tale, probably a myth, heard on the radio. His dinner friends related a mixture of personal and factual/scientific stories. Hong's professor tied his lecture together with a folktale. The lecture may also have contained scientific or historical tales. The chapters in this book contain several kinds of stories. Some are factual, scientific or historical stories about actual events or data (Green & Hennessey; Nanson). Others present fictional tales about imagined characters and events (Collison; Manwaring). Many include traditional stories, such as myths, folktales, and legends that have been around for a long time (East; Maddern; Ramsden): they have survived in the oral tradition, and their tellers – though not necessarily their recorders – are mostly unknown. Nearly all chapters involve personal stories that portray events in the authors' or participants' lives or in the lives of familiar people, places, or creatures. As Stith Thompson observes, however, story categories like 'traditional', 'literary', 'oral', and 'personal' are not closed but have porous boundaries. They overlap and flow into one another.[53] That said, when you seek information about stories in books or online, the categories can be useful.

Stories are generally thought of as more or less complete narratives with a beginning, a middle, and an end.[54] Their events happen in time (temporality) and the actions have consequences (causality). Stories also concern something that can be conveyed to other people, and they can be repeated, as demonstrated by the stories recounted by our four story-givers. Here is an example of one story that includes reported speech and blends features of traditional, fictional, and personal stories. It is also a story within a story. Sometimes recounted events stretch credulity and it can be hard to know who or what to believe.

The Stranger in the Inn

Long, long ago some peasants who knew each other well were sitting by the fire in a shabby inn. It was a cold, miserable night. They talked about all manner of things, barely noticing the stranger, wrapped in a ragged coat, who was leaning against the wall by the inglenook. Then one of the peasants groused that it was time they stopped complaining and said what they really wanted. His neighbour said he wished his daughter would get married and give him a son-in-law to help in the fields. Another wanted some tools. A third needed money to pay off a debt. After everyone had spoken, only the stranger was left. He hadn't said a word. They prodded him to at least wish for something.

He said, 'I wish that I was a powerful king who reigned over a big country. Then, one night, my enemies would storm my castle and I would flee wearing just my nightshirt. I would run and run over hills, through thick forests, careful to avoid men and beast. Then, at last, I would arrive here, in this inn, by your fire.'

The peasants looked at him and said, 'And what good would that do you?'

He replied, 'At least I'd have a shirt.'[55]

This story has several remarkable features. It is set on a wintry evening. A group of peasants has gathered around a fire in a local inn. People know each other well, but there's also a ragged stranger present, who brings the unexpected and the possibly dangerous to an otherwise familiar occasion. The peasants talk about everyday life and the things they desire. When they realise the stranger hasn't spoken, they pull him into the conversation. What new ideas might he bring? The story within the story starts. Even though we've recounted the stranger's tale minimally, it's easy to imagine how the dreadful events he describes might enthral his listeners, especially if he recounts them with well-chosen words, startling sounds, and evocative gestures. The beggar's simple punchline – 'At least I'd have a shirt' – is simultaneously unexpected, strangely disappointing, and quite unsettling. It galvanises the listener to think about what the significance of those last words might be and to reconsider the whole story in the light of them.

Viewed through a pro-environmental lens, this story has several attractive features: it suggests some true-to-life aspects of subsistence farming and is about people who can barely make ends meet, it introduces the topic of war and its ravages, and although the punchline has a humorous quality it conveys the desperate plight of a refugee. It's also very easy to imagine these peasants sitting by their fire as they while away the time, share their wishes, and listen to the stranger's story. Just as the stranger's story connects with the concerns of his listeners, so the story as a whole is likely to connect well with the concerns of people who are either already struggling to make ends meet or willing to contemplate what this struggle might feel like.

Like that stranger, our contributors aim to tell stories that connect with where their listeners are at. The beggar in this story may hope for a shirt. Our contributors hope their listeners will be able to develop a new, more caring relationship with their environment. Here it's important to reiterate that every told story is a performance as much as a spoken text. The way in which a story is told affects its meaning and impact. It is the common desire of anyone who tells a story, whether at home, in a meeting or workshop, or in a performance context, that their listeners will be affected by their story. Anthony Nanson, for example, says, 'I want the audience to feel gripped by a quality of tension both within the story, and between them and me. I may want them to be amused or scared or thrilled, but, more importantly than that, I want them to feel moved and I want to provoke them to think about the story and its implications. It's more important to me that I get them thinking than that I impart a simple clear message; quite often I want them to feel torn in their sympathies between characters who are in conflict.'[56] We may wonder if the stranger and the peasants in 'The Stranger in the Inn' hoped similarly to stir their listeners' thoughts, or whether they desired something else, such as the simple meeting of an acutely felt need.

Common usage of the word 'story' makes it easy to assume that all stories will include a place, a time, a situation, one or more characters, and some complications that terminate in a clear outcome that returns the listener's perspective to the present.[57] As 'The Stranger in the Inn' demonstrates, to achieve this stories don't have to be elaborate. In everyday conversation, for example, many stories are in fact quite minimal, such as: 'I wish my daughter got married,' or fragmentary, like: 'I need a coat.' The story's details may then be worked out during back-and-forth conversation, or be left unspoken.

Most chapters in this book discuss how to tell and explore fully-fledged stories, such as the tale recounted above. Others introduce minimal stories or 'pseudo-narratives' – things that could be said to represent a story, such as a map, a tree, a cloud, or a bench (Cree & Gersie; Hurley & Gersie; MacLellan; Shaw). The authors delight in these other types of story because they poetically encapsulate information and invite elaboration, curiosity, talk, or comment. Moreover, minimal stories can often be highly memorable. Remember that skein of geese?

The story and the fire

Several contributors argue that the storytelling experience is enriched by the presence of a heart- and body-warming fire (Cree & Gersie; Maddern; Salisbury). As Maria Tatar observes, 'Storytelling … is a communal situation, where people are also getting warmth and comfort from the stories. The fire reminds us of the "ignition power" of fairytales, their ability to excite the imagination, and to provide light in the dark. And with the fire, you also have these shadows, where fearful things might lurk. The tales not only have this magical, glittery sparkle, but also a dark, horrific side that stages our deepest anxieties and fears.'[58] The manner of a story's telling can raise its dark side or suppress it, and tips its meaning either way.[59] The ultimate impact of the story both on the listener's own experience and on their subsequent behaviour in the world depends on what the teller conveys and what the listener does with it. Tatar emphasises that the story itself is probably less important for its lasting effects than the interchange it stimulates. Our four story-givers agree.

The role of stories in meaning-making is at once personal, social, and cultural.[60] Though privately experienced, meaning is constructed, experiential, and interactive. All told stories, like all acts of meaning-making, are sensitive to their context: the culture, the socio-historical moment, the relationship between teller and listener, the agenda with which the story is told, and the place of the telling. We think it's important to explore these contexts when reflecting on a story's meaning (Schieffelin, this volume). Each of our four story-givers emphasised that the story's telling constituted a defining moment in their life. Nisha called it a turning point – an illuminating spark. Simon called it 'a bridge'. Louise said that the memory of the story of the geese gradually closed the gap between her vague intention to change jobs one day and a growing clarity that she actually wanted to do this. The image of that skein of geese turned her unfocused desire into a guiding vision. Maybe Odo was aware that Louise needed his story in order to do what in her heart of hearts she desired to do. Then again, most interactions between people are spontaneous and unpredictable. Either way, it's very likely that his story of that skein of geese was a gift. Regardless of our contributors' explanations of why they choose this or that story, or how they use it, or whether or not they're being paid to tell the story, all of them believe that this is what a story above all needs to be – a gift.[61]

So far we have drawn attention to the persuasive (and therefore potentially manipulative) aspects of storytelling and have mostly talked about stories as if they were all useful. They are not. It is important to bear in mind that stories, and traditional ones in particular, can perpetuate negative views of gender relations, contain derogatory stereotypes of outsiders, elders, or disabled people, and portray cruel treatment of animals. Other tales can validate unjust power relationships, greed, violence, or destructive environmental practices. In choosing stories, it behoves a facilitator or storyteller to explore stories' explicit and hidden messages, and then decide whether to avoid certain stories, subvert them with a new take, or set them up for critical discussion (see Lupton, this volume).

Furthermore, it matters to remember, as Jack Zipes points out, that stories by themselves do not have 'a magic power of healing the woes of children and the community'.[62] Although a particular story may be transformative for some people or situations, this does not mean that stories in general will be so in any troubling context or for everyone who hears them.[63] While the use of stories and story-based activities can enable people to share knowledge and experience and thereby shape their future in a sustainable direction, the same stories and activities may also make some participants more resistant to change. The emergence of real change often needs people to talk together about what they care about.[64] However, change is only actualised if these conversations are conducted in a change-promoting manner.[65]

On facilitation, participation, and story-based activities

We use the term 'facilitator' to describe any person who is responsible for the optimum functioning of a group. In our usage the term encompasses roles such as outdoor guide, workshop leader, coach, teacher, nature interpreter, or manager. We assume that people in these roles will have some understanding of how to facilitate the development of children or adults in their workshops or events, and will know what can be achieved, and how. The word 'participants' refers to the visitors, pupils, students, employees, guests, members, or residents who are present at a workshop or event. We chose this word to emphasise that our contributors expect participants to engage actively with each other, with their surroundings, and with what goes on in the group.

The ability to facilitate a group in a joyful, adroit way is both an acquired competence and an art. Skilled facilitators know how to help their group to formulate achievable and yet challenging goals, can enable the participants to move forward psychologically and socially, involve shy or forceful people in the process, endeavour to resolve interpersonal conflict productively, and can ensure that decisions are made in a fair, transparent manner. We strongly recommend that people who are not yet experienced in group facilitation but would like to try out some techniques from this book should initially work alongside colleagues who have such skills.[66] Co-working is particularly helpful on issues such as:

- participant involvement in setting ground rules;
- working with the participants to formulate achievable aims in tangible, action-oriented terms;
- deciding the right working space, duration, and other logistics;
- knowing how to safeguard a group's atmosphere and purpose;
- selecting the most appropriate review and evaluation methods.

The list of controllable factors that can influence the outcome of a workshop or other event is pretty long, never mind the weather, the skein of geese passing in the sky, or the daily news. Here we outline some key ones to bear in mind when reading our contributors' reflections on their practice.

Group size

A group's size has multiple effects on its ability to function, including: the level and quality of individual contributions; the option of consensus decision-making; the time needed to complete tasks; methods used to engage each participant personally; and when to use subgroups that stay within the common work-space, or breakout groups that move to other spaces where they become temporarily invisible to the other small groups. A group's size also influences the techniques and processes that can be used to facilitate the participants' capacity for mutual attention and interpersonal feedback, as well as the event's overall spatial arrangements and therefore the kind of communication it promotes or curtails. For example: twenty people sitting or standing in a circle can usually hear each other comfortably and remember each other's contributions. In a circle with forty people the participant's ability to hear another person speak is diminished and they will only remember what some people said. When someone in a group of ninety people tries to get their point across they rarely speak in a relaxed or even audible manner; very few people, apart from the facilitator and a speaker's immediate neighbours, will pay close attention to what another person says.

Duration

Most of the performance events discussed in this book were one-offs, though some were repeated in different locations with other audiences.

The duration (per session and over time) of the applied storytelling activities varied. Some one-off sessions took a few hours, others a whole day. Some groups comprised a series of sessions spaced out over a few months or a year. The length of time that people expect to be together influences their experience and thus the event's outcome. It would be wrong to assume that the impact of one-off events will be more limited than that of long-term events or ongoing groups. Remember Simon's night on the terrace with his friends? The person who told the story on the radio in all likelihood never knew what effects he or she had set in motion. But something certainly was, and because we've recounted Simon's story here the ripples of that broadcast continue.

Who attends?

Quite often most or all participants are strangers to each other. Sometimes they have met before: they live in the same village, attend the same school, are members or employees of the same organisation, or are at the same conference. Some adults and children attend in a private capacity. Others do so for professional reasons. For many it's a mixture of both. Eric Maddern, for example, discusses a half-day workshop for professionals at a forest conference. Fiona Collins describes a one-day story-based adventure that happens each year during the summer gathering of people committed to re-wilding a valley. Kelvin Hall's audience comprised people who knew each other through a shared interest in horsemanship. Malcolm Green and Mary Medlicott worked with teachers and children in local primary schools, while Jon Cree and Alida Gersie engaged with change consultants working for different organisations.

Storytelling and active listening

Another factor that influences the outcome of the storytelling discussed in this book is that audiences and participants can be rather preoccupied or stressed. In this plight they tend to listen in a distracted or absent-minded way both to the facilitator/storyteller and especially to each other. Such listening leaves 'the one who spoke' (especially if this is the other person in a pair exercise) feeling unacknowledged, however much the facilitator tries to compensate for some people's apparent lack of interest. When distracted listeners become aware of what they're doing they can feel ashamed, disappointed in themselves, and above all uneasy that when it's their turn to speak they will receive the same kind of listening that they offered. A lack of mutual interest can set in motion a downward spiral of inattentiveness.

To counteract the unhelpful phenomenon of inattentive listening, many facilitators employ creative variations on the technique of 'active listening' to support both teller and listener in their communicative process (see also 'response-tasks' below). Participation in these techniques needs to increase people's ability to convey clearly their intentions, experiences, and ideas, to relate to the communication of others, and to participate in associated conversations.[67] While listening to a story, irrespective of whether this is told by the facilitator or another person present, the listener needs to be able to sustain: (1) interest in what is being communicated; (2) an understanding of the teller's intention; (3) a sense of anticipation regarding likely developments both within the story and in the listener's relationship with the teller; and (4) the ability to manage their felt responses to all the above. This complex set of interaction and conversation skills involves capacities such as: dealing with uncertainty; being able to request and give information; identifying familiar and new ideas or knowledge; staying on topic; dealing constructively with interruptions and communicative breakdown; knowing how to repair communicative intent; and ending interactions in a productive way. Our contributors engage with these pragmatic aspects of human communication in numerous innovative ways – that feel natural and yet are highly effective in facilitating communication about complex topics such as loss of biodiversity, population pressure, carbon footprint, and living through droughts or floods.

Productive communication depends on a lively capacity in both teller and listener for active listening, and on a willingness to use this when talking about sustainability-related issues that evoke difficult feelings and demand solutions involving changes in familiar ways of doing things. Simply put, 'active listening' is a form of listening that the speaker or teller experiences as good listening. They feel heard, understood, and empathised with (more about empathy later). To generate a persistent active listening habit in both speakers and listeners, many facilitators use active listening exercises, such as response-tasks (see below), especially at the beginning of a session and later whenever the habit of actively listening flags. The active listening techniques used in this book are creative translations of what listeners need to do while actively listening to another person's talk.

Exercises in the technique of active listening involve the following pattern of procedure. A speaker is invited to talk for limited time to a listener who has agreed to feed back in their own words to the speaker what they have heard him or her say. The feedback is used to confirm the accuracy of their mutual understanding of what was actually said. Before starting the exercise, the speaker and the listener acknowledge to each other that they will assume that the listener tried their best to paraphrase the speaker's communication in ways that would enable the speaker to feel understood – even though they will not always get this right (from the speaker's perspective) and there may be disagreements about what was or was not said. The speaker also needs to listen carefully to what the listener says. To do this exercise well, both parties need to stay aware of their emotions. Each, in listening, simply notes without judgement where they may disagree and continues to dedicate their attention to the other person.

The benefits of doing an 'active listening' exercise in a group are predictable. As soon as speakers feel they are heard, they open up and try to find solutions to social and other difficulties they previously thought unsolvable. Use of this technique can be particularly important in situations where stress predominates. As Ben Haggarty observes, 'The process of Active Listening sustains and develops attention. Without attention, there can be no care.'[68]

Overwhelm, environmental problems, and the inability to think or act

Climate change, pollution, deforestation and other habitat destruction, soil loss, overharvesting of game and fish, overconsumption of water, all exacerbated by a world population increasing by 75 million every year and a consumption-oriented globalised economy – these interacting trends have a growing negative impact on people, communities, and environments worldwide.[69] The rising intensity and frequency of drought, floods, famine, poverty, economic instability, and extreme and unseasonal weather make timely adaptation both urgent and difficult. In order to be effective, adaptation must occur rapidly at several overlapping and interconnecting levels at the same time: individuals, social groups, institutions, infrastructures, and governments.[70] Many people find it nearly intolerable to actively listen to stories about these environmental realities. Part of the reason for this is that it is hard to face the fact that people's or an environment's resilience – their capacity to return to normal following damage from catastrophic events such as forest fires, floods, or wars over resources – can be severely compromised and even wholly lost as a result of such events.[71]

Consequently, many of us cling to a stubborn hope that species, ecosystems, individuals, households, communities, and organisations will 'of course' be able to recover from environmental damage. Our human response to troubling environmental information is often like that of Hare, the great culture-hero in the Winnebago Trickster Cycle.[72]

When Hare Heard of Death

> When Hare discovered Death he ran back to the place where he lived. He shouted and cried: 'My people must not die!' And then he suddenly thought: 'All things will one day die!' He imagined cliffs and crags. They fell away. He imagined big mountains. They fell apart. He imagined the place below the earth. All that lived in the soil stopped scurrying about and died. He imagined the skies high above and the birds that flew stopped flying and fell to earth, dead. He entered the place where he lived. He reached for his blanket, and rolled himself into it. He lay there and wept. There will not be enough earth for all that dies, he thought. There is not enough earth for all that dies. He buried himself in his blanket. He made no sound.[73]

Hare's overwhelmed response to his realisation that death is ubiquitous and inevitable raises two important questions for the practice of storytelling and active listening in the environmental field. The first of these is the question of what we can do now to comfort the Hare in all of us, so that we can face up to the actuality of environmental calamities, and their implications, in a centred state of mind. The second is how to enable people to tell stories about the disruption of the earth's ecosystems in such a way that their listeners can take in and engage with what is told (Cree & Gersie; Shaw, this volume). Inherent in both questions are issues of psychological and social resilience.[74] Alastair McAslan has spelt out some shared elements in different definitions of 'resilience'. Generally speaking, resilient people and organisations are able:

- to absorb and recover from shock;
- to face threats and events that are abnormal in terms of scale, form, and timing;
- to adapt to changing and often threatening occurrences;
- to marshal their will to survive;
- to rally round a common cause and a shared set of values.[75]

But something else is needed besides the skills of resilience and active listening for the Hare in all of us to get up and move from disengaged overwhelm to engaged concern. These are the capacities for sympathy and empathy.

Sympathy and empathy

'Sympathy' is often defined as a relationship of felt affinity between people or other beings in which what affects the one affects the other in similar ways. Hare's sympathetic response to his realisation that all living beings die was to simulate his own death. As the story says, 'He buried himself in his blanket. He made no sound.' 'Empathy' on the other hand is the capacity to feel oneself into the other's position (the other may be human or another sentient being) and to do so more or less accurately from the other's perspective. An empathic response only deserves to be named so if the recipient of that response affirms its accuracy. Empathic behaviour has four main components.[76] It involves: comprehending the feelings or stance of another individual or creature; resonating with those feelings; being able to distinguish one's own from the other's feelings; and feeling an inclination to act on behalf of the other's situation and, more often than not, doing so.

Empathy shares the first two components with sympathy and differs from sympathy by the presence of the final two components. To put it another way: in a sympathetic response the emphasis is on the listener's feelings about a problem that has been expressed by another person or creature; in an empathic response the emphasis is on the listener's accurate interpretation of what the other is actually feeling and on their ability to convey this understanding to the other in a precise, meaningful manner. The listener then feels motivated to use this understanding to help the other resolve their troubling situation, and often does so. If, for example, the peasants in 'The Stanger in the Inn' had responded empathically to the beggar's tale, they might have asked, 'Is this really how things are for you, and, if so, what can we do to help?' Normally, however, the development of an empathic response to the plight of characters in stories is not resolved in the story but left to the listener (see Nanson, this volume). How this response takes place is what this book is about.

A long history of social research identifies empathic capacity as fundamental to pro-social behaviour. Individuals who possess high empathic capacity are more likely to be altruistic – to volunteer to help others, to be engaged in community organisations – than those with a low capacity. We noted earlier that increases in people's ability to respond empathically to serious environmental problems are urgently needed. The contributors show how certain oral storytelling activities can directly lead to increases in people's empathic capacity and pro-social and pro-environmental behaviour. They also address why simply telling stories by itself may not suffice given that people's ears are so often fortified against stories, particularly when they contain bad news. We've explored why active listening to told stories can counteract some of the response-curtailing effects that 'bad-news' stories have. We believe, however, there is even more that can be done.

From overwhelm to storymaking

There is ample evidence that people's capacity to make and tell stories underpins their ability to deal better with troubling news or life events. It's also known that this ability is compromised when bad things happen or are about to occur. In such circumstances we are lost for words, and yet we often need words to prevent even greater problems occurring before it is too late, or to sort out the consequences in the best possible way.[77] Our resilience in the face of difficulty is enhanced if we have a strong pre-existing capacity to make and tell stories and an established ability to respond to stories to which we have actively listened. The reasons behind this are manifold.

In oral storytelling the boundaries between making a story and telling a story are hard to draw. Strictly speaking, every told story becomes a made story in the process of its telling. We therefore reserve the term 'storymaking' for an intentional creative process by which individuals create entirely new stories by themselves or in collaboration with others.[78] Our contributors enable their participants to do so in various ways. Besides storymaking activities that involve singing, stepping, talking, doodling, or writing, they use drama games that help in the development of a story's characters, settings, goals, difficulties, helpers, challengers. They may also invite people to record answers to a series of precisely formulated questions (Collison; Cree & Gersie; Green; Hurley & Gersie, this volume). The answers form the building blocks for a new, self-authored story. Once adults and children discover how to use these questions, which are based on key story components, they generally find it easy to make up, remember, and tell stories.

The following questions are an example of how this works:

- When and where does the story take place? (setting)
- Who is/are the main character(s) in the story? (protagonists)
- What is going on, or what needs to happen? (context and problematic)
- What motivates the character(s) to do something about this? (motivation)
- Who will help the character(s) to achieve the goal? (helper)
- Which challenges are encountered – if any? (obstacles)
- How are any challenges overcome? (resolution attempts)
- How does the helper help? (resolution attempts)
- How are things ultimately resolved? (outcome)

The answers the participants give to these questions create their story outline.[79] With this outline as a foundation, they then make a complete story. When people have learned how they can use their answers to story questions to develop a whole new story, and have gained a strong internal awareness of some basic story structures, they'll discover that it's possible to create a story around otherwise free-floating bits of information, such as:

- sea levels are rising
- ice caps in retreat
- heatwave causes 10,000 deaths
- severe drought for third year running
- forest fires threaten urban areas
- save the world

Such a story connects the information contained in headlines like these with a narrative context or setting in which there are characters who are affected by the information, protagonists who surrender to circumstances or respond constructively (or do a bit of both), and action sequences that clarify the process of addressing the difficulties implied in the information. Participants who learn to make stories at will thereby gain the capacity to deal with troubling pieces of environmental information that come their way, and learn to view them as integral parts of narratives that invite rather than preclude goal-oriented action – by them individually or as members of a group, and in one or all domains of their life.

Response-tasks as creative forms of active listening

Once people have gained a stronger capacity to place information into a narrative frame and develop from this a communicable tale, they also need to be able to convey their stories to others, and to elicit and receive feedback that facilitates further development of themselves, as well as their relationship with the respondent and the story or subject under discussion. All acts of communication during the process of storytelling happen in the interplay between the situation or place of telling, the teller's intention for their story, the story's content, and how the listener receives or interprets both intention and content and then feeds their response back to the teller. Many things can go amiss in this process, and many things can go right. Empathic attunement and accuracy of interpretation between teller and listener may or may not be achieved. This depends on the quality of the listening the story's recipient has been able to muster, and whether or not they've been able to shift from sympathy to empathy. In our experience there can often be a mismatch between a teller's intention, the story's content, and the recipient's interpretation of both. This divergence hampers the development of empathic attunement and the entailed capacity to act in a pro-social and pro-environmental way.

Our contributors therefore pay a great deal of attention to how they can enable people to discover what it means to them to be entailed in dynamic, reciprocal relationships with the more-than-human world as well as with the stories they themselves and other people tell. To facilitate this process of empathic alignment many contributors use 'response-tasks'. The use of these is not only a real source of delight to participants; it also develops the competencies that underpin reflective capacity and empathic attunement (Collins; Collison; Cree & Gersie; Gersie; Green; Ramsden; Salisbury).

In the 1970s Alida Gersie coined the term 'response-task' to describe a series of creative techniques that enable storytellers (or anyone who wants to communicate something in story form) and their listeners to develop their experience of 'what it means to be involved in reciprocal relationships with a story and thereby with each other in a transparent, delight-giving way'.[80] Before telling a story the facilitator or teller gives a specific task to the listener which will focus the listener's attention on a particular aspect of the story as it is told, i.e. not on the teller or on their telling of the story. Response-tasks may take the form of making a painting about something specific in the story, doing some writing, making a gesture, developing a dramatic scene based on the story, or creating some sounds. Because the task involves the listeners in making a highly specific response, this answering activity is called a 'response-task'.[81]

The selection of both the focus of the response-task and the creative modality in which the response will be expressed is of paramount importance. In groups that have a learning or developmental focus, the facilitator formulates the response-task. In situations where every participant will tell a story, the facilitator may use the same response-task for all stories, or vary the task from story to story. The responses are presented to the stories' original tellers after they have been made (painting or writing) or through being performed (dance, drama, sound). The group then reflects on their making, giving, and receiving, and participants may share their responses to the responses they've received. Response-tasks can be formulated as an exercise for individuals, pairs, small groups, or the whole group, depending on what the facilitator aims to achieve.

Here are some examples of response-tasks that have proved useful to our contributors:

- Please think of a natural gift that the main character in the story might welcome, and make a representation of this by drawing, making, painting, or writing something (which will later be given to the teller).
- Please note one word or short phrase in the story which touches you in a positive way, and write one sentence about this (which will later be given to the teller).
- Please identify what you think the character in the story really appreciates in their environment and make a representation of this by drawing, making, painting, or writing something (which will later be given to the teller).
- Please describe in a brief sentence what gave the character the courage to change their situation (this sentence to be later shared with the teller).
- Please draw or make a painting of an inner obstacle that the character needed to overcome and add one word that conveys what helped him or her to do so (this painting to be later given to the teller).
- Please show in a posture how the character felt at the end of the story and then show what this posture might look like if they felt even better (these postures to be later shown to the teller).
- Please create a brief song or poem to commemorate the events in the story (which will later be shown or read and given to the teller).

Response-tasks, active listening, and empathy

Participation in response-tasks (as maker and recipient) rapidly teaches people the practice of active ways of listening and an empathic understanding of what an accurate response to another person's stories can be like, both as an act of commitment to interaction and as a creative procedure. It also helps the participants to relate in greater depth to all manner of stories, their own and those told by others. The tellers' sharing of their response to the responses in the whole group enables the participants, as both tellers and listeners, to learn that people's responses and judgements are often based on personal history, an attempt to understand what is meant, and by and large benign intentions. They also discover how their responses compare with those of others and how different responses affect the original teller in different ways. Before long their intense involvement in structured responsivity helps them to understand that although a teller may experience many responses as constructive, attuned, or insightful, others (maybe their own) can be felt as irrelevant, hurtful, or out of tune with the teller's intent despite the response-maker's kind intentions.

This systematic process of listening and responding enables the participants to fine-tune and develop, in a surprising and satisfying way, their empathic capacity in a situation where reciprocal actions are expected. Thereby they develop quite rapidly from the more primitive ability to utter a self-focused sympathetic response, towards the fullness of an empathic response. A strong empathic ability enables them to be more compassionate towards themselves, towards others, and towards the more-than-human-world.

Reflective learning

When combined, the three creative techniques of storytelling, story-making, and participation in response-tasks help people to become reflective learners. In our approach to emancipatory education these techniques constitute a mutual, dialogic process through which facilitators and learners jointly investigate the reality they inhabit. They do so by means of stories that they hear or make and connect with their lived experiences. They learn to relate to the content of such stories not as 'facts' to be accepted, but as examples of human problem-solving that they need to examine. Freire observes that people cannot be truly human apart from communication. To exist, humanly, is to name the world, to change it. Dialogic encounter between oneself, stories, others, and the environment that we inhabit, and that inhabits us in return, depends on the establishment of equal, horizontal relationships between all that is and all who are party to a 'learning' event. It speaks for itself that these relationships need to be permeated by deep mutual respect, humility, and hope, of which, Freire says, mutual trust will be the logical outcome. This trust needs to stand the test of time. It is contingent upon a steady consistency between words and actions. To say one thing and do another undermines trust and reduces hope.

Storytelling performances and story-based workshops or training events that aim to bring about change in a sustainable direction, irrespective of whether they happen with world leaders or inner-city gangs, will be most effective when undertaken from this dialogic perspective.[82] In applying somewhat similar ideas to outdoor environmental education, Andrew Martin and Bill Krouwel describe such learning as 'a complex, dynamic interplay between all aspects of the human experience', culminating in 'a multifaceted beauty'.[83] And, as our contributors demonstrate, it is beautiful indeed.

Visitors to a nature reserve or staff on a training event need to be able to expect something positive from being there. They also need to be able to believe that timely action to prevent environmental calamity is possible and worthwhile, that the people who speak in favour of such action are trustworthy, and that they themselves have a role to play. During the kinds of story-based problem-posing events that are discussed in this book, people learn to learn together. They jointly develop their capacity to feel richly and to perceive critically how they exist in the environment in which they find themselves. They thereby come to see this environment not as a static reality, but as reality in process, in transformation. David Orr says, 'the plain fact is that the planet does not need more successful people. But it does desperately need more peacemakers, healers, restorers, storytellers, and lovers of every kind. It needs people who live well in their places. It needs people of moral courage willing to join the fight to make the world habitable and humane.'[84] We believe that this need can in significant measure be met through story-based approaches that build on Freire's ideas.

The ripple effect of this work

Given the urgency of the need for pro-environmental action, it is tempting for an organisation to focus exclusively on the immediate results of a story-based event. Although such outcomes are necessary and do exist, it's important to be aware that the kind of change that emerges from a story-based event is mostly gradual and frequently delayed. As some contributors show, the full fruits generally emerge some time afterwards (Collison; Cree & Gersie; Gersie; Hurley & Gersie; Medlicott). According to our four story-givers, 'the experience of hearing that story' percolated for some time in their inner world before it activated major change in their behaviour. They emphasised that the stories they heard would not leave them alone. 'It was as if Marianne's little story kept calling me back,' Nisha explained. 'Maybe it was the thought of those potentially wasted blackberries, or the glow on her face when she spoke about baking those pies.' Nisha didn't really know. Simon observed that the story-talk at that dinner had an important effect on him, not only in the pro-environmental changes in his behaviour, but also, and maybe even more importantly, because it affirmed his hope that positive change can emerge from such humble events as having dinner with some friends.

Yet one cannot assume that if Louise, Nisha, Simon, and Hong had been asked to state their reaction to the story at the time they would have granted it anything like the significance they do now. It is also likely that any evaluation of the occasion by the original tellers would simply have elicited that the listeners listened intently and appeared to enjoy the story and the subsequent chat. Neither teller nor listener could have foreseen the many productive consequences of these formal and informal story-telling occasions over the long term.

However, there are some clues in remarks made by our story-givers to the potential long-term efficacy of story-based work. Hong, for example, noted that the story his professor told about the dragon-slaying girl felt 'like a symbolic breath of fresh air'. He added, 'It was as if the story opened a window I didn't even know was there.' We think that a story's quality of 'welcome relief', which is hard to define but clear when it's present, is crucial. We further know that when a story is succinctly and evocatively told, and comes from deep within a teller, it invites strong identification from the listener. For example, Hong also remembered that it was as if he were on that mountain, as if he defeated that dragon. Each story-giver felt that the teller wanted them to become fully engaged with their experience of the storied events. 'It was', Louise recalled, 'as if Odo wanted me to see, hear, and feel those flying geese just like he had done, but in my own way. That's what was so wonderful about it.' And Simon's friend had called that story he heard on the radio 'irresistible'.

The reflections of our four story-givers illustrate what we have called a story's 'ripple effect'. Over time this effect may manifest within the person, in their actions in the world, and in their relationships with others and otherness. Some of these consequences will be immediate and clearly identifiable. Others may be delayed or only strongly visible to others at a later time. Some stories touch one person and mean little or nothing to someone else. Our contributors undertake this story-based work in full acceptance of the fact that change arrives in the same anticipated, and yet unexpected, manner as the passage of a skein of geese.

Give change a chance

When people learn to remember, create and share stories about their actual or potential environmental situation, their motivation to contribute to changing their situation often improves. This is because: they may now feel empowered; know what it's like to feel actively engaged in something; can hear, analyse, and interpret other people's tales better; and aren't so quickly overwhelmed by confusing data or persuasive stories. In other words, chances are that their enhanced capacities for skilled recall of a told story, for critical enquiry into stories, and for formulating empathic as well as enquiring responses to a received story will make them into more competent, active, and critical citizens.

After participation in several environment-focused story sessions, many children and adults feel more able to speak up within their groups of reference and beyond. The development of a clearer take on themselves and others boosts their self-confidence and increases their willingness to contribute to their wider society in relation to their environmental concerns. They also feel more comfortable about sharing their stories and experiences with others. They now can and want to act as green changemakers because they have learned what sustainable relationships are, what matters about them, and what it takes to maintain or restore fair dealing in all relationships, between humans themselves and between humans and the more-than-human world. Moreover, they have discovered that doing so can be really enjoyable.

Alida Gersie
Anthony Nanson
Edward Schieffelin

Notes

1 Ben Haggarty, personal communication, 10 January 2005.
2 Capra & Stone, 'Smart by Nature'.
3 Gersie, *Earthtales*; Nanson, 'Composting Dragons'; Whybrow, *The Story Handbook*; Brody et al., *Spinning Tales Weaving Hope*.
4 Gersie & King, *Storymaking in Education and Therapy*; Maguire *The Power of Personal Storytelling*; Pellowski, *The World of Storytelling*; Sawyer, *The Way of the Storyteller*; Sobol, *The Storytellers' Journey*.
5 Bauman, *Story, Performance and Event*; Birch, *The Whole Story Handbook*; Birch, 'Who Says?'; Lord, *The Singer of Tales*; Ryan, 'The Contemporary Storyteller in Context'.
6 Wackernagel & Reed, *Our Ecological Footprint*.
7 Global Footprint Network, 'Ecological Footprint Standards 2009'.
8 Porritt, *Capitalism as if the World Mattered*; World Economic Forum, *Global Risks 2010*; Turner, 'A Comparison of *The Limits to Growth* with 30 Years of Reality'.
9 Blackburn, *The Sustainability Handbook*; Blewitt, *Understanding Sustainable Development*. See also Devall & Sessions, *Deep Ecology*.
10 Stibbe, *Handbook of Sustainability Literacy*, p. 10.
11 Freire, *Pedagogy of the Oppressed*.
12 Vare & Blewitt, 'Sustainability Literacy'.
13 Roszak et al., *Ecopsychology*; Rust & Totton, *Vital Signs*.
14 Martin, 'Between Teller and Listener'.
15 Hopkins, *Transition Handbook*. See also Zolli & Healy, *Resilience*.
16 Carson, 'Environmental Storytelling'.
17 Jenkins, 'Game Design as Narrative Architecture'.
18 <http://www.worch.com>; <http://www.witchboy.net>.
19 Graham & Bird, 'Down the Garden Path'.
20 Nanson, *Storytelling and Ecology*.
21 <http://www.franstallings.com>.
22 Strauss, *Pecos Bill Invents the Ten-Gallon Hat*. See also Strauss, *Tales with Tails*; Strauss, *The Passionate Fact*; Caduto & Bruchac, *Keepers of the Night*.
23 <http://www.scottishstorytellingcentre.co.uk>.
24 <http://www.gdcvault.com/play>.
25 Nanson, *Words of Re-enchantment*, pp. 79–86.
26 Nanson, *Storytelling and Ecology*.
27 Rideout et al., *Generation M2*.
28 Louv, *Last Child in the Woods*.
29 <http://www.rspb.org.uk>; <http://www.woodlandtrust.org.uk>;

<http://www.conservation.org>.

[30] <http://www.foeeurope.org>.

[31] <http://earthhour.wwf.org.uk>.

[32] <http://www.projectaspect.org>.

[33] <http://www.greenpeace.org/international/en/news/Blogs/makingwaves/rainbow-warrior-enjoys-the-calm-between-the-s/blog/38136/>.

[34] Vare & Blewitt, 'Sustainability Literacy'.

[35] Gersie, *Earthtales*. See also Jenkins, 'Game Design as Narrative Architecture'.

[36] Finnegan, *Oral Tradition and the Verbal Arts*; Ong, *Orality and Literacy*.

[37] Prendergast & Saxton. *Applied Theatre*.

[38] MacDonald, *Traditional Storytelling Today*.

[39] Harvey, 'Staging the Story'.

[40] Haggerty, *Seek out the Voice of the Critic*.

[41] Haven, *Storyproof*.

[42] Buber, *I and Thou*.

[43] Jordan, *Nature and Self*; Gersie, *Reflections on Therapeutic Storymaking*, pp. 154–169.

[44] Lipman, *The Storytelling Coach*.

[45] Ramsden & Hollingsworth, *The Storyteller's Way*.

[46] Birge Vitz et al., *Performing Medieval Narrative*, p. 1.

[47] Quotation from <http://www.welcome.ac.uk>.

[48] Green et al., *Narrative Impact*.

[49] Lakoff & Johnson, *Metaphors We Live by*; Gladwell, *The Tipping Point*.

[50] Gottschall, *The Storytelling Animal*.

[51] Macy, *World as Lover*, p. 180.

[52] Genette, *Narrative Discourse*.

[53] Thompson, *The Folktale*.

[54] Genette, *Narrative Discourse*.

[55] Based on oral retellings as well as a version in Benjamin, *Selected Writings*, Vol. 2, p. 812.

[56] Anthony Nanson, preparatory paper, Tales to Sustain, Burnlaw Centre, Northumberland, 24–27 September 2009.

[57] Lakoff & Johnson, *Metaphors We Live by*.

[58] Lambert, 'The Horror and the Beauty', pp. 37–41.

[59] Gladwell, *The Tipping Point*.

[60] Bruner, *Acts of Meaning*, p. 62.

[61] See Hyde, *The Gift*.

[62] Zipes, *Creative Storytelling*, pp. 219–226.

[63] Gersie, *Reflections on Therapeutic Storymaking*.

[64] Hartigan, 'Beyond the Humpty Dumpty Economy'.

[65] Wheatley, *Turning to One Another*, p. 23; Shaw, *Changing Conversation in Organisations*, p. 33.

[66] Brandler & Roman, *Group Work*.

[67] Dewart & Summers, *The Pragmatics Profile of Everyday Communication Skills*.

[68] Haggarty, personal communication.

[69] For example: Wilson, *The Future of Life*; Flannery, *The Weather Makers*; Williams, *Deforesting the Earth*; Diamond, *Collapse*; Ellwood, *No-Nonsense Guide to Globalization*.

[70] Speth, *Red Sky at Morning*.

[71] Adams & Jeanrenaud, *Transition to Sustainability*.

[72] Radin, *The Trickster*.

[73] Gersie, *Storymaking in Bereavement*, pp. 34–35. See also Radin, *The Trickster*, pp. 23–24.

[74] Armitage & Plummer, *Adaptive Capacity and Environmental Governance*. See also McIntosh, *Rekindling Community*.

[75] McAslan, 'Community Resilience'.

[76] Catterell, 'A Neuroscience of Art and Human Empathy'.

[77] Devall & Sessions, *Deep Ecology*.

[78] Gersie, *Reflections on Therapeutic Storymaking*, pp. 8–44.

[79] See also Corbett, *Jumpstart Storymaking*.

[80] Gersie & King, *Storymaking in Education and Therapy*, pp. 297–338.

[81] Gersie, *Reflections on Therapeutic Storymaking*, pp. 113–133.

[82] Blewitt, *Understanding Sustainable Development*, pp. 21–24.

[83] Martin & Krouwel, 'Rejuvenating Outward Bound Programme Design'.

[84] Orr, *Earth in Mind*, p. 11.

PART I

CORE IDEAS AND TECHNIQUES

CHAPTER I

This chapter introduces the key principles behind
pro-environmental workshops with adults or children in
diverse educational, organisational, or nature conservation settings.
It describes:

a one-day programme for adults or children in the outdoors;

~

nature-based creative techniques that develop people's emotional
and sustainability literacy;

~

a rationale based on Fromm's ideas about biophilia and Freire's
practice of experiential education;

~

suggestions for circle time and action time that support a
group's pro-environmental goals;

~

one traditional story and accompanying creative explorations.

From the participants' perspective a pro-environmental workshop
is successful when, after the event, they feel a more sustained
love of life, find it easier to collaborate with others, and
possess heartfelt knowledge of what it takes to
behave in a sustainable manner.

Storytelling in the Woods

*The uses of story to create links between emotional literacy,
ecological sensibility, and pro-environmental behaviour*

JON CREE AND ALIDA GERSIE

> If we want the chance of a sustainable future we need to think
> relationally. That's it. Full stop.
>
> Stephen Sterling

Ecological sensibility is more than the human capacity to cherish the uniqueness and interrelatedness of all living beings. As a moral awareness it entails our willingness to acknowledge that people form but one community among other interdependent communities of plants and creatures, and that we carry the responsibility to pursue our lives in such ways that this interdependence is sustainable for all in the long term. The difficulty is that in order to be 'ecologically sensible' we need to think and feel relationally. This in turn requires us to be 'emotionally literate'. In sustainability-oriented workshops with policy-makers, teachers or social workers, business leaders, and kids with challenging behaviour we help the participants to explore three issues:

- how to know and recognise what they are feeling (emotional literacy)
- how emotions link with needs and values
- how these in turn affect the motivation to act in a sustainable way

This chapter unpacks these ideas and shows how we translate them into multi-layered story-based activities in the outdoors which support the participants' ability to engage in more sustainable ways of living.

PART I. EMOTIONAL LITERACY, STORYWORK, AND ACTIVE LEARNING

The terms 'emotional literacy' and 'emotional intelligence' are often used interchangeably.[1] We employ both terms to refer to someone's ability to recognise, name, and understand their own and other people's feelings and to become aware of the needs that are bound up with these. Candace Pert and other body–mind scientists show how our mind and body are intricately linked through an exquisite array of receptors, senders, neuropeptides, and neuro-anatomic exchange processes.[2] Though they may not be familiar with Pert's ideas, emotionally literate people are aware of this linkage between body and mind. They can express, respond to, and manage a range of feelings in ways that work for them and their important others. This matters especially for the socially more complex emotions of anger, surprise, sadness, guilt or shame, fear, delight, and joy. Within any given culture, people tend to agree on what they consider to be emotionally appropriate behaviour, on the importance of listening to others, on the value of empathy, and on why emotions should be expressed in ways that make cooperation possible and create a sense of community. In our workshops, these ideas are explored by participants in terms of their physical and social experience of themselves in the world around them.

To facilitate this type of embodied environmental learning we often use traditional or local stories. Some may be unfamiliar to the group, others well known, like the tale of Chicken-Little. When an acorn falls on her head Chicken-Little believes that the sky is falling. Her panic alarms one animal after another and soon they are all running as fast as they can to the castle to tell the King about it. On the way they meet Fox, who genially offers to show them the route. Instead of leading them to the King's castle, however, Fox takes them to his own den, where he kills and devours them all. As a contrast to this story we often tell a similar one from the Indian Jataka tales. Here Young Lion stops an equally panicked group of animals to enquire what's going on. Hare tells Lion that he heard a terrible thud, that the earth is breaking apart and they're all running to save themselves. Instead of scheming to kill the terrified creatures, Lion asks Hare to lead him back to the place where he heard the dreadful noise. Once there Young Lion shows Hare that a falling nut caused the panic and the earth has survived intact. The Jataka tale ends with each animal happily going to where they want to be.[3]

We'll return later to the value of telling both versions. Here it suffices to say that we may use these tales to explore the animals' over-hasty responses to the unexpected event. We can then think about what might have enabled them to respond more productively (such as emergency preparedness, or knowledge about what happens when you warn others about an imminent calamity) and which emotional, social, and practical skills the animals would have needed to do this. We also use the stories to clarify some patterns and processes by which nature sustains life, such as networks of relationships, dynamic balance, and flow.

Our holistic approach to groupwork is deeply informed by the principles of accelerated learning.[4] From this latter perspective, working holistically means engaging everyone physically, intellectually, emotionally, and spiritually: that is, doing things that involve their hands, head, heart, and spirit.[5] The holistic approach also helps us to support group members in their attempts to manage the uncomfortable feelings aroused by uncertainty and by stepping out of a habitual mindset. Cloë, a boisterous teenager in trouble with the law, once said that, having learnt in our workshop how to make some 'weird things that didn't really make sense', she now felt much better about trying something new. She had also gained more confidence in herself, and her relationships with other people, and discovered that she loved 'being outside'. She was amazed how quickly she had learnt to explore something in depth simply because she was allowed to use her hands to do so and was then encouraged to briefly stand back to think about it before carrying on. She was very happy about this. Not only because she was 'never-ever' bored, but above all because the experience had showed her that there was more to her than she had thought. Her thoughtful words mattered to us too.

In the field of experiential and active learning, 'doing something' is often separated from 'reflecting', both conceptually and practically.[6] During the 'doing' period, participants are meant to be doing something creative, exploring something practically, or actively moving about. During 'reflection' they are meant to sit and talk, though the talk may include structured debate, brief mutual interviews, or prompts. In our approach to active learning, these posited distinctions between action and reflection are more fluid. We structure our activities in such a way that the participants 'reflect while doing' and 'do while reflecting'. As such they learn to think on their feet and walk their talk. This is important, we think, because it is much easier to adopt new behaviour when we can remain mindfully present in our actions and interactions.

We believe that playing with stories, storytelling, and story-based activities are essential components of this active learning strategy. They bring several pedagogical advantages. When hearing a story, for example, listeners need to temporarily suspend disbelief, maintain operative attention, and use different forms of knowledge. For Cloë, listening to the stories, learning to make some up, and then doing things with the stories helped her to think and act differently. They made her think, she said, 'about what I did and didn't know. I learned to concentrate when I wanted to. The stories also made me wonder about things and, best of all, they stopped me brooding.'

During a period of 'reflective action', which we call 'walkabout time', we use exercises that stimulate the participants to explore or show their emotions, to quickly make something new, to step back from this once in a while, and to use others' feedback when proceeding with the exercise. During 'circle time' or active reflection, the participants share feelings, impressions, or ideas, give further feedback, and identify issues or behaviours that promote or delay progress towards the workshop's goals. They don't do this only by sitting and talking. Every period of walkabout time or circle time encompasses a cycle of action and reflection-upon-action. We'll illustrate below what these ideas mean in practice when we discuss a typical one-day workshop. But first we want to highlight a tricky issue that confronts many facilitators of outdoor learning: namely, how and when to deal with matters concerning the environmental crisis.

Out in the natural world, workshop participants often say that they 'connect with real life' or 'with something deep' within themselves. The Harvard biologist E.O. Wilson has pointed out that at least 90 per cent of (the period of) human evolution was spent honing our emotional intelligence, well-being, and innate relationship with all that lives. He observes that 'the knowing of other living creatures elevates the very concept of life' and that regaining excitement about the 'untrammelled' world is 'a formula of re-enchantment to invigorate poetry and myth'.[7] We work outdoors also because most of our participants rarely venture into the natural world in their everyday life. Richard Louv points out that 'nature' has become something to watch, to consume, to wear – or to ignore.[8] For many children and adults the outdoor world is now more abstraction than reality – a tragic reversal of how human life has been since it first began.

However, once our participants reconnect with themselves, with each other, and with a more natural environment, they discover that 'mysterious little known organisms live within walking distance of where they sit and that splendour awaits them in minute proportions'.[9]

Here things can get a little complex for environmental groupwork facilitators and nature wardens, who often have multiple groupwork goals. Besides enhancing people's self-esteem and introducing them to the delights of the outdoors, we also are expected to awaken awareness of environmental problems and strengthen people's willingness to live more sustainably. In discussions with colleagues we've learned that while the first two goals (raising self-esteem and enjoyment of the outdoors) are relatively easy, the second two (awareness and motivation to change) are more difficult, especially in one-off sessions. Although participants readily learn to enjoy the outdoors, they're not as keen to hear about human-caused environmental complexities. This is often because they may not yet have the internal capacity to process the feelings that these man-made troubles arouse.

We have found it counter-productive to try to address such issues with participants who feel detached from each other and from themselves. In order for this detachment to ease, they first need to get to know each other, shed some of their own emotional load, discover the group's strengths, and above all have some fun. When they do something new together and share something personal in a friendly, accepting atmosphere, they quickly get a sense of the group as a welcoming temporary community – a psycho-social home of kinds. Once their needs for connection, for soothing, for playfulness and feeling a sense of resilience are met, they are keen to develop a deeper, more layered relationship with the more-than-human-world (see note in the Introduction). Only then do they become more willing to explore the complex reality that our environmental troubles are intricately linked with our reluctance, or even our refusal, to engage in sustained pro-environmental behaviour.

In our workshops we therefore gradually embed work on emotional literacy within the larger framework of ecological and sustainability literacy. 'Ecological literacy' enables group members to understand the basic principles of ecology and how these affect their place in the world. 'Sustainability literacy' gives the participants the skill, knowledge, and value base to be active citizens in creating a more sustainable present.[10]

To facilitate this multi-level learning we consciously structure each group as a temporary learning community, as carefully and joyfully as we can. This is achieved by means of a wide repertoire of action-based creative techniques, by safeguarding the group's agreed goals, needs, and boundaries, and by ensuring that everybody receives equal attention and has an equal say. Our participants know that we expect them to collaborate in this. Central to our approach to our mode of 'active learning for change' is the development of a sense of connectedness and a feeling for the dynamics of initiating and maintaining relationships, for resilience, fun, and aesthetics. Aesthetics matter. Once people find something beautiful right here, right now, life – and all that lives – begins to sing.

PART 2. A ONE-DAY SUSTAINABILITY-ORIENTED WORKSHOP IN THE OUTDOORS

The above-mentioned ideas inform our down-to-earth approach to group-work practice. We'll now give an overview of a typical one-day event for a group of about thirty participants.

We begin with circle time, during which we introduce the setting, fine-tune the day's goals, and explain housekeeping issues such as the timetable, emergency procedures, first aid, and the need for pro-environmental behaviour on and off site, including clearing up after ourselves. We also form agreements about how people want to deal with confidentiality, touch, safety, responsibility, and respect.[11]

After this we introduce several quick-fire activities to get people moving, meeting one another, and exploring the site. Each activity lasts a few minutes and achieves several things at once. Some activities enliven the senses (sound, sight, taste, smell, movement). Others help participants to use their voice and body, facilitate shifts in attention or mood (from a directed to a soft focus, from stress to delight), or invite verbal or movement responses to something or someone. Sometimes everyone does the same thing at the same time (like pointing to something of interest in nature). At other times people work in pairs or by themselves. They may explore their body-space, share a nature-memory that will be retold by someone else, or take turns calling out animal names beginning with 'P', for example, or the names of round fruits or red vegetables. Depending on the kind of warm-up that people need, we may ask them to make and throw imaginary snowballs, imagine running through a rainstorm, inhale deeply to smell the air, hum a comforting song, suck on an imaginary slice of lemon, create the sound of a waterfall, or pretend to splash in a shallow river.

What we ask people to do depends on their emotional, social, and developmental needs, but we always include some games around feeling-words like 'happy', 'upset', 'grateful', 'content', 'bored', 'anxious', or 'pleased'. For example, people may be asked to walk the workshop space randomly and then on the cue of 'Stop' greet the nearest person with a hello and share something that has delighted them this morning and something that has evoked another feeling. They then continue moving, and on the cue of 'Stop' make eye contact with another person and point to the part of their own body where they felt that feeling of delight and where they felt the other feeling they've identified. This immediately gets us 'into our bodies' and thinking about feelings. Embodiment is a cornerstone of emotional literacy work. Moreover, the symbolic and direct communication of everyday stress and blocked emotions helps ease emotional constraints they may experience. Ample research, especially that of Pert, has shown that the troubling impact of everyday stress or blocked emotions can be eased through symbolic or direct communication as entailed in these activities.

At this stage we often hand out pencils and crayons plus portfolios or sketchbooks which the participants can keep and take home. Sometimes they personalise the cover with a sketch of a landscape, plant, or animal. People use their portfolio/sketchbook throughout the day to record things that matter to them.

Circle time in action

Towards the end of these introductory activities we re-form the circle to focus on what we've done so far, on the group's social interactions and how they feel or what they need. We'll draw attention to the kinds of feelings that are common at this stage, and promote some understanding of how or when such feelings arose. We often ask questions such as:

- Does anyone else feel like that or notice that?
- Did you feel anything else at the same time as feeling ... ?
- If you'd felt that feeling a bit more strongly (or weakly) what would you have called that, or what would you have done with that?

This normalising process quickly expands people's emotional vocabulary, clarifies interpersonal perceptions, and increases tolerance for mixed emotions. It also helps participants to realise that feelings and needs are integral to being alive and that relationships involve the encoding and decoding of emotions, perceived needs or demands, and other communicative messages. The group is now ready for the next activity.

A place in the woods

Participants are asked to locate a 'magic spot' in the woods that 'speaks' to them, preferably beneath a tree. Once there they need to sit down and be beneath that tree for about 10 to 15 minutes. We ask them to be still and to focus on the breath that connects them to the rest of life by staying with its 'here-and-nowness'. The key to this exercise, we say, is both to be alert and to enjoy solitude, sitting, stillness, and silence. If being still is a challenge we suggest they imagine having a veil of silence that they can bring down to close their mouth and can remove altogether when they want to talk again. We explain that we'll beat a gong or blow a flute when it's time to rejoin the circle. Before they leave their place, we ask them to restore it to how it was before they sat there.

They then set out into the woods to find their tree.

Afterwards, back in the circle, people first share their experience with someone on either side – but only if they wish. We then open up the sharing to the whole group. An overworked organisational consultant noted that at first 'just sitting there' made him feel agitated, but that he 'sat through that'. He then noticed a small spider crawling away. Its departure made him unexpectedly sad. His sadness, he observed, after a while made him feel alive. A female interim manager added that beneath 'her' tree she felt relaxed 'for the first time in months'. Some schools Jon has worked with now start their teaching day with such 'tree to be me' time. During a recent visit a five-year-old boy eagerly told Jon, 'I love my tree cause I can tell it anything and it listens and it tells me things and I listen. Today there were ten robins telling the tree lots of stories. My tree is always there and it is good.' His teacher later told Jon that the boy's parents were going through a difficult separation, which was badly affecting the boy and made the tree-time very important to him. Many participants comment that soon after they sit by 'their' tree their stress eases. Once participants, of any age, feel more present to themselves, their capacity to recognise, tolerate, and name some emotions increases.[12] This stress-release response is backed by numerous studies that examine the role of the natural world in restoring our well-being and the ability to attend to something. As William Bird notes: 'The countryside can be seen as a great outpatient department whose therapeutic value is yet to be fully realised.'[13] The 'tree' exercise also helps people realise that, even though all did the same activity, each person has unique things to say about it. Suzie, a troubled teenager, noted that these things had 'for once nothing to do with me'. This enhanced her ability to think about the meaning of her experience, and to review her understanding in the light of what other people contributed. This new cognitive/emotional skill underpinned her growing ability to deal more effectively with the otherness of others.

Once everyone has said something about the morning so far, we close this session. At this point some people get their portfolio or sketchbook to make a quick note or a drawing. Others have a stretch. A few chat together. Some go on a quick run. People normally don't check their mobiles, as we have made an agreement to let that go for the day. Then follows a short break with refreshments.

Memories, meaningful thematics, and motivation

After the break we again reflect on the day so far. At this point the participants frequently share some 'nature' memories. We hear about Grand-dad and his allotment or Uncle Tom 'who took me fishing', about sneaking into a local park after dark for some star-gazing or canoodling, about not being allowed plants at work, or feeling locked in when seeing a bird through the school window. These 'headline-only' stories express the connections that are arising between feelings, desires, motives, and actions. This matters because once these links are revivified we can more easily enable the group to identify some themes that are particularly meaningful to them.[14] Here are some examples:

- Once we're outside we have a great time. Why don't we do it more often?
- Our parents grew a lot of vegetables. Why don't we?
- We want to spend more time outdoors.
- We want classrooms or offices with fresh air and good views.

During the identification of these emotionally charged themes people realise that the outdoors matters and that it's impossible to be non-emotional. They also learn that their emotions not only influence their everyday behaviour; they also inform how they think about the future and consequently what they might try to make happen to achieve future goals.

Telling a story to facilitate critical enquiry

After this thematic clarification we often tell a story that we'll later work with. As noted above, we tell stories because it is so much easier to examine important themes or issues through the de-familiarising potential of a traditional story than through straightforward discussion. The old story's narrative frame enables us to examine a character's motives, to identify their needs or wants, to explore alternative points of view, or to challenge assumptions that might otherwise be taken for granted. In the stories of Chicken-Little and Hare, panic infected every animal they met – until, that is, the animals encountered either Fox, who exploited their vulnerability and killed them for supper, or Young Lion, who, as an early incarnation of the Buddha, simply calmed them and asked some questions that led, in Paolo Freire's terms, to critical consciousness ('conscientisation'): that is, he enabled them to surmount their panicked interpretation of their reality. This generated new viewpoints, reflection, hope, and action. In many ways Freire's consciousness-raising questions resemble those used by Young Lion in the Jataka tale:

- Who makes the statement?
- To whom is he/she making it?
- On whose behalf is he/she making it?
- Why is this statement made here and now?
- Whom does it benefit?
- Whom does it harm?
- What can we do to explore its truth?

There is, however, one crucial difference. Fox and Young Lion ask rather similar questions to establish what the animals 'feel they need'. Once they know this, each behaves in a fundamentally different way. Fox pursues self-interest. Lion reassures the animals that they will not perish.

Few traditional tales encourage, in and of themselves, concern for others, green behaviour, or ecological understanding. The development of the listener's awareness of such things depends primarily on what they do with a story, rather than on the story itself. At the heart of our storywork are: the illumination of the characters' behaviour and how this connects with our own needs and values; the evocation of a desire to pursue behaviour that harmonises with these; and the acquisition of the skills to do so.

Here is an example of a tale we like to tell.

The Woodcutter and the Three Eggs

There was once a poor woodcutter who spent his days cutting and selling wood. Although he worked long hours, he earned little money and was barely able to feed and clothe his family. One night, the woodcutter dreamt he saw a beautiful spirit smiling and waving at him from a hole in a huge tree. The next morning he went into the forest to cut wood, hoping to find the tree he had seen in his dream, wishing that it housed the tree-spirit he had dreamt about. Just before dusk he found a large tree with a hole in its trunk and decided that this must be the tree that housed the tree-spirit. From then on, every time he worked in the forest he left a small present for the spirit. Often he talked to the tree-spirit, telling it about his life and family. Unbeknown to him, the tree-spirit grew fond of him and decided to give him a present in return for all his care. The next day, when the woodcutter came to place his gift at the foot of the tree, he found a bird's nest that contained three golden eggs. The woodcutter was astounded and knelt beneath the tree in gratitude. He knew his days of poverty were ended, that his family would no longer have to worry about money.

As he ran home to show the eggs to his family, a bird swooped down and snatched one of the eggs in its beak and quickly flew out of sight. The woodcutter was upset but he knew that even two golden eggs that remained would be of great help to his family. Thirsty he knelt down to scoop some water from a stream. As he drank, one of the eggs fell into the water and was swallowed by a hungry fish. The woodcutter mourned the loss of the second egg yet he knew that even one egg would help his family. Carefully holding the one remaining egg, he hurried home. As his family gathered round, their cries of joy attracted the attention of a greedy neighbour. Watching through the window, he saw the woodcutter place the egg in a jar of grain for safekeeping. When the woodcutter and his family were asleep, the neighbour crept into the house and stole the last of the three eggs.

When the woodcutter woke up and found the third egg missing, he felt sad and ashamed. He went to the tree-spirit to tell her all about it and to apologise for his carelessness. That day he chopped wood with a heavy heart. At dusk he slowly began to make his way home. Carrying his load of wood, he heard a sound above him. He looked up and saw a tree full of ripe fruit. He decided to take some home for his family. As he was picking the fruit his hand touched a bird's nest, and when he looked into it he saw his golden egg. With a heart full of happiness he shouted thanks to the tree-spirit. At home a surprise awaited him. His son had gone fishing and caught a beautiful fish. When his wife opened it to clean it for dinner, there inside lay a golden egg. The greedy neighbour, hearing the shouts of joy, came to the house to hear what had happened. Their good news filled him with terror. How was all this possible? That night, when they were all asleep, he crept again into the wood-cutter's house and returned the third golden egg to its place of safekeeping in the jar of grain.

The woodcutter sold the three golden eggs for enough money to keep him and his family comfortable for the rest of their lives. But he never forgot the source of his good fortune and continued to bring presents and talk with the tree-spirit for as long as he lived.[15]

Exploring the story in creative depth

After this tale we often invite people to do one or more activities to explore its content and impact. We choose which exercise to use according to the needs of the group. Here are some examples of what we might do.

I.

In a pair or group of three the participants have about 20 minutes to create in the woods a sculptural representation of the events in the story, using only natural materials and some googly eyes (small eyes used in craftwork), paper, string, and scissors. We emphasise that the natural world will help them with their representation of the story and also with keeping to a positive outcome to the events. They may place different parts of their story around the woods but in that case the scenes need to be connected with rope or wool to provide a visual storyline. We ask them to place some cards with feeling-words at certain points in the story to reflect 'the emotion of the scene'. Once their story in the woods is complete they return to the circle. Then the whole group goes on a story-walk to view each 'picture' in turn. We talk about the characters' needs or feelings as well as our own while viewing these 'nature-picture' stories.

2.

Alternatively we may ask each participant to imagine a creature that could live in the forest near the woodcutter's village. At this point the participants are likely to wonder: What kind of forest is it – tropical, montane, temperate, coniferous – and which animals live in such a forest? We explain that for this exercise they can accept whatever forest their imagination conjures up and choose whichever creature comes to mind. We encourage everyone to choose any character that's not in the story, i.e. not the bird or the fish. We then ask people if they have decided who this character might be. Once everyone has affirmed that they have chosen an animal, we ask them to accept our suggestion that their chosen creature witnessed everything that happened in the story and has something to say about these events that reflects his or her norms or values. We give the group members some time – though not too much to ponder what their character might want to convey. Then we pass a story-stick around the circle to invite each 'being' to have their say. When all have spoken on behalf of their animal about the story's events, we ask the group to be silent for a while. We then open the space for reflections.[16]

3.

In another possible activity we help the whole group to identify the tale's core scenes and to sequence these. We then divide the group into pairs or small groups and invite each pair or small group to choose one of the scenes. If two groups choose the same one, that's okay, provided all scenes are covered. We then invite each pair or small group to imagine and create the ecological soundscape of their chosen scene as they imagine it might have been at that moment and in that place. Once they've explored and rehearsed their imagined soundscape, we invite the pairs/groups to share their work by sequencing the soundscapes according to the storyline.

We may then do a similar 'representative sequencing' exercise with pairs or small groups creating the physical movements of a scene, with people working in either the same or different pairs or small groups. We might then ask each pair or small group to create a single phrase to express their take on a scene's core emotional content. These phrases can then be joined together in an expressive, choral-like way, for example by asking other pairs or small groups to repeat or sing each phrase.

If people have made anything 'material' in the woods, we ask them now to disassemble their makings, to recycle or discard materials in our bins as appropriate, and to restore their chosen site to its former shape. To leave nothing behind and carry off only their memories.

After the exercise(s) we meet for circle time in which people quietly ponder what they did or witnessed. After that they work on their portfolios. We then consider the story from different perspectives – intuitively, sensorily, ethically, spiritually, socio-culturally. Each raises different questions: What was that forest really like? How many trees could the woodcutter cut in a day? How did that affect the forest? What motivated him to visit the tree-spirit? Were the eggs really meant for him? What made him decide to be honest about the loss of the three golden eggs? How did he explain what happened? What was the tree-spirit's response when she heard about the loss, and why? Did the woodcutter make any reparation for having lost the eggs? What happened after the story's end? What might have blocked his intention to continue to live simply? What might have strengthened it?

At this stage we take care to address the story's links with the participants' own needs, motivations, and actions. This often involves active exploration using dramatic techniques such as role play, forum theatre, and hotseating.[7] This work quickly instigates talk about issues such as work or unemployment, home finances, luck or misfortune, honesty, what makes for good family or community relations, the unpredictability or messiness of life, knowing what you want, or the pursuit of a dream. We may also explore the woodcutter's situation in the context of logging, biodiversity, resource depletion, family size, relations with poorer or richer neighbours, and transport. Another thing that often emerges is the tension mentioned above between feelings about the beauty and wonders of the natural world and feelings about the human-caused threats to it. Given this rich diversity of responses to the tale and the exercises, it's no wonder that we like to tell this story and work with it.

Developing mutuality with a tree

After another, somewhat longer break, we reassemble the circle for the day's final exercise. Taking a leaf from Joseph Cornell's work on sharing nature with children, this activity speaks to the participant's relationship with something that lives in the immediate environment.[18] We ask everyone to reflect on the day and especially on their time in the presence of their tree. If we've told 'The Woodcutter and the Three Eggs' in a mixed wood we'll identify some of the common trees there – such as hazel, oak, rowan, birch, ash, cherry, and hawthorn – and hand out corresponding tree identification cards that contain some ecosystem information. We then ask them to return to their tree for about 10 minutes and, by alert sensory watchfulness (sight, hearing, touch, smell, and intuition), get to know its living essence in relation to its environment. This is both an intuitive process and based on precise observation.

Back in the circle we share these experiences and situate them within the heartfelt ecological frame of relationships, connectedness, and context. By now most participants will feel aware of themselves as living within nested systems. This makes it easy to clarify the group's collective knowledge about their trees' function in our community and ecosystem. To deepen this knowledge we may offer some activities that develop embodied awareness of the trees' environment, including soil, water, sunshine, wind and weather, and other plants and creatures. When talking about specific trees – let's say a rowan (also known as 'mountain ash' or 'dogberry') – we might ponder its age. Was it self-seeded or planted? Depending on the season, birds (such as chaffinches, waxwings, blackbirds, thrushes) may have enjoyed its berries or a red deer nibbled its foliage. Have lichens grown on its bark? Someone may recall that in the old days people said that if you had a rowan walking stick you never got lost. Another person may wonder if its extreme hardiness explains why people believe that a rowan planted near a dwelling will ward off malevolent beings.

With our collective knowledge of trees revived, each person then revisits their tree one more time. This is what they're asked to do:

1. They bring themselves into full awareness of the encounter between themselves and their tree as tree.

2. They ponder how the tree supports their well-being.

3. They consider what they can do in return to support the well-being of this tree, of other trees like it, or of its ecosystem.

4. In their mind's eye they consider how they might be able to convert this 'support' into a manageable, specific action that they could realistically perform within the next 60 days.

5. They ponder whether they want to develop this idea into an intent and, somewhat like the woodcutter's gifts to the tree-spirit, whether they want to give to their tree 'their gift of intent to perform a specific pro-environmental action'.

6. They either make or don't make a heartfelt commitment of intent.

7. They then say goodbye to their tree and return to the circle.

The participants are often very thoughtful upon their return from this activity. We do not intrude upon this with premature comments or interpretations. Sooner or later someone speaks. Our collective learning and sharing then takes what shape it needs to. Participants are often surprised by the intensity of their feelings and their desire to ensure their tree's well-being. We reassure anyone who did not make any inner commitment to constructive pro-environmental action that it is better to withhold a commitment than to make one when we're pretty sure that we cannot keep it. At some point the right time will arrive for a natural break. We agree its length with the group.

Review, preparation for the journey home, and goodbyes

After the break, we return to the circle to review the entire day's activities and processes. We revisit our expectations for the day, what we did, our feelings, needs, and motivations, and we look at how these developed during the day. We also evaluate what worked well, what could be improved, what we learned, which questions we'll continue to ponder, and which actions we plan to implement, and when. We then discuss how we'll say goodbye to each other and what each person will do to ease their return to their home, school, and/or workplace. After clearing up we thank each other and the woods for being there. We then say our actual goodbyes. We take about an hour for this process.

Some further thoughts

In this chapter we have shared some core ideas and activities that inform our work. We introduced the familiar folktale of 'Chicken-Little' and its less familiar Indian counterpart about Hare, we did so to highlight the tendency to react impulsively to something unexpected, and to draw attention to a key moral difference in Fox's and Young Lion's responses to the animals' panic. Both wanted to know the cause of the animals' fear. Feigning helpfulness, Fox lured the animals to their death to satisfy his immediate need. Young Lion put an end to the animals' fear and preserved their life. In 1964 Erich Fromm defined 'biophily' as the profound love of life and living.[19] He placed the life-enhancing urge of 'biophily' alongside 'necrophily', our destructive pull towards violence, deadness, and death, pointing out that each of us faces their unceasing internal and external dynamics.

By modelling the delight of having compassionate relationships with each other and with the natural world, we try to create a motivating environment in which change in the direction of sustainable living can occur. This includes being thoughtful about energy, waste, water, food and drink, and the need to restore the sites of our exercises individually or collectively. We attend to these issues because we think that sustainability involves a constant, thoughtful, and often fun interplay between people and the more-than-human world. From this perspective our negotiation of a clear working contract at the beginning of the workshop signals that we are serious about the need for the participants and ourselves to maintain an inspired self-discipline in all our relations with other people and with the natural world.

In the course of a workshop day like the one outlined above, our participants become aware that doing something expressive in the outdoors meets many key emotional and social needs, such as those for understanding, creativity, and participation. Most are moved by the fact that being mindfully present in the outdoors is so deeply satisfying. Harry, a stressed single dad of three boisterous kids, said, 'It may sound stupid, but I've realised for the first time that nature's always there. I only have to turn to it to feel part of something greater than myself. I feel so moved by that. I never have to feel that alone again.' Harry's sense of belonging resonates with the experience of Debbie, a teacher, who wrote to Jon about the Forest School area she co-created outside her primary school: 'Our site is evolving and changing day by day and it really feels part of me, which may seem strange. Every day when I go to check how things are going, it is like going home.' She continued, 'The children now use words such as "sustainability" and "biodiversity" with complete understanding. This high level of thinking and comprehension would not have been achieved without Forest School.'

When our workshops offer the participants a lively experience of ecological sensibility, emotional literacy, and a participative take on the world, they soon enjoy a vibrant sense of fun alongside a passionate openness to others and otherness which is wonderfully gratifying. This deep sense of homecoming to themselves and to the natural world will underpin their ability to pursue self-motivated, ecologically considerate behaviour. Our activities and the way we conduct the group aim to generate a restorative response that frees the participants to care for themselves, for others, and for their surroundings. Their revived 'capacity to care' gives them an affinity with all that lives. This affinity is not only unforgettable; it is the prime motivator for engagement in sustainable action.

Notes

1 Thomas & Killick, *Telling Tales*.
2 Pert, *Molecules of Emotion*.
3 Cowell, *The Jataka*, Vol. 3.
4 Meier, *Accelerated Learning Handbook*.
5 McIntosh, *Rekindling Community*.
6 Boshyk & Dilworth, *Action Learning*.
7 Wilson, *Biophilia*, p. 139.
8 Louv, *Last Child in the Woods*.
9 Wilson, *Biophilia*, p. 139.
10 Stibbe, *Handbook of Sustainability Literacy*; Stone, *Ecological Literacy*.
11 Gersie, *Reflections on Therapeutic Storymaking*.
12 Kaplan & Kaplan, 'Preference, Restoration, and Meaningful Action'.
13 Bird, 'Natural Thinking'.
14 Freire, *Pedagogy of the Oppressed*.
15 Gersie & King, *Storymaking in Education and Therapy*.
16 See Gersie & King, *Storymaking in Education and Therapy*, for this activity and related ones.
17 Boal, *Games for Actors and Non-actors*.
18 Cornell, *Sharing Nature with Children*.
19 Fromm, *The Heart of Man*.

CHAPTER 2

The authors, who are storytellers and naturalists, describe
how they deeply familiarised themselves with a small region of
hill country in order to develop 'stories of place'. Here they share:

different ways of getting to know the place, such as ritual walking,
silent sitting, journal keeping, plus other techniques to see the landscape
with new eyes;

~

how they subsequently crafted stories from these ways of 'being in place' which they
then performed for the local community;

~

three stories (fictional, observational, and traditional) that
emerged during their work.

They also explain how a new inner stillness empowered them as
storytellers and environmental facilitators to be more present to
the people they work with, and how this enhances their
ability to effect pro-environmental change.

By Hidden Paths

Developing stories about a local environment
while bearing its ecological challenges in mind

MALCOLM GREEN AND NICK HENNESSEY

How do people get to know a place? Why should they want to? How may they be changed by a place and how may it be changed by them? How may exploring its stories affect their relationship with it? This chapter outlines a 14-month project in which we, two environmentalist story-tellers, explored how a meaningful relationship with a particular locality may be articulated through story. Our aim was to choose a defined area, spend as much time there as possible, and, on the basis of our experiences, devise a performance in which we would tell stories of the place to different audiences. However, the project's investigatory focus was on the *process* of getting to know the locality and then shaping that knowledge into story. To facilitate this, both of us kept detailed field journals.

We decided to work in a location Malcolm already knew quite well, a small area two miles south of Haltwhistle, in the North Pennines Area of Outstanding National Beauty in northern England. Predominantly open moorland, with a wooded river valley running through it, the area included a small village, a primary school, and several outlying farms, and so gave us the opportunity to investigate it through both the people and the natural environment.

'One of man's oldest dreams', says Barry Lopez, 'is to find a dignity that includes all living things. For a relationship with a landscape to be lasting it must be reciprocal.'[1] This implies that respectful awareness of such reciprocity between people and place should be a cornerstone of sustainable living. We wanted to explore how story and storytelling might foster this sense of reciprocity – in our audiences, yes, but first in ourselves, for facilitators of any kind who wish to promote an 'ecological feeling' must model that sensibility in themselves. Gaston Bachelard describes the spaces our intimate lives inhabit as 'scintillating, felicitous (and) eulogized through our immersion in them'.[2] To enter a place is an act of intimacy and to explore it is also an exploration of our own nature. From the outset we aimed to proceed in a spirit of awareness, dignity, and reciprocity, and to treat each creature, person, or object within the place as a significant part of the whole.

Getting to know the place

First and foremost we sensuously immersed ourselves in the area and cultivated what Lopez calls 'techniques of awareness'.[3]

We walked a lot, getting a sense of the place in our bodies, and of our bodies in it, perceiving the place through muscle, breath, sights, sounds, and smells. Sometimes we proceeded very slowly, stopping, using all our senses, covering only a hundred yards in an hour, undoing our habitual tendencies to rush to get somewhere. We got down on hands and knees to look closely at things, for place includes much that lies beyond one's ordinary gaze. We would sit still and observe a single object in nature and notice the relationship formed between object and observer. We would close our eyes and move our body in response to the environment. We talked about what we saw, our perceptions, ourselves, exploring the ways our complex emotional selves are also the medium through which a place is encountered. We became aware of the impact our emotional states had on our perceptions of the place. When we were calmly present, nature would reveal something that was otherwise hidden.[4] We were continually astonished by the worlds that opened up. Malcolm noted such a moment in his field journal:

The Birch Tree [journal entry]

It was a grey, drizzly day I was walking along, more concerned with my own inner thoughts than what was around me, when I stopped wearily by a birch tree. The tree was on the opposite

bank of the burn ... It was tall and freely branched with those
fine delicate birch leaves fluttering in the wind. It dared to be
healthy in that rocky, wild, windswept place. I felt confronted
by its unmoving, unselfconscious, perfect presence in the landscape. And at that moment felt myself pulled into its world ...
felt my own feet on the ground and my own head in the air and
slowly it seeped into me that I was too, another being, absolutely
perfect in the landscape ... For that moment, at least, I knew I
belonged. I nodded gratefully to the tree and walked away.

We also interviewed some local people. In these face-to-face encounters
we became conscious of the agendas we brought with us, which anticipated, and at worst predetermined, the answers we received. We learnt
to ask open questions that let people feel free to share their memories
and experiences: 'How has technology changed the way you work with
the land?' 'In what ways did your community meet up together?' What
we asked and how we asked it had a big impact on what we heard. It was
important to bring to the people who lived in the area the same respect
and openness we sought to bring to the physical landscape.

From encounters to story

The conversations revealed the changing nature of people's relationship
with the land as remembered in stories passed down from as far back as
200 years ago. Many stories were anecdotal, even fragmentary, without
a clear resolution, but they were the stories that had emerged from lives
lived in this area. Thus there were anecdotes of poaching salmon, of out-
witting bailiffs, or of the auctions for the poor at the Methodist church.
All of these would contribute material for the stories of the land we were
beginning to compose. We investigated also the area's folktales and legends. And the land itself told its story through its lumps and bumps and
remnants of past habitation and reminded us that human habitation constitutes only a fraction of a place's stories.

Note-taking and journal writing remained our key practices, not just
for gathering information but also to explore ideas and reflect on our experiences and to find the beginnings of narratives in the diverse material

we gathered. Visiting the same localities regularly, we recorded the changes we observed over time. We asked ourselves questions about how the landscape came to be the way it is. While looking at something, we would sometimes write a continuous stream of consciousness in response to it, taking care neither to premeditate nor to edit what we wrote. We made similar freeform notes of our internal conversation while walking a route, which helped us to understand the relationship between a journey and a story, and how an encounter with landscape provokes a narrative.

We read and discussed what we'd written to see what narratives were emerging. The most promising of these we developed into stories that could be told. Most of the work of story composition was done away from the place. This distance provided space for the imagination to work upon the raw material of experience and information. We gradually evolved four different categories of stories, which occupied a loose continuum. At one end were events rooted in our own direct experience. At the other were events largely created from our or someone else's imagination. The four story categories are: personal, fictional, scientific, and folktale. Though the boundaries between them are fluid (see Introduction), each offers a different way of expressing something about our chosen area and our encounters with it.

Personal stories

These stories emerged directly from our observations and encounters. In them we tried to be true to what we had experienced and thereby to express some insight into what it meant to dwell in the area.[5] The most compelling ones came from moments when we had made ourselves open or vulnerable in such a way that we became more intimately a part of the place and implicated in what we observed. Here's one that Malcolm wrote.

The Nest

It is June and it has been raining hard all day and the river has swollen bigger than I have ever seen it, inundating vast areas of the low-lying land. I crouch under a small hawthorn by a turn in the river. Sand martins miraculously dart between the raindrops, taking food to their young. My clothes are soaked. Rivulets of water stream down my back. I have given up on dry feet and watch the water swirling peaty brown around my legs and through the dense stems of new bracken.

I hear a persistent thin piping noise. I look up and there is a willow warbler edging its way up and down a bracken stem. Calling calling calling. Twisting its head and looking deep into the water as if trying to enter. There is such earnestness in the little green bird's endeavours. It climbs up the stem and down again. The bird is so close I could almost reach out and touch it. It seems to have lost all fear.

It flies off across the river, but is soon back again. It flies back and forth across the swollen river many times, always landing on the same bracken stem. I'm sure that if it could dive into that churning water it would. I wonder what is there. What is it looking for?

At last I guess. I wade over to the bracken stalk and immerse my hand in the water. At the base of the stalk I find what I expected. I carefully lift it out. A small nest with five speckled eggs. I put it on a mound and walk back. The bird comes, momentarily lands on it, but is soon away. I realise what a futile effort I've made. The bird could no more sit exposed like that than I could sit in a burning house. I take the nest back in my hand. It is neat and beautiful and I place it back in the water. It belongs to the river now.

The next morning the river has subsided. The nest is gone, but I find one small egg. It breaks in my hand. An almost fully formed young one inside. No wonder the mother was so determined.

Localised fiction

In these stories we created an imagined scene inspired by something seen or heard: by an abandoned millstone in a quarry, the ruins of a Romano-British settlement, a plaque on the lip of the valley, the remains of a prisoner-of-war camp, and by conversations with local people – about young men poaching, a steamroller hitting the Methodist chapel, a drunken man finding God. They evoked a relationship between people and place that was outside our own experience. They led us to research some relevant subject matter and explore the wider context of historical events that may have impacted on the area. We imagined possible encounters that reflected the relationship between people and place. We created characters and placed them in a historical moment when something happened that could epitomise that relationship. The challenge was to transform the information we'd acquired into a well-shaped story while at the same time representing the place, its history, and its people as authentically as we could. Through exercising our imagination like this we became, in effect, a part of the area's stories.

Here's one example. A local resident had told us that the map displaying the boundaries of newly enclosed land had been kept under a particular pew in the church. From this small snippet of information, contextualised by research into the period, Nick devised the following story.

The Awarded Ways

On 1 August 1859, Joseph Forster of Barnstonhead, Thomas Teesdale of Parsonshield, Sowerby the keeper, Thomas Bell the waller, John George Frederick Hope-Wallace, the laird of the Featherstone estate, and Clarke the land agent gathered in the Burnstones Inn, Knaresdale, to discuss the 'Awarded Ways' – access ways through the newly enclosed land. As Forster began to read the agenda, old Maggie Nixon entered the room.

'I've come to speak and I've come to be heard.' Three weeks before, Mrs Nixon's husband had died and now she had to care for their sheep on her own. 'The first time I walked them up to the moor, what did I find between me and the common land but a wall – a wall blocking me from my God-given liberty to graze sheep on the open land!'

'It's the way the world is going,' Clarke explained. 'It's the future of farming, the bright future of the countryside. Whilst it may seem a curtailment of your liberties at first, you'll soon find that the Enclosures Act has great benefits for us all.'

'How can there be great benefit when I can't feed even my own?'

'We can't stand in the way of it, Mrs Nixon.'

'If I can't stand in its way, tell me how I may get round it! Where can I walk in this land of God's that you've chosen to take from the meek?'

The men took her to the map under the front pew in the church. When they had rolled out the great map, Mrs Nixon saw there the familiar curves of the burn, the bluff, the tracks and roads, and then she saw the straight lines of the walls that sliced and split the land. She slumped down on the pew with her head in her hands.

'God save us from your laws and maps! And God save us from your bright future!'

Scientific stories

Scientific narratives can be off-putting, but when put alongside more familiar forms of story they can convey something of the complexity, sensitivity, and scale of natural processes that have occurred in a place and made it what it is. We explored scientific narratives about geological events and the life cycles of organisms. Close to where we camped during our visits we found the fossil of a lepidodendron – a giant clubmoss that had stood in a forest 300 million years ago, on a continent situated at that time far away in the tropics. The fossil was at once a symbolic and physical manifestation of the immense history of the place. We developed a story, too long to include here, that condensed the whole period of time from the Carboniferous to the end of the last ice age, including eventually the arrival of humans in this part of the world. This story communicates vast stretches of time that the imagination struggles to absorb in any other form, and, in doing so, puts our human presence in the place in perspective.

Folktales

Our research threw up a few local folktales that told us something about the time in which they were collected, but that we thought unpromising for our specific exploration. There was one tale, however, that really captured the atmosphere of the moors: 'The Deurgar', originally collected in the Simonside Hills a dozen miles to the north. The truth of this story lies in the realm of metaphor. Its meaning cannot be pinned down. The story leaves the listener with a sense of things outside our ken that prompt deep questions to think about.

The Duergar

One morning, a man looked out of the window at a hill and decided he wanted to know that hill. So he walked through the village, crossed the river, and took the path up the steep slope. He walked all day until, as the sun began to set, a mist fell, and he was lost. Stumbling through the mist and heather, he came to a small stone hut. There was no answer to his knock, so went in. He was delighted to see a raging fire in the hearth, and pulled up a chair to get warm. As the last daylight faded, a little old man came in, bent as a root and brown as the earth. The two men stared at each other. When the fire was nearly spent, the young man threw on a log. The old man gave a mocking a laugh. The log burned swiftly with a pale heatless flame till it was all but ash. The old man picked up another log and cracked it across his knee, shattering it into countless splinters. He put one of these on the embers and to the young man's astonishment it burned with great heat and colour. Time and time again the old man fed the fire with tiny fragments of wood, each burning long and hot, till the last was spent and the room was dark again. One more log lay by the hearth. When the young man reached for it, he heard the old man laugh. Then suddenly he was gone, and the hut too, and the fire, and the young man was alone on the moor in the misty moonless night. Soon enough the sun rose, the mist lifted, and the young man headed for home, but as he walked he wondered what that long night had brought him, and what he was left with.[6]

Performance and process

The performance in which the project culminated stitched together stories of these different genres within an extempore frame narrative that told the story of our project through the unfolding year. All the other stories were thereby contextualised within the account of our personal experience. Although we did shape this personal narrative somewhat to fit the performance's structure, it was the basic authenticity of our account that engaged the audience, drew their imagination into their local landscape, and enabled them to make sense of the whole.[7]

Many people who attended the shows told us that they perceived the landscape with a new and heightened awareness afterwards. In enabling us to give something back to this locality in return for what we received from it, we see the performance as an act of reciprocity. But the process was the chief motivation of the project, and the greatest impact of the work was on ourselves.

Stillness and sustainability

We entered the place with no need to use the land to make a living like the farmer or the gamekeeper. We had no management agenda like the conservationist and no destination like the rambler. We lacked the knowledge that comes from dependency on the land, and frequently we questioned our right to say anything about the locality. But we developed a different kind of knowing, one that transformed our own perceptions. Our purpose was simply to be present and *do* nothing, and so enter into a conversation with the place. This was a challenge, arriving as we did from elsewhere with rushing minds from rushing traffic, but when we managed to stop and be still, a relationship of reciprocity developed between us and the place and the beings that inhabit it. From this stillness the stories emerged. Through our having become intimately part of a place, our inner imagined landscape brought forth our experience of the natural landscape, so that when we now come to tell stories we are – in some sense – more able to give voice to place.

Such inner stillness is a quality that we believe storytellers and environmental facilitators need to cultivate in order to be truly present for the people they work with. Ruth Sawyer writes, 'The best of the traditional storytellers I have known have been those who live close to the heart of things – to the earth, the sea, wind and weather ... those who knew solitude, silence. They have been given unbroken time in which to feel deeply, to reach constantly for understanding.'[8] The absence of a utilitarian agenda gave to the time that we spent in the field a sacred quality – and allowed the place, for us, to acquire a sacred quality too, a bit like the sacred places that indigenous people have honoured in many parts of the world. The stillness we were privileged to experience in our 'sacred place' has helped to sustain us as storytellers and environmentalists; at the same time, we believe, the recovery of a sense of the sacredness of place is key to sustaining a healthy reciprocal relationship with the land and its creatures. Stories and storytelling are a vital part of this, for through them a connection is made between our outer and inner landscapes.

We invite you to try out the methods we've described to get to know a chosen area in reach of where you live, in order to nurture your own connectedness to place and thereby bring deeper stillness and ecological feeling to the groups of people you work with. To focus the intention of the process, we suggest you define some tangible outcome. This need not be a performance; it could be a batch of stories to use in field interpretation, or a piece of writing, or the adaptation of the process for use in groupwork to enable others to discover a deeper, reciprocal relationship with a place.

Notes

[1] Lopez, *Arctic Dreams*, p. 405.

[2] Bachelard, *Poetics of Space*, p. xxxv.

[3] Lopez, *About This Life*, p. 114.

[4] See Abram, *The Spell of the Sensuous*.

[5] Berry, *Jayber Crow*.

[6] Summary of oral retelling. Inspired by Grice, *Folktales of the North Country*, pp. 130–133.

[7] Garner, *The Voice that Thunders*.

[8] Sawyer, *The Way of the Storyteller*, p. 29.

CHAPTER 3

How do you choose stories that will inspire constructive
choices about the way we treat our environment? Eric offers four
traditional stories carefully selected to serve four different purposes:

to bring a group of different professionals together so they can usefully
communicate with each other;

~

to challenge adults to think about something they might prefer to ignore;

~

to promote values and qualities we need to nurture if we are to live sustainably;

~

to clarify a problematic situation and stimulate thought by presenting
an unresolved dilemma.

We learn how these stories and purposes relate to the challenge of
sustainability and to particular organisational and educational
contexts in which these and similar stories can be used.

The Sustaining Story

How to choose stories for storywork and inspire constructive choices in relation to issues of environmental concern

ERIC MADDERN

As a storyteller my core audience has been in schools and festivals, but I've also worked at historic sites, forests, parks, zoos, and museums.[1] My primary aim has always been to bring these places alive with folktale, myth, and legend, sometimes also drawing on history and science. I've found that a well-chosen tale often elicits a positive, heartfelt, even transformative response. Something is touched deep down. It can be like a wake-up call.

Sometimes I look for a story that will inspire ecological awareness. It helps, when looking, to be familiar with a wide range of stories (see Ramsden, this volume). But in the end what matters most is not how many stories you know but how much you care about the ones you know. A story you love can be told in many ways to a variety of audiences for different ends. That doesn't mean any story will work any time, anywhere. You need to develop a sense of the impact of the story and an intuition about the right time to tell it. This comes from trying stories out in many settings. Of course, listeners will respond differently depending on their background and needs. But usually there is a sense of shared communion in a story audience.

Familiarity with a story means you can, to a degree, improvise, varying the pace, the point of view, and the particulars. Sometimes you may even step outside the story to offer asides, give commentary, and embed the tale in a larger conversation (see Manwaring, this volume). The more conversant you are with a story, the more it becomes part of you and the freer you are to play with it creatively.

In this chapter I give examples of traditional tales I've told to serve four different purposes relating to the task of sustaining and restoring the world:

1. to unify disparate groups of people so they can usefully talk to each other;

2. to challenge people to think about something they'd prefer to ignore;

3. to promote qualities we need to nurture if we're to live sustainably;

4. to clarify a situation and stimulate thought by presenting a simple unresolved dilemma.

A story to bring people together

Some time ago I took part in a conference, held on the edge of an English forest, about how woodlands can and should work for people in Britain. Several 'tribal' groups had gathered here. There were *foresters* who saw trees as timber, an economic resource to be grown, felled, and sold; *scientists* for whom forests were primarily carbon sinks helping to moderate climate change; *conservationists* who loved biodiversity and sought to maximise it; *historians* who studied how forests change through time; *amenity providers* who believed that access to the woods (as outdoor classrooms or recreational spaces) nourishes people's awareness and well-being; and a *storyteller* who told tales about trees.

Groups with different professional agendas can find it difficult to see beyond their own perspective and accept and value other views. They use jargon that can obscure as much as illuminate. I was asked to lead a warm-up to help the participants go beyond their professional allegiances and find areas of overlap where their interests and understanding met. It struck me that each 'tribe' represented part of a greater whole – the world of working with trees. I wondered if that greater whole could be represented by one tree, and whether taking a fresh look at a single tree might prove instructive for this multiplicity of tree workers. A simple Welsh folktale about looking at trees came to mind.

The Tree with Three Fruits

There was once a young man called Baglan. His saintly teacher, Illtud, recognised Baglan's virtue and sanctity and sent him with a brass-handled crook to find a tree with three fruits. There he was to build a church. Baglan set out, following the way his crook led him, looking for a tree with, he expected, apples, pears, and plums. But nowhere did he find one. At last he stopped under a great spreading oak on a hill and dozed off. When he woke he heard the sound of a sow rooting among the acorns with a litter of piglets. He smiled. Then he looked up and saw wild bees flying in an out of a hole halfway up the tree. Mmmm, honey! His thoughts were interrupted by the song of a blackbird warbling at the top of the tree. He leapt to his feet as he realised that this was the tree with three fruits. Not apples, pears, and plums at all, but piglets, honey, and birdsong![2]

With this story ringing in their ears, I asked everyone to go into the forest and take 20 minutes looking, with a soft, unbroken focus, at a tree of their choice; they were to simply register thoughts and feelings that arose. They returned from this experience to find a diagram of a tree drawn on the whiteboard. The roots were labelled 'piglets', the trunk and branches 'honey', and the leaves, flowers, and fruit 'birdsong'. I invited everyone to report back something they'd thought or felt while looking at their chosen tree. We discussed where the gist of each statement should be scribbled on the tree picture: near the top, the trunk, or the base. Not all of their observations fitted into this simple threefold classification. Nonetheless we agreed that 'timber', 'firewood', 'monetary value', 'carbon store', and 'ecosystem services' should be rooting in the acorns with the pigs. 'Moss', 'epiphytic ferns', 'lichen', 'symbiosis', 'shade', 'flowers', 'insects', and 'wildlife' flitted in and out with the bees. And 'play', 'music', 'peace', 'proportion', 'strength', 'memory', 'reassurance', 'heart', 'transcendence', and 'community' perched up among the blackbirds.

I then invited people to talk for five minutes with one or two others about any connections between the statements they'd offered and the three parts of the tree. During feedback to the whole group, we came to see that the piglets symbolised Economy, the capacity of the forest to provide sustenance to human communities. The bees represented Ecology, the capacity of the forest to provide interconnected niches for a myriad of wild beings. And birdsong in the flowers and foliage stood for Education, the capacity of the forest to expand the mind and uplift the spirit. These three E's were the forest's three fruits. Next I invited the participants to separate into their 'tribal' groups to reflect on their affiliation with these three fruits. The result was: the foresters considered themselves primarily affiliated with Economy, the conservationists and scientists with Ecology, and the amenity providers with Education. All played a part in the greater whole.

A tree does not compete with itself; rather its parts complete it. So it is in the human world as well as the world of the forest. The telling of this story and the subsequent activities facilitated a respectful communication between these diverse professional groups.

A story to challenge

Later that evening I told stories and sang songs beside a fire in a forest clearing. The first story I told is grim and does not have a happy ending. Some find it uncomfortable or even dislike it. Yet it's such an apt metaphor for what we're doing to the world today that I feel impelled to tell it. It's a 'wake-up' story. In choosing to tell a tale like this, I take inspiration from the idea that traditionally the bard was both a 'poet' and a 'prophet' – a 'poet' whose talent included storytelling and a 'prophet' whose duty it was 'to speak boldly to the people, and even to the king, of things they might not wish to hear'.[3] That prophetic role is unfashionable these days, yet it has a long pedigree and remains, I believe, an important service of the arts – including storytelling – to society.[4]

Inevitably a storyteller's choice of story is influenced by his or her values. It's important to be conscious of those values as well as the practical reasons for choosing a story. That night by the fire I told the following ancient Greek tale because it alerts us to the insatiable hunger of consumerism and because at its heart is the story of a tree.

Erysichthon and the Curse of Insatiable Hunger

Erysichthon was a king who wanted to build a great feasting hall. He ordered men to cut timber from across the land but they couldn't find trees tall enough to span the roof. The only place where such trees grew was in an ancient grove sacred to Demeter, Goddess of Plenty. Erysichthon, who only mocked the gods, ordered his men to fell those trees. But when they reached the most sacred one of all, a prodigious oak festooned with offerings and circled by dancing nymphs, the men refused. Erysichthon furiously seized an axe and began chopping. A voice cried, 'I am the spirit of this tree and I curse you!' But he kept cutting until the great tree shuddered to the ground. The nymphs fled to Demeter, bewailing the desecration. The ripening harvest shivered as the goddess listened. Then she condemned Erysichthon to an insatiable hunger.

Hunger is an emaciated goddess who has to do Plenty's bidding. Demeter commanded her to possess Erysichthon's belly: 'Let everything I pour down that fool's gullet only deepen his emptiness.' So Hunger flew to the house where Erysichthon lay asleep, planted her shrunken mouth upon his, and breathed into him a hurricane of starvation. Erysichthon dreamed of banquets but could see only death. His stomach wrenched him awake. He called for food. Great platters were brought but they weren't enough. He called for more but nothing satisfied him. His gullet was like a bottomless void. He consumed his entire wealth. He even sold his only daughter to feed his hunger. Nothing was enough. He became an ugly, monstrous, ravenous brute. Finally the inevitable happened. He began savaging his own limbs and in one final feast he devoured ... himself.[5]

In my view Erysichthon's story illustrates how civilisation drives us to cut down the most sacred tree, to extract the last drop of oil, all for the sake of satisfying what is an insatiable hunger. With the advent of agriculture and city life it seems humanity came to see nature as a resource to be exploited rather than a sacred gift to be venerated. We were blinded by our pursuit of ever-greater wealth and cursed with an endless craving so severe that we became willing to sell our kin into slavery, as Erysichthon did his daughter. If we consider that the air we breathe blows round the world and much of the food we eat is flown round the world, it is difficult to say where one person begins and ends. As we devour the world so we are, in a way, devouring ourselves.

This story may not be comfortable to hear but it can prompt discussion about humanity's impact on nature, about what we mean by 'resources', about consumerism and whether or not our cravings are insatiable, about what is meant by 'sacred' and what it means to 'mock the gods'. It offers a way to acknowledge the destruction caused by the ceaseless consumption of resources and to reflect on what is the right thing to do.

A story to inspire

Telling the story of Erysichthon is like presenting 'the problem'. It needs to be followed by one or more stories that are hopeful and uplifting, that offer, in part, a solution. For this purpose I'm drawn to short 'wisdom tales'. They come from many traditions, are easy to learn, often have one striking image, and vividly encapsulate a positive value. Such values may not be explicitly about sustainability, but they help to build a picture of how we need to live in order not to devour the Earth. For me they include courage, creativity, friendship, resilience, nature, community, and vision.

The following simple folktale illustrates another vital quality we need in these troubled times: compassion.

The Most Beautiful Thing in the World

A king was growing old. He had three daughters. To decide who should wear the crown after him he gave each one a bag of gold and asked them to bring him the most beautiful thing in the world. The oldest visited wonderful markets, looking at beautiful things. She found a painter finishing a glorious picture, decided it was the most beautiful thing, and paid for it with her gold. The second daughter visited jewellers, seeking a precious gem. She found a gleaming pearl, decided this was it, and bought it with her coins. The youngest daughter wandered among her father's people, seeking beauty but finding only sadness and need. Many were ragged and hungry, homeless and weary. Wanting to help, she gave away one gold coin after another. As bellies were filled and new homes were built, joy spread across the city. When it came time for the daughters to present the most beautiful thing in the world, the king was impressed by the painting and the pearl. But when the youngest daughter hung her head and said, 'Father I have nothing beautiful to show,' her father replied, 'You're wrong, my dear. News of your kindness has come to me daily. You've shown the most beautiful thing of all – a kind heart. So you will wear my crown.'[6]

The youngest daughter didn't seem to care much about the crown. She cared more about the people she saw suffering around her. She gave away her wealth to help them without a thought for her future. Not only was she moved to acts of generosity by her compassion; she also acted selflessly and courageously with the faith that it was the right thing to do. With inequality increasing in many places today, perhaps the lesson for us now is that generosity is far more beautiful than greed.

A story to make you think

Another kind of story I use to strike a more uplifting note is the 'dilemma tale'. These often clarify a complex situation in simple metaphorical form. The ending is usually unresolved, leaving the listeners with a dilemma, a discussion to have, a decision to make. In many communities these stories were traditionally used as an educational tool.

Bird in the Hand

Once, just outside a remote village, lived a wise old man. Whenever people from the village needed advice they would take their question to him and he invariably had a wise answer. Everyone in the village was happy to have him living nearby, except for one youth who, for some reason, was irked by the old man always being right.

'He can't be right all the time,' he thought. 'I'm going to play a trick and prove him wrong.' He came up with a clever plan. In the woods he captured a small bird and, cupping it in his hands, went to the old man. 'Old man,' he said, 'you are very wise. Can you tell me, is what I have in my hands alive or dead?'

Now the old man knew the boy had a bird in his hands. Perhaps he saw a telltale feather flutter to the ground. Perhaps he picked up the vibration of the bird. He also knew that if he said the bird was alive the boy would crush it in his hands and it would be dead. If he said it was dead the boy would open his hands and the bird would fly away. So, in his wisdom, the old man said, 'The answer to your question is in your own hands. It's up to you whether that bird lives or dies.'[7]

I told this story at the launch of Somoho, the Soweto Mountain of Hope, during the Johannesburg Summit on Sustainable Development in 2002. The audience included both local people and delegates from around the world. At the end of the story I added that the earth is like that bird. We have it in our hands. It's fragile. If we take too much without giving back we'll crush it. But if we nourish and nurture it then it will take wing and fly. Each one of us can make a difference. Many in the audience came up afterwards and were clearly touched by the story.

When I told the same story at the annual gathering of an environmental organisation, the director approached me afterwards with a smile and his hands cupped as if holding a bird. 'Yes,' he said. 'That's it! That's it!' A simple strong image like that can have a lot of power.

Conclusion

There are many reasons for telling stories: to convey a wise insight, to shock people into a new awareness, to create sympathy, to inspire action, and simply to give pleasure. And there is a whole 'tree of tales'[8] to choose from – myths, legends, folktales, history, science, personal experience, and more (see Hennessey & Green, this volume). Finding the right story for a particular occasion is not an exact science. Finding one that nudges an audience towards action to sustain and restore the world is an intuitive and personal art. I've given examples of ways I've done it in this chapter. You'll find your own. But above all perhaps what you'll discover is that storytelling is, in itself, an act of sustainability. It's timeless, lightweight, and independent of technology. It consumes nothing. It needs only a willing listener. And a voice to tell.

Notes

[1] Maddern, *Storytelling at Historic Sites*.

[2] Summary of oral retelling. Full text in East & Maddern, *Spirit of the Forest*.

[3] Nanson, *Words of Re-enchantment*, p. 163.

[4] Heinrich, 'The Artist as Bard'.

[5] Summary of oral retelling. Sources: Ovid, *Metamorphoses*; Hughes, *Tales from Ovid*; Callimachus, *Hymn to Demeter*.

[6] Summary of oral retelling. Source: Walker, *Most Beautiful Thing in the World*. I heard this story from Cath Little, who changed the sons in the original story to daughters, as she wanted a story to inspire girls to think about inner beauty.

[7] Summary of oral retelling. Sources: Jaffe & Zeitlin, *While Standing on One Foot*; Kornfield & Feldman, *Soul Food*.

[8] Tolkien, *Tree and Leaf*.

CHAPTER 4

Many nature wardens, teachers, and group facilitators try
to help group participants make up stories that develop strong,
enjoyable connections with where they live or work. Gordon
explores how this can be done. He offers:

innovative ideas about how to make up new stories on the basis of a
traditional story pattern to impart interest and significance to a place
both now and for the future;

~

stimulating activities that tap into the richness of adults' or children's creativity;

~

a rationale for why it matters to do this work from an environmental perspective.

Gordon suggests that strong links exist between our enjoyment of
a place and the motivation to behave in more sustainable ways.
The made-up stories bear witness to what this means.

Stories in Place

Exciting story-based activities to help children and adults
discover and connect with the environment where they live

GORDON MACLELLAN

I t is easy to be right. To know what other people should do, what they
ought to know, what message we want a story to convey. This is as
true for environmental issues as for anything else. Most of us have a
list of principles that we think others should follow or ideas they should
believe. But I am wary of telling or creating stories that teach specific lessons. It is also very easy to be wrong. Good stories aren't that controllable.
People will take from them what they will, and the lesson one person
finds may be completely different from that found by another. The giant
who squashed his young friend might be a monster for one person but
might for someone else just be the extreme end of the spectrum of the
game that went too far and 'someone got hurt. Doesn't mean the giant
was bad.' Virtuous stories tend not to work for me. Stories are there to
engage, to entertain, and to appal or enchant. They are also there, I'd say,
to challenge people into thinking for themselves and to offer moments
of empathy with a hero, a villain, a monster, Jack-the-Lad, or Jill-the-Lass.

I therefore look for stories that will give people something to think or
talk about, stories that offer choices, wake emotions, and shake loose a
certain dark humour. And somewhere in all that I will try to wake people
up to the need for 'sustainability' without telling them what they already
know about reusing, recycling, repairing, alternative transport, energy
conservation, Old Uncle Tom Cobbly and all. The thread that guides me
through this maze is the experience of 'home'.

'Ecology', the science that lies behind our understanding of the world
and our place in it, comes from the Greek 'logos' and 'oikos': the knowl-

edge of home. Concepts from ecology are the springboard of my story-work around sustainability, in the sense at least that this work can remind people of the importance of home, of place, and of their connection to all that lives. In other words, I set out to strengthen people's relationships with the world around them.

'Homes' are a good place to begin. Traditional tales, and stories made during workshops, remind people of their homes and the value and importance of place. Be it house and home, or street, neighbour-hood, town, community, or wider landscape, 'home' calls to the emotions and offers starting points, physically and emotionally, that most of us share. You may anchor a new story in people's homes or neighbour-hoods, or simply in a nearby field, hedge, or tree, in expectation that such a story stands a good chance of being retold to friends and family. Seeing the tree or opening the door will remind our storymakers of their compositions. In this chapter I shall focus on ways and whys of drawing stories out of the immediate environment to explore emotional connections between people and the places they live in. These activities are not meant to produce finished products; they are starting points, to try on your own or with a group, to find pathways into stories from the place called home.

Making new stories

To create a new story with a group, we might start by simply finding or noticing three things. We don't plan in advance or try to anticipate what will happen; we just pick something up and start talking. 'The first clue to this adventure is this' (moss: a giant's eyebrows). Then add something else as we wander: 'A dry twig, like this one, snapped behind me and ...' Stories can overlap to incorporate each other's finds. I may feed in prompts: 'Make sure the next thing tells us something about our hero' – or a villain, a problem, a treasure. My suggestions about clues guide things in the most general of directions; the specific stories grow with the participants. With a group in the English county of Staffordshire, the following story grew out of moss, twigs, mud, and a sense of danger:

The Giant Stone

A boy was walking home across the fields near Longnor, where he lived, when he heard a twig snap behind him. Looking back, he couldn't see anything special but there were shadows by the hedge and shadows in the trees behind the hedge. He kept walking. A bit faster now. He heard a rustle, a sigh, a thump. Looking back, he saw one of the shadows step away from the hedge. He saw the feet first when they thumped on the ground and then the big hands with fingers as thick as branches and then the giant's face with red, glaring eyes and a huge nose. The boy ran. He ran as fast as he could down the hill towards the river. He heard the giant run after him, great thumping footsteps to his quick stamping ones [Sound effects!]. He ran as fast as he could but the giant was getting closer and closer. He could hear his own breath and his heartbeat pounding. He could hear the giant's breath like a snorting bull or a train running him down. He splashed through a puddle and then squelched across a swampy bit of grass by the river. Behind him came a splash and an angry shout and a noise like an elephant having a bath. The boy stopped and looked back. The giant was sinking in the soft, swampy ground! He sank up to the tops of his shoes and as he tried to pull his feet out he kept sinking – up to his knees, his waist, his chest! The boy ran forward, wondered if he should help. The giant was up to his shoulders, his neck. As the mud reached his chin, the giant closed his bright, red eyes and the boy turned and ran home. He dragged his mum down to the field to show her the giant, but when they got there, there was only a great round boulder in the middle of the swamp. The boy thought he could see a shape like a nose, maybe ears. Those rushes might be hair. The moss might be eyebrows ... A mouse was living up the hole that might be a nostril and a rabbit was hiding in one of the earholes. And there was no giant. Just a faint footprint. And of course that rock had always been there! His mum dragged him home again. But that night, and for the rest of his life, the boy found that if he crept out of his house late at night, and took some cake with him, the giant would wake up, eat the cake, and the boy and the giant would share news of today and stories of long ago. And if you don't believe our story you can walk across the fields near Longnor and find the Giant Stone. If you're lucky there's a rabbit on the giant's head to give him a warning, for the giant will never open his eyes and talk to you unless you take cake and juice and sit beside him and share a picnic.

What comes out of this story? Something about the unpredictable, and about when to intervene in times of trouble, and that any feature of a landscape can have a story. There is also something about the power of secrets, and the experts or grown-ups who don't believe what we know. Making up new stories like this one gives a group the chance to explore their experiences in the outdoors imaginatively. As adults, or experts, or environmentalists, we may not be wrong in our plans and hopes and guidelines for environmental action, but we may be limited in our im-aginings of how other people experience the outdoor world. Both newly made and traditional stories can set people free to speculate about what they experience: wildly, creatively, hopefully.

Talking about stories of home

I would like the stories a group makes to remind them of the power of walking down their home street, or to evoke the exile's longing for home, or to foster understanding of a new landscape. To begin storymaking, we may play with the strength of an opening sentence. We can grow first lines from weather and observation: 'On a cold, windy day, when even the crows weren't flying, a boy walked alone along the street ...' 'In this dull, grey town, where no one ever smiled, there was once a girl who laughed too much ...'

In a session with some teenagers I set out to make and tell stories about their hometown. We began by talking about trees in streets and parks which they knew as individuals – trees that were important to them. The stories that grew out of those first ideas were very revealing about loneliness and the support these young people found in the branches of trees. Their classmates received these tree stories with remarkable gen-tleness. I had planned that this activity would lead into looking at the structure of stories, but the group sidetracked into a discussion about some trees they had planted the year before and about their dawning re-alisation that this had set stories in motion for children a hundred years from now. They hoped the children of the future would find a similar sense of friendship in these new trees. This then fed into a conversation about the school's eco-committee and whether and how its policies made a difference, both to the trees and to the quality of life of current students and maybe to future generations'.

When I work with issues of place, I often notice this natural evolution from discussion of what matters here and now to concern for the future, as well as a shifting focus from the personal to the general and from the intimate to the technological.

Story-poems from the here and now

The immediate environment, the world we can walk through, see, listen to, touch, smell, and fall over in, is probably our best source of inspiration for stories. Story-poems can grow even more quickly than stories out of our experience of that environment, and they can offer a chance to ex-plore and express the emotional connections between people, places, and wildlife. Emotions do not need to be described vividly to be conveyed in a story or poem. Simply describing the moment can offer your listeners their own opportunity to form an emotional connection. In the making, the telling, and the listening we may meet the possibility of a reconnec-tion, of new environmental awareness.

Story-poem exercise

Stop for a moment and step outside these words. Look at where you are, where you live, work, travel, or play. Think of this immediate environ-ment as a place where adventures happen. Feel your way into your sur-roundings. We are all storytellers. We can all enjoy our words. So take some paper and a pen and write a quick list of words inspired by where you are. Focus on your senses: sight, sound, touch, taste, smell. Then let some words join other words and make short phrases, sentences, one-line images. 'Sitting by this wall, I hear ...' Sort your phrases into a sequence you like. Shape a brief story-poem of place. Think of it as a spell to get someone else to sit where you sit and to breathe this place.

Here are three examples of story-poems written by workshop participants:

The darkness in the city at night.
Darkness between the streetlamps.
Light gleams on puddles.
There are cars but the street feels quiet.
I am as quiet
as the street,
as the shadows,
as the fox trotting across the end of the road.

Barefoot is the only way to really walk this path.
Rough and risky.
No shoes or sandals can convey the timeworn smoothness of
polished limestone,
the pattern of warmth and coolness marked by the moving shadows
of the day.
Barefoot connects me with centuries of other feet
and paws and hooves and snake scale-bellies and snail-slimy feet
that have used these stones,
this ancient path up into the hills,
worn it to this 21st-century polish.

Empty windows, no one watching the lawns and the long drive now ...
the curved bridge was built for carriages and only has our feet and
baby-buggies now ...
children played here once and still play here now –
different children, different centuries, different games, same laughter.

These story-poems have value in themselves, and it's great to hear them read out, but some may be potential seedlings of longer stories. Listen for the words that open the doors of imagination: watch for them in people's faces. Don't be afraid of anger, or sorrow, or endings that fade into uncertainty like the mist. Don't judge a poem or story by the applause but by the laughter that swallows the punchline or the silence before any clapping starts. Encourage the group members to quietly reflect on the impact of the story-poems and suggest refinements, sharing this with the poems' authors either in speech or written on slips of paper.

The Counting Ghost

I was sitting with a group of children by an old packhorse bridge, working on poems about the river and 'What do people do here?', when we started telling this story about another school visit at another time:

> Children on a school trip, enjoying an old packhorse bridge, an uneven, mossy-stone, arching span over a river, one child or one packhorse wide. Exciting! Under the bridge there might be trolls. Children take photos. But as they sit down to draw the bridge in their sketchbooks they realise they are not alone, that another child is with them on the riverbank. Sitting quietly on a stone with bare feet and ragged clothes is a boy about the same age as them, tears in his eyes as he counts the stones of the bridge. The children crowd round and talk to the new boy, discover that he came on a school trip, just like they have, and just like them he enjoyed playing on the bridge and just like them he sat down and looked at the bridge. But his teacher told him he couldn't go home until he had counted all the stones in the bridge and whenever he nearly got to the end of the counting he got confused. Had he counted this one twice? Had he missed out that one? So he has been sitting here for ages and ages, and the children, looking at him, thought longer than that … How can they help? They rummage in pockets, find sweets, sandwiches, a football, a mobile phone, a magic marker, and some playground chalk … [Expand the list!] Choosing the chalk rather than the magic marker, they count with the tatty

boy, while Amina and Bilal hang over the edge of the bridge and chalk a cross on each stone as it is counted. At long last, after a hundred years of counting, the tatty boy counts all the stones of the bridge and, as the last stone gets its chalk cross, he stands up, smiles at his new friends, and disappears.

After a story has been told, we may discuss what it says about how we behave towards one another and relate to the world that supports us. What does 'The Counting Ghost' have to say? Something about compassion regardless of stereotypes (ghosts aren't always scary), readiness to help, and that solutions can be improvised and adventures happen anywhere. The discussion may initially have nothing to do with climate change, food security, or transport policies. The twenty-first-century ecological context – the obstacles to surviving in one's larger home – grows out of more personal reflections.

Charting possibilities for the future

Here is an activity for making stories with a group about ways the place where they live may change in the future:

Group story-making exercise

On big sheets of paper, let the group or subgroups brainstorm ideas about a central question such as: 'What should our town be like in a hundred years?' or 'If we were the river, what would we want to change?' Encourage everyone to scribble, scrawl, or draw as many ideas as possible without editing or censoring unless they absolutely have to. Then shape those ideas into short phrases and sentences: 'Feeding fields. Watering cattle. I want to run all the way to the sea. I want to feel fish swimming through me and crocodiles and children and hippos.' Ask the group how these sentences might fit into a story? Might they be the voice of the future, or a secret message hidden on a pirate's map, or the words a hero hears as the wind blows through the rushes. Make up a story together as a group or in subgroups, and talk about the stories.

When working in South Africa I was very taken by some conversations with young people from township schools. We had told stories, created story-poems, and made puppets on the theme of what they would like to change about their lives. Initially, no one talked about better houses or water or food. The most important thing to change was the opportunity for their whole family to be together. For these young people 'room for all the family' was the most important sustainability goal, more appealing than effective sanitation.

We then explored possible futures with an exercise like the one above. One group worked with 'Future Environments', about the freedom of a river to run clear and be full of fish again. Another group worked on 'Future Families', about people's freedom to gather together. By rooting their ideas in the here and now these young people mapped ways in which their world could, or should, change. They generated desired possibilities. For them 'sustainability' was more about people and social change than about technological change. Any wish to know more about the latter grew out of desires about the former.

Home, hope ... and what about change?

I have noticed again and again that 'home' is a word that people respond to – usually positively or at least as a beacon of positive hope in the face of immediate troubles. As the South African example demonstrates, the sharing and discussion of stories in a group quickly show what the participants value in their homes as well as how such concerns might extend into wider action. When we look at the world around us, where does 'home' end?

But people's creation of stories about a place they know does not necessarily mean that they will make up powerful ecological stories. I go into this work hoping that the process will engage people more closely with landscapes that matter to them: either with the one we are working in or more generally in the world around them. I hope they may more easily recognise their neighbourhood as a place where adventures do happen and where they can find something they value.

Does this encourage people to change their behaviour in the direction of more sustainable ways of living? My role is often fleeting. Only occasionally is my input part of a longer-term programme. By the end of a project I may be able to tick a set of boxes about knowledge imparted, pro-cesses explored, discussions held, but I cannot realistically claim that I effected change. And the people involved may not recognise the impact of the experience for years, if ever. So I do not expect that every session will generate more sustainability-oriented citizens. I find it rewarding enough when stories we shaped the year before are still being told in a school, or that someone still tells the tale of the Giant Stone near Longnor. In the end my work is about installing hope and inspiration: both for the people I work with and for myself.

CHAPTER 5

The Hindu image of Indra's net of jewels conveys the
idea that everything in the world is connected to everything else
– a schema that is becoming ever more manifest in ecological science
(and network theory). Ashley presents:

his experience that, with the right intention and methodology, almost
any story you ask a group to work with can speak to the particular
current needs of each participant;

~

structured creative activities that facilitate this process;

~

four traditional stories.

He describes why this work can nurture the kind of cooperative fellow
feeling among the individuals in a group that we need when
facing up to the challenges of sustainability.

Jewels on Indra's Net

*How experiential storywork can generate a deep sense of the
world's interconnectedness which can set people on a path
towards more sustainable behaviour*

ASHLEY RAMSDEN

Calling to us from all sides is a complex and delightful truth: the
interdependence of all that is. The science of ecology has charted
the web of dependencies and feedback loops among the earth's organisms and non-living constituents. The new science of network theory
has uncovered webs of connectedness almost everywhere one looks: in
the chemistry of living cells, in the brain, the immune system, finance
markets, our social networks, and of course in the internet.[1] This idea
of universal interconnectedness is not new. Myths from many cultures
conveyed the theme long before the discoveries of modern science. In
Hindu mythology, for example, it is portrayed magnificently in the image of Indra's net:

Indra's Net

Indra, king of the gods, wished to show his subjects the wisdom
of the world he created, so he ordered that a net be spread above
his palace as spacious as the sky. Wherever the net's threads
crossed, Indra placed a multifaceted jewel. The smallest change
in any part of that infinite net sparkled in every jewel.[2]

This tale has a strikingly modern resonance when we think of the way some little incident, posted on Facebook or YouTube, can flash around the world to affect the daily lives of countless people.

The challenge of sustainability involves, like Indra's net, a complex of ecological, economic, moral, and political patterns of interdependence. How this situation will unfold depends upon the collective interactions of people's responses to the challenge, whether these be competitive or cooperative.[3] Awareness of all this – of what Thoreau famously called 'the infinite extent of our relations'[4] – can be very important when a facilitator conducts a sustainability-oriented workshop with, say, staff in a national or multinational organisation, schoolchildren in a National Park, or families in the community. In this chapter I give three examples of how interconnectedness affects my work with stories to show how one story can address many different themes, how the participants' search for meaning underpins their ability to make sense of a story, and how I've used this notion to address the theme of 'isolation' in order to develop group cohesion.

Let's begin with a story, different versions of which are found on either side of the US/Mexican border. It tells about Mr Wolf, who in some versions is Mr Coyote, but, wolf or coyote, the same thing invariably occurs.

Señor Lobo

Señor Lobo, Mr Wolf, was hungry and out hunting. He had just spied a juicy lamb that would do nicely for his lunch when suddenly he heard a howling pack of dogs. They had picked up his scent and were after him. Mr Wolf started to run. The dogs gave chase. Over the fields he ran and up into the woods. In and out of the trees he ran, the dogs coming closer and closer. Soon he was up into the hills but still the dogs were after him. Mr Wolf was getting desperate when suddenly, as luck would have it, he spied a cave and leapt inside; a cave just big enough for Mr Wolf but too small for those big dogs.

Inside the cave Mr Wolf caught his breath and smiled with pride. As a matter of fact he was so pleased with having escaped that he began to speak to himself. 'Feet, feet,' he said, 'what did you do to get me here inside this cave?'

And the feet answered, 'Mr Wolf! Why, we brought you all the way here. We ran faster than we have ever done before. We carried you as we always do everywhere.'

Mr Wolf was pleased with his feet and praised them. 'Fine feet, wonderful feet, loyal feet.' Then he spoke to his eyes: 'Eyes, eyes, what did you do to get me here inside this cave?'

'Mr Wolf! Why, we showed you the way across the fields and through the forest. We were the ones who spied the cave. We are always looking out for you.'

'Yes, fine eyes, good eyes, marvellous eyes, you serve me well.' Then he spoke to his ears: 'Ears, ears, what did you do to help me?'

'Mr Wolf! Why, we heard those dogs coming. We were the first to warn you. We are open night and day, listening to protect you.'

'Ah yes, ears, fine ears, sharp ears, glorious ears.' Mr Wolf was so pleased with himself that he decided to pat himself on the back. It was then that he caught sight of his tail. 'Tail, tail, useless tail, what did you do for me today? I bet you did nothing. I bet you just hung around back there like you always do bringing up the rear.'

Well, the tail was not happy to be spoken to like that so it stood up on end and answered back, 'Huh, Mr Wolf, if that's what you think of me then let me tell you that, yes, I waved myself in the air, I beckoned to the dogs, I showed them where you were going! I called out, "He's over here, he's over here!"'

When Mr Wolf heard this he was so furious that he tried to bite his tail. Round and round he went trying to catch it, but the cave was too small so in the end he turned on it, snarling, 'Get out, get out!' and he pushed his tail outside. But unfortunately Mr Wolf was connected to his tail and the further he thrust it out of the cave the more he followed after it. Now those dogs had not gone away and when they saw Mr Wolf's tail emerging from the cave, they grabbed hold of it, pulled him out, and tore him to pieces. That was the end of Mr Wolf and it is also the end of this tale![5]

Like Señor Lobo, most animal characters in old stories are, first and foremost, just themselves. But often they are also pointers to other themes or issues. They may speak indirectly about society, about interpersonal stuff, about our personality, or about our relationship with ourselves. The award-winning illustrator Ed Young dedicated the Chinese version of his book *Lon Po Po*, about Little Red Riding Hood, 'to all the wolves of the world for lending their good name as a tangible symbol of our darkness'.[6] In this vein, let's see how 'Señor Lobo' can facilitate the exploration of some issues related to interconnectedness.

When I put this story to work, whether for an organisation or a community group, I first tell it and then allow an open space for people to discuss how it speaks to them. This discussion often leads in several directions simply because the story touches on a spectrum of themes: hunger, survival, praise, recognition, blame, exclusion, death – to name a few. Each group I work with is different. Teenagers, for instance, may decide to use this story to explore body-image issues. We might then talk about parts of ourselves we are fond of and parts we struggle with. There are many personal stories to be told here and I would be sure to share some of my own. The sounding of personal stories in a safe context often provides the first step for healing what is broken or isolated. Over time I have found that when we experience our own body through a distorted, troubled lens, it is harder to be aware of the bodies of others, whether people, animals, or plants, as worthy of care, let alone preservation. That's why, from a sustainability perspective, this kind of healing matters.

I've also used the story as a lens to help members of a community group or staff in a company look at how they work together. In any such 'group' there will be those who are good at getting things moving (the 'fine, fine leg people'), those who can see what's happening or where things are heading (the 'fine, good-eyed folk'), and those who are great listeners (the 'sharp-eared ones'); but who are the tail people? Maybe they are the staff in *that* department, *those* difficult neighbours, a disrespected minority group, or individuals in a family whom everyone is keen to avoid. But the wisdom of the story can go deeper than that. Once we contemplate, for example, the many functions of an animal's real tail we find new treasures. Tails of animals are used for many things, such as keeping balance, expressing emotions or attitudes, brushing away insects. Is it any wonder that in disregarding his tail Mr Wolf brought about his own demise? I sometimes think that in human life 'tail people' are the whistle-blowers, those who flag up things that are not right.

Many years ago, while working in storytelling in organisations, I was invited with my colleagues to do some consulting with a major oil company. At a dinner I attended for the top management, the company director spoke extensively of the company's successes and its anticipated profits. At question time, one brave manager raised his hand and asked, 'Sir, what will we be doing about alternative energy sources?'

The director replied, 'Let me ask you one question: How did you get here tonight?'

Sheepishly the questioner replied, 'In my car.'

'Precisely,' his boss powered on. 'Any more questions?'

No one raised another hand. No one had the guts or the presence of mind to stand and say, 'Excuse me, sir, but maybe the question to be asked is: "How would you *like* to have got here tonight?"' Though this did not happen, the questioner did create a tail-alert moment. He was ahead of his time and could acknowledge that his company needed to take greater responsibility for the effects of its work on the environment. His colleagues' collective inability to follow up on the response he received to his question was an opportunity missed.

'Señor Lobo' could have been usefully put to work to enable this company to deal with its contested priorities, to raise awareness about biodiversity, to explore how best to protect endangered species, how best to deal with the destructive impact of climate change, how to develop more sources of clean energy, and many other issues of sustainability. These are a few leads for your imagination to run with for this tale.

Because 'Señor Lobo' can be used in diverse contexts and ways, it is one of those stories which 'speak to me'. Over time I have shared it with many people, and the story and I have come to know each other well. In my work, participants or listeners often ask, 'Ashley, where can I find a story like "Señor Lobo" that speaks directly to many important issues? In my own work I search and search and I've only found a handful.'

My answer contains several threads.

On story-finding and meaning-making

I first explain where I found the story and give my source. I then get real about the long search for the 'right' stories. It's a necessary form of session preparation. I too go through lots of stories in order to find the one that I want to tell or work with on a specific occasion. This despite the fact that I've heard, read, told, and worked with stories for decades. There's no alternative. In order to develop a repertoire of stories for your work you need to immerse yourself in stories: listen to them, read avidly, tell them, so that the story that calls you can in due course come your way.

I also explain that I only tell stories that matter to me. Any story I tell has to touch me in some way or another. I want to live with it for a while and I prefer to live with stories that serve many purposes. In fact I bet the shirt off my back that nearly any issue you throw at me can be addressed by 'Señor Lobo'. Who among us is not touched somewhere by issues of hunger, survival, praise, recognition, blame, exclusion, or death? To find the story that works we simply need to develop a different way of being with stories, one that involves the imaginative consciousness that recognises that nothing exists in isolation.

The medieval mystic Meister Eckhart is reputed to have said, 'When the soul wants to have an experience of something, she throws an image of the thing ahead of her and then enters into it.'[7] When we decide to attend or arrange a workshop to help us, for example, to tackle some difficulty relating to sustainability, or to modify the way we live upon the earth, we likewise send images ahead of ourselves. By this I mean that our imagination already carries our hopes, desires, and particular ways of responding to challenges and that these will inform what we do in the workshop. When I offer a workshop pertaining to sustainability or greener living, I rarely know the particular questions that participants will bring, or whether I can possibly answer their needs. But I believe that, as for the jewels in Indra's net, a larger connectedness will be at work between us which will link us in shared purpose and accompany us in whatever we are doing. I sometimes run a session that introduces the participants to this idea. I do so when I think that participants with whom I have ongoing contact are underestimating the fact that all of us are meaning-making creatures who tend to search for an answer to an important question wherever and whenever we can, and that we do this particularly with told stories. If we are told ahead of time that a particular story is likely to contain the answer to our question, we do so even more.

When I want to offer such a 'meaning-finding' session I begin by rummaging through my much-loved collection of storybooks and fairly quickly select a bunch of stories (one or more for each participant). How can I *trust* my choice? It is not as random as it might seem. While I may choose the stories rather intuitively, my intuition is informed by deep familiarity with these stories and a seasoned sense of how people connect with them. Indeed, when I choose this bunch of stories I try not to think too closely about their content lest doing so should prematurely influence the outcome of the work.

At the start of the workshop I place copies of the chosen stories, or the actual books, in the circle where the participants will sit. Shortly after the group has arrived I invite each member to take a story or storybook from the floor and then immediately put it aside. It is very important that they do not read their story at this stage. I then offer some exercises to prepare everyone for telling their story. After this I ask the participants to pick up and read their stories and practise telling it to themselves or to the wall until they know it well enough to tell it to another person (without notes).

When all are ready to tell their story, I say something like, 'I imagine that each of you came to this workshop with a question or concern in mind, hoping that you would find a story that addresses it. Please hold that question in mind now, but do not talk about it yet.' I then ask everyone to glance around the room, catch someone's eye, reach non-verbal agreement that they will work together, and go and sit together. Partners are not to tell each other their questions; they simply decide who shall be A and who shall be B. I clarify that A will be the first to tell the story they have prepared. Then I suggest to B that the story A will tell him or her will address the question or concern he or she brought to the workshop. I also remind B not to mention this question to A until the story is over. I explain that once A has finished their telling they will invite B to reveal their question, and then the pair will discuss the story's relevance to B's question.

Now they change roles: B invites A to attend to A's own question or concern, tells A the prepared story, and reflects with A on this story's significance for A's question. Once both members of the pair have gone through this entire process, and only then, I invite them to compare their experiences. Most pairs need about 50 minutes to do this exercise: about 20 minutes per person plus about 10 minutes to compare experiences.

Immediately after hearing the prepared story the listener will often exclaim, 'How did you do that?' or 'How did you know that this story was just what I needed? That's magic!' If it is magic, it is, I think, magic that arises from the structure of our world. It resides not only in Indra's net, and the patterns of connection revealed by science, but also in Goethe's perception that 'Every object truly contemplated awakens a new faculty'.[8] Does this process always work? No. I can't claim that these spontaneously chosen stories have a 100 per cent success rate in speaking to the listener's question; but neither will a carefully chosen tale. Why does the process work so often, but not every time?

The Arrow and the Target

Once there was a man who wished to be the best archer in the world. He sought out many masters, travelled to many countries, and his skill grew year by year. One day, searching for an even better teacher, he came upon a barn out in the country with targets on its sides and plumb in the centre of each one – an arrow. He asked around in search of the marksman and when he found him he enquired, 'How do you do this? Never have I seen such skill, such consistency!'

'It's simple,' the archer replied. 'First I shoot the arrow, then I paint the target around it.'[9]

I think that the listener's question-based attention to the prepared story is rather like the archer's drawing a circle around the arrow. Listening with one's question or concern already in mind makes it very likely that the listener will try to link the story to their question in a meaningful way. The process is also underpinned by the fact that I, with all the authority invested in me as facilitator, explicitly suggest that the listener can find an answer to their question in the story. This highly intentional cue primes the listener to activate their solution-finding powers. Consequently, most listeners will be able to find something of what they're looking for in the story they've heard. However, there's no guarantee that every participant will succeed in doing so. Some may think that the story was a kind of koan that has not revealed its wisdom immediately. Others may dismiss the story altogether.

Encouraging connectedness between people

Having considered the connectedness that can be found between a story and the diverse concerns that different people may have, I'll move on to consider how stories can help to enhance the sense of connectedness between people. In most groups, including ones that promote some aspect of sustainability, people sometimes (and this may mean frequently) complain that they feel isolated and disconnected from others, however hard they try. I've developed a way of working with the story 'The Golden Key', which is the last story in the complete *Grimm's Fairy Tales*, to help people in this plight to reconnect with their group. It might be good to try this exercise with friends before using it in your work.

After I've given each person a copy of 'The Golden Key' I ask them to read it quietly to themselves:

The Golden Key

In the winter-time when deep snow lay on the ground, a poor boy was forced to go out on a sledge to fetch wood. When he had gathered it and packed it, he wished, as he was so frozen with cold, not to go home at once, but to light a fire and warm himself a little. So he scraped away the snow, and as he was thus clearing the ground, he found a tiny golden key. Hereupon he thought that where the key was, the lock must be also, and he dug in the ground and found an iron chest. 'If the key does but fit it!' thought he; 'no doubt there are precious things in that little box.' He searched, but no keyhole was there. At last he discovered one, but so small that it was hardly visible. He tried it, and the key fitted it exactly. Then he turned it once round, and now we must wait until he has quite unlocked the lock and opened the lid, and then we shall learn what wonderful things were lying in that box.[10]

I then instruct the participants to hold the story in one hand and to read it out loud while simultaneously enacting every aspect of the events that unfold in the story. I encourage them to enter into this in a spirit of play: feeling cold, packing the wood, getting down to scrape away the snow.

Next I ask them to find a quiet place and again read the story to themselves, this time silently, making sure they feel the nuances of its every word and phrase. For instance, the story opens with the words 'In the winter-time'. If it had begun 'In the summertime', the feeling would be quite different. Similarly, notice that the boy is 'poor' and 'forced to go out'. Truly contemplating each word with emotional intelligence will unlock many things the participants may not have noticed at first.

Now I invite everyone to select one phrase or word that has caught their attention. They may be intrigued, for example, by a particular part of the story or be irritated by a specific bit of wording. They may not understand why their attention is drawn to a particular phrase. It doesn't matter. I simply encourage them to choose a word or short phrase to work with. For instance: 'frozen' or 'precious things' or 'now we must wait'. Then I ask them to add the words 'I am' before their chosen word or phrase: 'I am frozen' ... 'I am precious things' ... 'I am – now we must wait.' Note that the resulting phrases do not have to make grammatical sense. After this I ask everyone to stand up and move about the room to introduce themselves to as many others as possible using their 'I am' phrase.

I then invite each participant to pair up with one or two other people. I remind them that they chose their phrase because they felt some connection with it. As a wise storyteller once said, 'When we enter into a story we find the story inside ourselves.'[11] It's that story inside them that the participants will now need to find and, if it feels okay, share with their partners. At this stage I encourage them to be as open as they want to be about how their phrase links with what is going on in their life. I also remind them to ensure that everyone in the pair or trio gets opportunity to speak and that they need to share evenly the available time – about 20 minutes.

I then gather the whole group together and invite each participant to speak about the fruit of this exercise. I allow 30 to 40 minutes for this part of the workshop.

Without fail, this work with 'The Golden Key' generates a quality of encounter that enables group members to surmount – here and now, in this group – the feelings of isolation I mentioned above. Participants describe the process as honest, intimate, and meaningful. The essence of such groupwork is expressed for me in the beautiful words of the fourteenth-century Sufi poet Hafiz: 'I am hungry to know you.'[12] The process brings people together by creating a shared understanding of our common humanity. I have used it to help heal broken communities in the Middle East, Australia, and the UK. For people involved in green action, this deepened experience of connectedness with each other is empowering of the cooperative efforts that the challenge of sustainability demands.

The phases of engagement with this story represent different ways of learning, and so evoke different connections between the story and the person. First the group members read the story, taking it in at great, intuitive speed. In the second step they physically – kinaesthetically – climb inside the story by using the wisdom of their whole body. In the third step they focus on their emotional centre to discover yet more connections. Lastly they select one small part of the story to discover how that speaks to something that matters in their life. The story serves throughout as a medium through which to meet others and generate conversation, which in its highest sense the Sufis call 'sohbet' – the rare occasion when the veil of who we are as separate individuals lifts and we glimpse 'the light that is blazing inside each other's presence'.[13] I know of no medium that facilitates this 'lifting' better than story.

Conclusion

Richard Buckminster 'Bucky' Fuller was an American engineer, author, designer, and inventor. For the first four years of his life the world was a blur. Then he was given spectacles. Immediately everything became clear, focused, aligned. Bucky Fuller used this experience as a guiding metaphor for the rest of his life.

A story, I believe, can be like such a pair of spectacles. It can help us see things anew, clearly, so that the world makes sense to us: to perceive answers to the many questions and concerns that arise as we grapple with the difficulties of sustainability, and to see the authentic light of being in other people with whom we need to cooperate in that mission. In 2003 I spent some months in India. For three weeks I lived in a temple in Varanassi. There I learned every day about yoga and meditation from Ganga, the temple's custodian. Soon my head was spinning with so many new things that I felt quite lost. In my meditative life I had so far to go that I felt totally humbled. In desperation I asked Ganga one morning, 'Where shall I begin?' He smiled at me, took off the beads he wore about his neck, and laid them before me. 'Choose one,' he said. I did so.

'You see,' he said as I gripped a bead and by doing so lifted the necklace. 'Wherever you begin, the rest will follow.' It was another lovely image of the interconnectedness of all things that I bring to both the preparation and facilitation of a workshop. In my experience thoughtful storywork can nurture, in participants from widely different backgrounds, the consciousness that recognises that nothing and no one lives in isolation, that everything we do is connected in some way with everything and everyone else that exist on our beloved planet. That, I propose, is the common ground in which sustainable behaviour finds its renewable strength.

Notes

[1] Barabási, *Linked.*

[2] Oral retelling. Many sources; originally from the *Avatamsaka Sutra.* See also Cook, *Hua-Yen Buddhism*

[3] Wheeler, *The Whole Creature.*

[4] Thoreau, *Walden*, p. 136.

[5] Oral retelling. Source: Gersie, *Storymaking in Bereavement*, p. 120.

[6] Young, *Lon Po Po*, p. 2.

[7] Translated from Eckhart, *Die Deutschen und Lateinischen Werke.*

[8] Translated from Goethe, *Goethe Werke, Hamburger Ausgabe*, Vol. 13, p. 38.

[9] Oral retelling. Source: oral tradition; also appears in Cohen & Stewart, *The Collapse of Chaos*, p. 176.

[10] Grimm & Grimm, *Complete Fairy Tales*, p. 721.

[11] Livo & Rietz, *Storytelling*, p. 4.

[12] Hafiz, 'Because of Our Wisdom'.

[13] Rumi, 'Storywater', p. 171.

PART II

BECOMING FAMILIAR WITH STORIES

CHAPTER 6

Hugh explores Ovid's story of 'The Judgement of Midas'
through the lens of the relationship between human civilisation
and the wild. In so doing he raises such important topics as:

the ongoing destruction of nature by modern civilisation;

~

what happens when, during a time of spiritual uncertainty, a rational and
ordered civic worldview overwhelms an older, more ecstatic relationship with
the natural world;

~

how to think creatively and deeply about a traditional story in the light of
historical evidence to illuminate its ongoing message about
environmental problems of our time.

Hugh suggests how one small but significant change to this old
story would transform its environmental message for our time.

Apollo's Lyre and the Pipes of Pan

*Rethinking an ancient story to show how one small change
in the story transforms its environmental implications*

HUGH LUPTON

There is a tradition among the Traveller people that when a story is told, everyone who has ever told it before is standing behind the teller. The storyteller mediates between these ancestral voices whispering from behind and the concerns of the audience listening in front. The teller's words must honour the voices of the past, but if they are to be more than a diversion, if they are to make a difference, if they are to heal and sustain – as has always been the bardic function – then they must be aligned with the needs of the moment.

But the stories are bigger than we are; the ghostly tellers behind us far outnumber our audience. We must not overload the stories with our contemporary anxieties or weigh them down with information. We must trust them to speak for themselves ... and let them move the hearts and beguile the minds of their audience with their imagery and musicality.

It is also important for a teller to know something of the histories, cultures, and landscapes that spawned the stories he or she tells. For a long time I've been in love with ancient Greece, and I've told many of its myths. One of my sources is the Roman poet Ovid. At first I retold the tales much as Ovid told them, translating the names of the Roman deities into their Greek originals. Jove became Zeus once more, Minerva became Athena, Bacchus became Dionysus. But increasingly I became aware this wasn't enough. Something didn't quite fit; there was a curious mismatch between Ovid's narration and those Greek gods. I realised that Ovid was only one of the ghosts behind me, and that to make true sense of the material I had to look further back. Nowhere was this more apparent than in the story of King Midas.

The Judgement of King Midas

After King Midas had been cured of the terrifying affliction of the golden touch, he hated gold. Every day he turned his back on his palace and wandered deep in the forest. He followed tracks dappled with sunlight into the untamed places, far from the glimmer and glitter of golden statues, and the clink and chink of golden coins.

One day, as he wandered, he heard music. He followed the sound and stumbled into a clearing. Sitting on the trunk of a fallen oak was the goat-legged, horned god of the wild places. Midas saw great Pan and he was filled with panic. He crouched behind a clump of bushes, trembling, hardly daring to breathe. Pan was playing his pipes. The forest was alive with the sound of them. Midas listened, enchanted and terrified.

The god lowered his pipes from his lips. The forest fell silent. Pan began to boast: 'I'm the finest musician in the world! I'm the finest musician of them all! I'm a finer musician even than golden Apollo when he plucks his silver-tongued lyre!'

The words of Pan echoed through the forest. They were carried by the wind to the high slopes of Olympus. Nothing is hidden from the eyes and the ears of the mighty gods. The words were heard by Apollo. The shining god frowned and picked up his lyre. As swift as thought he flew down to the world.

Midas gasped. Now there were two gods in the clearing. Apollo and Pan stared and glowered at one another. Apollo was the first to speak: 'We will have a contest of music, you and I. The judge will be this mountain.'

Looming high above the trees of the forest was a craggy mountain called Tmolus. With one sweep of his hand Apollo gestured towards it. Two grey, stony, elephantine ears unfolded on either side of Tmolus.

Pan was the first to play. He lifted his pipes to his lips and blew. In his music were the baying and belling of stags, the howl-

ing of wolves, the thundering of hooves, the crashing of floodwater, the creaking and cracking of branches, the rilling and rippling
of streams, the humming of bees, the bright songs of birds. It was
a music beautiful and terrifying in equal measure.

Pan lowered his pipes and Apollo lifted his lyre and began
to play. To anyone who could hear it was as though the strings
of his lyre were the threads upon which the whole world is woven. It was as though every note was an element, every melody
a formula. It was a music perfect in form and modulation. As
the shimmering, cascading scales rose and fell, the whole forest
held its breath. And when Apollo lowered his lyre and fell silent,
Tmolus, the mountain, opened its cavernous cave of a mouth
and pronounced, 'Apollo is the winner.'

The golden god smiled. This was as it should be.

But from behind a clump of bushes came another voice:
'No! Why should the victory go to Apollo? Why should the victory go to the plinkety-plonk of a plucked lyre when Pan's music
is the real thing? Pan's music is finer by far!'

Apollo turned and saw King Midas, crouching, shaking with
indignation. The golden god's smile vanished; he stared at Midas with shining, unwavering eyes. He furrowed his forehead
into a frown and vanished into the light.

With the frown of Apollo, King Midas felt strangely changed.
He reached up and touched the sides of his face. His ears had
moved – to the top of his head. He felt them with his fingers.
They had become two long, hairy, twitching, bristling – donkey's
ears. For one appalling moment he waited to see whether the
transformation was going to spread downwards. But no – just
his ears.

King Midas stayed in the clearing until the night came and
the sky glittered with stars. Then he folded his ears down the
sides of his face and crept back to his palace. He slipped through
a side door. He found a roll of purple cloth and wound it around
his head like a turban.

'There. No one need ever know.'

But a king's hair will grow, just as anyone's will. The days
became weeks, the weeks became months, and all too soon King
Midas knew he had to have his hair cut.

He summoned a barber to a secret room. When all the doors were locked he said, 'Can you keep a secret?'

The barber bowed. 'Yes, your majesty, I can keep a secret.'

'If you can keep my secret then you have a job that will last as long as I live. If you can keep my secret I will pay you every month with a purse crammed and jangling with silver coins.'

The barber bowed again. 'In that case, your majesty, I can certainly keep your secret.'

The King unfastened and unravelled his purple turban. The cloth fell to the floor. His hair flopped onto his shoulders. And from the top of his head two grey, hairy, twitching, bristling donkey's ears pointed up at the ceiling.

The barber stared, laughter and horror wrestling in his belly. He bit his lip and swallowed. He took out his scissors and razors. He cut and clipped and shaped and shaved. He oiled and combed and held up a mirror. The King flinched and nodded. The barber wrapped the turban around King Midas's head. The King dropped a purse of silver coins into the barber's hand.

'Remember, not a word to anybody.'

The barber bowed and left the palace.

For one day the barber kept the secret. But it was as though he had a mouse pouched in his cheek: every time he opened his mouth he thought the secret would jump out. For two days he kept the secret, but every word he spoke wanted to turn on his tongue into 'The King has donkey's ears'. On the third day he could stand it no longer. He took a trowel and went into the forest. He knelt on the ground and dug a hole. He leaned forwards and whispered into it, 'King Midas has donkey's ears. The King has the ears of an ass.'

He filled in the hole and made his way homewards. Unburdened of his secret, he felt comfortable at last.

But where he'd dug the hole a cluster of reeds grew from the ground. The wind blew through them and they whispered the secret. The birds of the forest heard the reeds whispering and they began to sing the secret. The birdsong echoed from village to town and soon enough the whole world knew: 'King Midas has donkey's ears. The King has the ears of an ass.'

Ovid set this story on the page two thousand years ago, about the same time as Jesus Christ was growing up in Judaea. For the Romans it was a time of outward stability. Their empire was approaching the height of its power. A new order, a civilised urbanity backed by military efficiency, was being imposed on Europe and North Africa. But at the same time there was a spiritual vacuum. Ted Hughes writes,

> The Greek/Roman pantheon had fallen in on men's heads. The obsolete paraphernalia of the old official religion were lying in heaps, like old masks in the lumber room of a theatre, and new ones had not yet arrived. The mythic plane, so to speak, had been de-frocked.[1]

In the same century that Ovid was writing, Plutarch reported that Pan had been pronounced dead, and Apollo was rumoured to have been glimpsed living in squalor in a filthy shack in Delphi where his oracle had once been. The old belief system was in decay and the Western world was awaiting the new spiritual impetus that Christianity would bring. But that impetus had not yet arrived. In the mythological hollowness of that time, we might recognise something of our own predicament in the early twenty-first century. Scientific rationalism has undermined all forms of religious belief, but has, as yet, offered us no replacement.

In his book, *Metamorphoses*, Ovid constructed an entertainment, sophisticated, savage, and urbane, from the old tales of the old religion, to delight his fellow Romans. How would they have been understood by his audience? How might they speak to us and the challenges our society faces today? I'd like to look at the ancestry of Pan and Apollo, to examine the defeat of one by the other, and to consider the implications for ourselves of the shaming of King Midas.

> In the Palaeolithic cave of Trois-Frères in southern France the creatures are not painted on the walls, but engraved – fixing for millennia the momentary turns, leaps and flashes of the animal kingdom in a teeming tumult of eternal life. And above them all, predominant ... watching, peering at the visitor with penetrat-

ing eyes, is the now famous 'Sorcerer of Trois Frères'. Presiding impressively over the animals collected there in incredible numbers, he is poised in profile in a dancing movement ... the antlered head is turned to face the room. The pricked ears are those of a stag; the round eyes suggest an owl; the full beard descending to the deep animal chest is that of a man, as are likewise the dancing legs; the apparition has the bushy tail of a wolf or wild horse, and the position of the prominent sexual organ, placed beneath the tail, is that of the feline species.[2]

Here, surely, we have the ancestor of Pan. We glimpse him again and again in the mythologies of the Near East and Europe – as Enkidu, as Cernunnos, and in his vegetative form as the Green Man. He is the sexually potent god of the herds; the wild, careless, unbridled, inexhaustible energy of life invincible.

In Greek mythology Pan is the love child of Hermes and a tree nymph. When he was born, his mother, seeing his horns and hooves and bearded face, deserted him. But his father wrapped the infant in the pelt of a mountain hare and carried him to Olympus. The gods and goddesses gathered round to peer at the strange child. First they laughed at him, then they loved him; Dionysus was especially smitten. They called him Pan (All) because he delighted all their hearts. But Pan was never an Olympian god. He lived in the wilds of Arcadia, where he guarded flocks, herds, and beehives and helped hunters find their quarry. The ancient god, grafted on to a new mythology, quickly found his old familiar territories.

Pan is portrayed as being in a state of perpetual sexual arousal. He pursued the beautiful Syrinx, who transformed herself into a reed and hid in a reed bed. Unable to find her, Pan plucked all the reeds and made a set of pipes. His music inspires rapture and terror. And when the Romans adopted the Greek pantheon Pan remained an outsider, inhabiting mountains, caves, and forests far from the haunts of people.

In his most archaic form, Apollo is one of the twin archer deities. His sister is the archer goddess of the moon. He is the archer god of the sun. Their pursuit of one another across the sky is described in hunter-gatherer mythologies across the world. In Greek mythology Apollo retains his association with the sun as Phoebus Apollo, but also becomes the god of prophecy and divination, the patron of music and the arts, the father of medicine, the leader of the muses, and the Lord of the Silver Bow whose arrows can bring plague and death. After the trinity of Zeus, Hades, and Poseidon, he is the most powerful of the gods. His cult overthrew the old order of Gaia, the Earth Mother, at Delphi when he killed the serpent Python in Gaia's sacred shrine. He became Pythian Apollo and his oracle there became the most important in Greece, though a trace of its origins remained: he allowed the priestess who spoke his oracle to be known as the 'Pythia'.

In another story Apollo desired Daphne and pursued her relentlessly until she was transformed into a laurel tree. The leaves of the tree became sacred to Apollo and were used to make the laurel crowns awarded to athletes and poets. Again and again in the stories of Apollo we glimpse a male god subduing an older goddess-based ecstatic religion. At Delphi, originally sacred to the earth goddess Gaia, Apollo took over the shrine after killing her son, the giant serpent Python. Thereafter, the ecstatic priestess of the oracle had to curtsey to the new maxim 'Nothing in excess'.

The Greeks understood the limitations of the Apollonian way. During the winter months Apollo's shrine at Delphi was given over to the worship of his half-brother Dionysus (who loved Pan), whose maxim could be described as 'Everything in excess'. But when the Greek gods were adopted by the Romans there was no such compromise. Dionysus became Bacchus, the tubby wine-besotted god of drinking. Apollo, on the other hand, the Romans took to their hearts. Robert Graves writes,

> The Romans conquered Greece and brought Apollo with them to Italy. They were a military nation ... but some of them began to take up Greek poetry seriously as part of their education in political rhetoric, an art which they found necessary for consolidating their military conquests. They ... understood that major poetry was a more musical and philosophical form of rhetoric than could be achieved by prose and that minor poetry was the most elegant of social accomplishments.[3]

By Ovid's time Apollo had become the god of rhetoric and reason, of civic order and the polite arts. Graves says, 'True poets will agree that poetry is spiritual illumination ... not an ingenious technique of swaying a popular audience or of enlivening a sottish dinner party.'[4] Apollo had superimposed himself on an older cosmology with a feminine force-field. His lyre was no longer the tortoiseshell-backed gift of Hermes, but a well-tempered and -tuned instrument whose harmonies echoed the harmonious whole of the body politic.

So, to return to 'The Judgement of King Midas', of course Apollo had to win the music contest. How could any civilised Roman think otherwise? The Roman project, after all, was to subdue the wild hordes and wildernesses of their conquered territories. Tmolus (who should have known better) pronounced Apollo's victory and only Midas disagreed.

Midas had already learned in his experience of the golden touch, thanks to Dionysus, that there is no life in the precious shining metal that drives commerce and defines wealth. From behind his bush he heard the two musics and had no doubt which rang more true. He spoke his mind to the golden god and Apollo frowned. Immediately donkey's ears sprouted from his head. He became part animal, like Pan. Every Roman listener would recognise this as a terrible and hilarious humiliation.

The Roman poet Pindar describes Apollo spending the winter months (when Dionysus was resident in Delphi) among the Hyperboreans, delighting in the sacrifice of great numbers of asses. 'In the banquets and hymns of that people Apollo chiefly rejoices and laughs as he looks upon the brute beasts in their ramping lewdness.'[5]

Why should the intelligent, beautiful, alert donkey become a figure of contempt? Why has 'ass' become synonymous with 'fool'? Why should the donkey's long ears, fine-tuned to every sound and sensation, become a device for shaming a king? For the answer to these questions we must look to Roman Apollo. It is the Apollonian way of thought that has driven a wedge of contempt between the civilised and the wild, between human and animal, between villa and cave, between lyre and pipe – and we are still reeling from the consequence.

When, at last, a new religion filled the spiritual void, when the Christian religion converted even the emperors of Rome, the old gods did not pass away. Pan did not die and Apollo did not retire to a squalid hut in Delphi.

Both of them, in all but name, found a place in the new cosmology.

As solar deity, son of Zeus (God), healer and shepherd, vanquisher of the serpent, Apollo was absorbed into the iconography of Christ, who in early Christian imagery is represented as a beardless young man, his face radiant like the sun, who takes his place in heaven as Christ Pantocrator.[6] And Pan? With his cloven hooves, his hairy legs, his goat eyes, his horns, Pan was identified with pure evil and relegated to the pit of Hell. James Hillman writes, 'Legends, images and theology attest to an irreconcilable conflict between Pan and Christ, a tension that has never ended in that the Devil with his horns and hooves is none other than old Pan seen in the Christian mirror.'[7] A thousand carvings, mosaics, frescoes, and stained-glass windows testify to these transformations of Apollo and Pan. What might it mean that the ancient Palaeolithic god of life invincible became a figure of pure evil?

The conflict does not end there. We find ourselves, like the Romans, in a time of spiritual uncertainty. Scientific rationalism has so permeated our culture that for most of us the Christian paradigm no longer convinces. Once again Apollo has jumped ship. The god of light has thrown in his lot with the Enlightenment. The Apollonian, rational, detached vision holds sway and a misguided faith has been building since the eighteenth century that our own cleverness, our empirical arts, can win us whatever we want. We are blinded to the effect our machinations are having on the wild world we depend upon. Graves describes Apollo wielding the atomic bomb as though it were a thunderbolt, 'for since the age of Reason was heralded by his eighteenth century philosophers, he has seated himself on the vacant throne of heaven ... as regent'.[8]

But we fail to hear the music of Pan at our peril. Although he may be suffering he cannot, ultimately, be defeated. His creatures may be depleted, his terrains enclosed, his forests felled – but at the same time his icebergs are softening, his waters are rising, his weather is becoming more extreme. *Panic* is taking a new form. The wild will triumph over us eventually. Our accomplishments will count for little when the human episode in geological history becomes a rust-red seam in the rock strata, or when strange fishes swim in and out of our coral-encrusted houses and unnamed creatures graze on hills where cities once thrived.

King Midas was right to give Pan the victory.

Hillman writes,

> Pan might ask us: Why are you civilised people ... so hard on the environment? Why do you blast, bulldoze and flatten so many acres of woodlands and hillsides? Why are there fewer and fewer lonely places where people may hide in nature and nature hide from people? Are you trying to eradicate my haunts? Put a final solution to the problem of Pan? ... You rape nature and call me the rapist ... You leave tracts of ruin, yet claim I am the god who favours deserted wilderness. Is not your day world becoming a suffocating nightmare? Your children having more and more trouble breathing? Are you not security obsessed, seat-belted against surprise, medicated against panic attacks? ... Science fears the return of Pan ... He is unpredictable and amoral. His urges live in the barren places of the psyche where the mind of civil engineering makes no inroads.[9]

Maybe we could risk the disapproval of some of the ghosts behind us and reconfigure 'The Judgement of King Midas' in the light of both our contemporary needs and what we've learnt about the background of this story.

> ... The mountain Tmolus opened his cavernous cave of a mouth and pronounced, 'Apollo is the winner.'
>
> The golden god smiled. This was as it should be.
>
> But from behind a clump of bushes came another voice: 'No! Why should the victory go to Apollo? Why should the victory go to the plinkety-plonk of a plucked lyre when Pan's music is the real thing? Pan's music is finer by far!'
>
> Pan peered into the bushes and saw King Midas, crouching, shaking with indignation. The horned god's face broke into an unfathomable smile. He looked at Midas with shining, unwavering eyes. He bowed his head and then vanished as suddenly and silently as a startled stag.
>
> With the smile of Pan, King Midas felt strangely changed.

He reached up and touched the sides of his face. His ears had moved – to the top of his head. He felt them with his fingers. They were his ears no longer. They had become two long, hairy, twitching, bristling – donkey's ears. The wild god had blessed him with the ears of a donkey. Suddenly he could hear the music of the forest. He cocked his new ears and closed his eyes. He could hear the baying and belling of stags, the howling of wolves, the thundering of hooves, the crashing of floodwater, the creaking and cracking of branches, the rilling and rippling of streams, the humming of bees, the bright songs of birds. He shouted with delight and jumped to his feet. Here was a gift beyond price, worth infinitely more than any golden touch.

Notes

[1] Hughes, *Tales from Ovid*, p. xiv.

[2] Campbell, *Primitive Mythology*, pp. 309–310.

[3] Graves, *The White Goddess*, p. 392.

[4] Ibid.

[5] Pindar, 'Tenth Pythian Ode', quoted in Graves, *The White Goddess*, p. 289.

[6] See, for example, Schapiro, *Late Antique, Early Christian and Medieval Art*.

[7] Hillman & Roscher, *Pan and the Nightmare*, p. 8.

[8] Graves, *The White Goddess*, p. 476.

[9] Hillman & Roscher, *Pan and the Nightmare*, p. 71.

CHAPTER 7

This chapter considers the gap between talk and action
in relation to storytelling and the desire for a greener world.
Anthony presents two stories of ecological history and explains:

how exercising restraint in the way one tells a hard-hitting, true story
of species extinction, such as that of the passenger pigeon, provides the
listener with cognitive and emotional space in which to find their own
response to the story;

~

why a wider scope of response becomes available to the listener when ecological
history is combined with the mythic imagination.

Anthony argues that hearing historical stories about species extinction
can nurture the listener's desire that further species should not become
extinct, as well as the willingness to act in accordance with this desire.

Jumping the Gap of Desire

*Telling stories from ecological history about species
extinctions to evoke an empathetic and questioning response*

ANTHONY NANSON

Compelling stories are usually propelled by a 'gap' between a character and the fulfilment of some desire they pursue. This 'gap of desire' is one source of tension by which a storyteller holds the listeners' attention. There's also a gap of desire between *talk* (including stories) about sustainability and *action* that does something about it.[1] If these two kinds of desire work together, if listeners to an ecologically motivated story empathise so deeply with the protagonist's desire that they carry something of that desire back into their lives,[2] you might hope the story's impact could make some difference to the world.

Different kinds of stories touch people in different kinds of ways. Imaginative, 'mythic' stories can have a potent transformative effect within a person's individual being,[3] but the challenge of the ecological crisis is to take action towards a physical reality external to your individual being. My experience as a story-listener is that, much though I feel nourished inwardly by myth, it is historical stories – about events understood to have actually happened – that have more radically impacted on the values by which I live. This chapter examines the potency of this genre, with a focus on the capacity of stories to mobilise concern about the extinction of wildlife.

My first experiences of the impact of orally presented historical stories involved themes of social justice. David Metcalfe's telling of the Albigensian Crusade against the Cathars in France reinforced in me how unacceptable is the persecution of people who are different from you; that I'd never endorse such behaviour; that such stories must be remembered. I realised the importance of stories like this one in times of resource scarcity, when there's heightened danger that people will demonise out-groups defined by ethnic or religious difference. Chris Sunderland's telling of the impeachment of Warren Hastings, for the East India Company's systematic extortion of wealth from native Indians, helped me understand the perennial temptation of the rich and powerful to manipulate law and privilege to take what they want. This story and others like it made me more politically radical and desire that such stories be known so truth can speak against power.

Receiving a story of this kind publicly, as one of many listeners, means receiving it *together*, so the outrage is shared and there's a heightened hope that people acting together might stop similar things happening in future. Moreover, the face-to-face relationship between audience and storyteller enables the latter's personal authority to reinforce the values at stake. Hugh Lupton's story *On Common Ground*, about John Clare, victim of and witness to the systematic enclosure of the English countryside, delivers a scathing indictment of the consequences of that development, not only in Clare's time but today too. It strengthened views I held to hear them publicly confirmed by someone respected by the audience: 'It's not just me who feels this, but Hugh does too and all these people who are applauding him.'

But it was in a book that, as a boy, I discovered stories of animal species that have been exterminated by human action or saved at the brink.[4] They awakened in me a desire that further species should not be lost. Since prehistoric times, humans have repeatedly driven other species into extinction, thanks to our capacity to exploit new ecological resources when we've exhausted old ones.[5] We are most prone to cause extinctions soon after we invade new territory, as when people entered Australia about 45,000 years ago, the Americas about 13,000 years ago, and New Zealand 1000 years ago, and again when Europeans colonised many parts of the world in recent centuries.[6] Fewer extinctions ensue when people have inhabited a region long enough for their culture to adapt to the ecology.[7] The ecological impact of European colonisation continues today as industrial civilisation relentlessly subsumes other cultures and seeks ever more resources to sustain its demands. More species become extinct every year and many others stand on the brink.[8] In 2006, for example, the Chinese river dolphin was declared extinct and today (2014) fewer than 35 Amur leopards survive in the wild.

Because of human beings' evolutionary predisposition to be ecological 'niche thieves',[9] and because cultural adaptation to ecology takes generations and in today's global economy is ceaselessly undermined, I'm doubtful that pragmatic, anthropocentric rationales for the conservation of wildlife can be adequate by themselves to prevent extinctions. Some species may provide vital ecological services or have potential to yield new drugs, but others may offer nothing we really need. Some species may give pleasure to those lucky enough to observe them, but others may be elusive or unappealing. The 'Wise Use' movement in the United States, in its lobbying for unrestricted economic activity, calls for the exclusion from that nation's Endangered Species Act of 'species lacking the vigor to spread in range'.[10]

So a deeper motivation is needed. Its basis, says the proponents of 'deep ecology', has to be an affirmation of other species' right to exist for their own sake, not merely as resources to serve human needs.[11] For me this involves a comprehension that each species has its own unique 'umwelt', or perception of the world,[12] and hence its own unique universe of being. The philosopher Arne Naess argues that what needs to be nurtured is an expanded sense of the 'self' that we identify with, to include not only a 'social self' (other people) but also an 'ecological self' (the rest of the ecosystem), so that we find joy in acting – we *desire* – to enable the flourishing of not only our own individual being, and our family, pets, neighbours, but also the habitats and wildlife encompassed in this ecological self.[13]

Listening to Metcalfe's and Sunderland's provocative historical stories, therefore, inspired me to apply my concerns about wildlife conservation to telling stories from ecological history. Here's a summary of one of them:

The Passenger Pigeon

The passenger pigeon was once the most abundant bird in the world. The early European settlers in North America were amazed by the enormous flocks, containing billions of birds, which could darken the sun and collapse trees under their weight. The native people had always hunted this species, but the settlers killed them in much larger numbers. Once the industrial revolution was underway commercial hunters used every means to kill the pigeons in astonishing numbers and sent the carcasses by railway to lucrative markets in the cities. Native people's protests were ignored, the pigeons granted no protection because they were so numerous. Rapidly they became less numerous. Not only were they hunted so intensively, but deforestation destroyed their food supply and breeding sites. Producing only one chick per season, they couldn't breed fast enough to replace their losses. Hunters obliterated the last large flock in 1896; all the carcasses were wasted when a derailment halted the train carrying them and the meat putrefied in the heat. Thereafter, sightings of wild passenger pigeons were few. The last one was seen – and shot – in 1907. The few captive birds in zoos failed to breed and died one by one. Till only one was left, called Martha. When she died, in 1914, the species became extinct. Her stuffed body is today in the National Museum of Natural History in Washington.[14]

When I tell this story, my matter-of-fact tone and the use of dates and statistics convey that I'm narrating events that really happened. My voice also conveys a moral commitment to the story. The palaeontologist Gregory Paul writes of the passenger pigeon that, 'realistically, their extinction may have been for the best', since a species that needed to live in such large flocks was incompatible with agricultural development.[15] My presentation of the story, in both structure and delivery, implies a mourning of this creature's loss and a challenge to the mode of development that necessitates such loss.

The story's 'protagonist' is the passenger pigeon as a species. Its 'desire' is to survive. In this it fails and the story ends downbeat. Although a species may seem a rather abstract 'character', I've found that many listeners do empathise with the species, as if it were a character, as the numbers in which it's sighted inexorably decrease through the story. When the species is reduced to a single named individual, the listener's emotional involvement tends to intensify: the species' desire to survive, a desire we're likely to share as we listen, is focused in an individual who we know will die without any chance of reproducing. I feel this shift myself in rehearsal, listeners have told me they've experienced it, and I detect it in the audience's quality of attention as I tell the story.

A similar emotional 'coup' is delivered by the story of the golden toad, which has a similar structure – the species is reduced to a single male who for two consecutive years waits in vain for a mate to appear at his pond – but this story involves a different set of ecological issues, since the golden toad was protected in a reserve and the reasons for its demise are complex and linked to climate change (see Metcalfe, this volume).[16] By contrast, the stories of both species of bison, which were saved from extinction by assertive conservation efforts, have an upbeat ending. It's good to tell such positive stories, because they encourage us about what can be achieved, but they're less challenging in that they permit the listener to feel reassured that endangered species do get saved. Downbeat stories like the passenger pigeon's do not resolve the conflict they contain in a pleasing way; they leave the listener the challenge of what to do with their frustrated desire for the species to survive.

Different listeners respond in different ways. One listener to 'The Passenger Pigeon' has said, 'It gets me every time.' Another said it elicits a sense of the finality of extinction and an enhanced regard for wildlife's well-being. Some have asked me, 'Why did you tell that story?' in a way that implies they're startled I should transgress an assumption that stories should merely entertain. One person, visibly shocked, responded, 'Is that the God's honest truth?' Another queried how I could be sure these past events really happened. Secondary-school pupils have told me that the story illustrates that you shouldn't exploit nature's resources beyond what it can withstand. When I told two ecological stories of this kind in a worship service, there was a deep silence and then the minister led us into prayer with the words, 'These things happened ...'

I welcome this diversity of response. In telling the story I do hope that my listeners will empathise with the passenger pigeon's doomed desire to survive and that thereby they may desire that other endangered species won't share the same fate, but I don't expect everyone will respond to the story as I do. I don't try to force my listeners to feel what I want them to feel; such an imposition of effect is where propaganda diverges from art and education. There's a delicate, paradoxical, balance to be held between the storyteller's commitment to the story and their respect for the listener's authentic response; it mirrors the way that storytelling involves the listener co-creating the story in their imagination (see Manwaring, this volume).

This requires restraint. Firstly, restraint from spelling out the significance of everything, so the listeners have the chance to formulate this for themselves. Secondly, restraint in the manner the story is delivered, since much of the spoken word's impact upon the listener is imparted by sonic qualities of the voice.[17] When telling extinction stories I rein in my feelings, and use a calm, neutral voice, neither ranting at the audience as if what happened is their fault, nor giving vent to my sorrow. I give the listeners emotional space in which to discover within themselves the emotion I haven't provided.

Thirdly, the use of pauses provides gaps of time for the listener's mind to work in. After saying, 'That was the last time anyone shot – or saw – a wild passenger pigeon,' I pause, to mark that point in history, to allow a whiff of possibility that in the story the species is now extinct, but not so long a pause as would convince people it is, before I continue, 'There were still a few in zoos. But they didn't breed well in captivity, and one by one the captive birds died.' Pause more emphatically. 'Until there was just one left.' That line is the 'coup'. It's an emotional torpedo; those words seal the species' doom. As I speak them I'm more careful than ever to sustain an intention of compassionate restraint. 'They called her Martha. She was hatched in Cincinnati Zoo in 1885. People came from all over the United States to see her – the last of the passenger pigeons. She lived on to the age of twenty-nine. She died on 1 September 1914 at 1.00 p.m.' Another pause as '1.00 p.m.' delivers another coup – the exact moment of extinction – before I conclude the story.

These dimensions of restraint – in content, voice, and pace – open up a space of uncertainty and possibility which is one and the same as the gap of desire: it's where the impulse of desire within the story may give rise to an authentic impulse of desire within the listener – what Jack Zipes calls a 'gestus' towards the coming-into-being of the world as you desire it to be.[18]

Extinction stories are so hard-hitting that, deployed in isolation, they might do little more than be depressing. I like to juxtapose them not only with opportunity for discussion but also with other stories. Ecological history includes diverse other kinds of stories besides ones about individual species. Let me now tell you a very different story, which puts the theme of wildlife extinction in the larger context of ecological change (in Britain) over thousands of years. It's a story in which I try to combine the inward potency of myth with the outer reality of ecological history.

The Coming of the Wildwood

Once upon a time, thousands of years ago, most of the land was covered with ice. There was just ice and snow, and here and there a crag of bare rock jutting through. In the white and blue air, nothing breathed, only the wind that whistled across the emptiness.

Away to the south were plains of hardy grassland, where herds of mammoths and reindeer and woolly rhinoceros roamed. And behind these herds came men and women, who hunted them. Tall people they were, who walked with their heads held high.

These people made their homes in caves and rock shelters, and in the deepest, darkest recesses of the caves they made images to honour the spirits of the animals they killed for meat and clothing. And the most sacred of all the animals they hunted was the bear – who like humans could stand on her hind legs and like humans made her home in caves.

The years passed ... like raindrops falling in a stream ...

The land grew warmer. Each summer, the ice melted a little bit more than the winter's freezing. The ice retreated northwards, leaving behind bogs and pools of meltwater and a litter of boulders. In this watery wasteland, trees began to grow. The wiry birch came first. Then the willow. Tiny trees they were, no taller than my knee. Here and there you might have seen the scarlet-berried rowan, the spiky juniper, and the slow-growing yew.

The years passed ... like raindrops falling in a stream ...

And the pine trees came. Like a pall of darkness the pine-wood swept across the land, and the mammoths and the woolly rhinos vanished as if they'd never been. Inside the dark wood, new creatures lived: the stag, the boar, the elk, and the aurochs.

Men and women feared the dark wood. They made their homes along the rivers and lakeshores. In small pools of fire-light after dark you could hear the sound of human voices ... but for mile after mile after mile in the woods beyond there was only the wind in the trees and the grunts and cries of the night creatures. And in the deepest, darkest shadows of the wood, the bear yet lurked; no longer honoured by the people, but feared as the strongest and wildest of the wild beasts in the wood.

The years passed ... like raindrops falling in a stream ...

The land grew warmer still, and new kinds of trees appeared: alder by the rivers, and tall stately elms, and armies of oak. These trees spread their branches wide and opened the wood to shafts of golden green sunlight. Deer nibbled at the leaves around the edges of glades, where flowers of many colours bathed in the sun.

The light made men and women bold. They entered the wood – and with their mastery over stone and bronze and iron they cut down trees for firewood and for timber to make their houses and boats and weapons. With their mastery of fire they cleared space for their goats and sheep and cattle and their crops of barley, wheat, and rye. They hacked away bigger and bigger swathes of woodland until most of the land was open to the sky, and dotted with villages, towns ... and cities.

At last just a few sizeable tracts of wildwood remained, now protected by the King as royal forests so that he and his men could hunt the stags and boars that still roamed among the oaks. None of the common folk could lay a hand on any game or timber – unless they wanted that hand chopped off. But in the deepest, darkest shadows of the wood you might, just possibly, have heard the groan of a bear.

As the years went by, even these tracts of forest were whittled away, to make space for more crops, more houses, more factories, more roads, till today just a few ragged scraps and slivers of woodland are all that's left of the wildwood that once covered the land. The bears are gone. There's nowhere left for them to live. Gone too are the boar, the elk, and the aurochs.

But where a patch of ground is left alone, without nibbling sheep and not covered with concrete, where acorns and nuts fall and take root, then bushes will begin to grow. With time the bushes will give way to trees. And if we let the trees grow – and if we wait long enough – then the wildwood will return.[19]

The desire line of this story – the wildwood's impulse to flourish – is less forceful than that of 'The Passenger Pigeon'; the story depends for its effect on repeating patterns of description and a rhythmic, entrancing voice to awaken an inner experience (see Manwaring, this volume) evoking a sense of deep time and hence of humankind as a force of nature in large-scale ecological change. Sometimes a colleague will play a rainstick to intensify the refrain, 'like raindrops falling in a stream'. In imparting a mythic rather than straightforward factual impact, the story avoids specifying dates or locations and simplifies complex science. For example, I make no mention of Britain's physical continuity with northwest Europe during the ice age when the North Sea was dry land, and I elide any distinction between the cave bear (prevalent during the ice age) and the closely related brown bear (which survived into historical times). I also make poetic assumptions where there are gaps of scientific evidence, for example about woolly rhinos surviving long enough to encounter *Homo sapiens*, and about the prevalence of cave art in Britain.

The 'multivalency' of this mythic style of storytelling (see Shaw, this volume), together with the diversity of ecological motifs in this story, invites a wider scope of response than a more focused and factual story like 'The Passenger Pigeon'. The bear motif, for example, is used to convey the idea of animals being sacred and to symbolise the vanishing of the wild, as well as to communicate the actual extinction of bears in Britain. The story ends on a hopeful note by hinting at the possibility of rewilding the land. Except for the aurochs, the extinctions of British wildlife *since* the ice age are not absolute, since the lost species survive elsewhere and could in theory be reintroduced. But of all these species the bear is the least likely to ever be allowed back.[20]

In discussion, prompted by open-ended questions, 'The Wildwood' has elicited from secondary-school pupils diverse views about land use: some desired the land to be safe, productive, and convenient for people; some were inclined to mourn the loss of wilderness and megafauna; others favoured a balance between these conditions. One boy spontaneously brought up the topic of wilderness restoration: his father's neighbour wanted to reintroduce on his Scottish property locally extinct animals like bison and wolves, which his father was concerned should be securely fenced in.

Wherever feasible I make space for such discussion after telling stories. It gives the listeners a chance to formulate in words their response to the stories and thereby advance their own understanding of the world and themselves and their values and desires. From the inner 'space of possibility' opened in each listener's mind, it develops a social space of congruent and contesting desires, which may spark new permutations of desire and reflects the real-life need to negotiate between competing desires in matters like land use.

Hard-hitting historical stories can be juxtaposed to good effect with the consolatory power of myth. *The Liberty Tree*, performed by Hugh Lupton and Nick Hennessey, contains three true-life stories about the suppression of dissent in England, which elicited in me the same moral outrage as the stories of the Albigensian Crusade and Warren Hastings. By embedding these stories within the fanciful story of Robin Hood, the storytellers not only sweetened the pill but made connections between the imaginative inner world and the outer world of history. Near the end Lupton asks what's the point of dissent if it's repeatedly crushed by forces of ruthless self-interest, and then shifts perspective to show us the heroes of myth and history coexisting in some timeless space, sitting round a fire beneath the night sky. This enigmatic scene moved the impact beyond the political, to elicit a feeling of otherworldly hope – that in some way, beyond understanding, all our efforts count, however intractable the world's challenges seem.

David Phelps has done something analogous with 'The Passenger Pigeon'. It moved me to hear this story told by someone else, to feel the emotional shift as the focus narrows from the species as a whole to Martha as an individual; but Phelps then segued into 'Why Owls Stare', a Choctaw tale about an owl who argues with a pigeon about whose people are the more numerous. When the pigeon flock arrives they're so numerous they darken the sun. The 'pigeons' must be passenger pigeons! I felt an eerie consolation, in a way that doesn't weaken the tragic historical story, that this extinct species endures in the imagination thanks to the tradition of a people whose world it had been part of.

Let us return to the gap of desire. How does the impulse of desire evoked by a story translate into action in the physical world? My experience, and that of people I've questioned, is that the impact of stories is cumulative: rarely does a single story directly trigger a change in behaviour. I believe that the accumulation of desire arising from multiple stories over time really can drive change, both in individuals and in society as a whole. My own desire for the survival of wildlife, intensified by working with stories of ecological loss, has caused me to support conservation charities, avoid products that exploit endangered creatures, and make my garden hospitable to wildlife. The converging desires of many people become part of public opinion, initially resisted by vested interests, but able to eventually change public policy in ways beyond the scope of individual lifestyle choices.[21] Such a change saved the bison from going the way of the passenger pigeon. The ecological crisis is so vast in scale that our collective response requires the quilted, paradigm-shifting impact of an expanding matrix of stories, of diverse genres, mediated in diverse ways, imparting different kinds of impact. In this enterprise, stories of ecological history have a potent part to play.

Notes

1 Rueckert, 'Literature and Ecology'.

2 Brooks, *Reading for the Plot*.

3 Gersie and King, *Storymaking in Education and Therapy*.

4 Silverberg, *The Dodo, the Auk and the Oryx*.

5 Kingdon, *Lowly Origin*.

6 Martin, 'Prehistoric Overkill'; Day, *Doomsday Book of Animals*.

7 See Nabhan, *Cultures of Habitat*.

8 See Wilson, *Diversity of Life*.

9 See Kingdon, *Lowly Origin*.

10 Craig Allin quoted in Grumbine, 'Wilderness, Wise Use, and Sustainable Development', p. 386.

11 See Naess, 'Deep Ecological Movement'.

12 Lopez, *Arctic Dreams*.

13 Naess, 'Self-Realization'.

14 Summary of oral story by Anthony Nanson. For a full text and further discussion, see Nanson, *Words of Re-enchantment*.

15 Paul, *Dinosaurs of the Air*, p. 314.

16 See Nanson, *Words of Re-enchantment*.

17 See Stallings, 'Web of Silence'.

18 See Zipes, *Creative Storytelling*.

19 Oral story by Anthony Nanson devised as part of Fire Springs' production *Robin of the Wildwood*.

20 Taylor, *Beyond Conservation*.

21 Stearns, *Global Outrage*.

CHAPTER 8

Drawing on forest advocacy and anthropological fieldwork
in Papua New Guinea, Edward shows how the underlying
environmental significance of indigenous stories may be unpacked
through ethnographic knowledge of the indigenous culture.
This chapter describes:

how to apply anthropological methods and thinking to unpack indigenous
local and traditional stories for what they may say about sustainability;

~

how environmentalists can use indigenous and other traditional stories – as
informed by ethnographic knowledge – to question Western assumptions
about sustainable relations with the natural world;

~

two traditional stories.

The chapter shows how ethnographic knowledge not only informs
our understanding of indigenous stories, but can enhance
the way we tell them as well.

Listening to Stories with an Anthropological Ear

Why it matters to explore indigenous people's own understanding of their traditional stories when using such tales to promote sustainability in a Western context

EDWARD SCHIEFFELIN

Many who work in the field of sustainability are attracted to stories from indigenous peoples (hunter-gatherers, subsistence cultivators) on the assumption that such peoples live in 'harmony with nature' and so may have insights to offer on sustainable living. There is often, in fact, truth in this. But if we want to tell these stories to stimulate new ways of thinking about sustainability, we would do well to consider that tales of culturally different peoples may not mean what we take them to mean. How, then, can one find out what the original tellers of a tale meant to convey? The anthropologist's method for discovering this lies in ethnography, the study of indigenous culture. A telling of the story informed by ethnography as well as knowledge of the region's ecology can give us our best means of presenting the original tellers' perspective on their world to a non-indigenous audience.

In this chapter, I explore two traditional stories from the Bosavi (or Kaluli) people of Papua New Guinea from an ethnographic perspective. My aim is to show how one may come to understand the cultural context that gives these stories their significance and to convey the meanings and implications the stories had for those who originally told them. Finally, for the environmentalist and activist, I address how this knowledge can facilitate ways of telling these stories which will open up the indigenous message of sustainability the stories can hold for us. This method of deepening our understanding of stories from other cultures can also be used to deepen our understanding of our own.

A forest people

The Bosavi people live in a vast tropical rainforest in central Papua New Guinea. When I first met them in 1966 they had had very little contact with the outside world and lived, in most respects, their traditional way of life. At that time, the 20 or so Bosavi communities each lived in a large communal longhouse separated from each other in the forest by a one- or two-hour walk. They lived from hunting, fishing, gardening, and pig husbandry – and from the starch flour extracted from wild sago palms. Their lives were patterned by the cycle of shifting cultivation. Every two years or so, when gardens were exhausted and local forest resources became scarce, a community moved to establish a new longhouse and gardens in a fresh place. The old site was abandoned to re-forest and recover over the next 20 or so years.

Bosavis had a deep knowledge of the forest plants and animals. They knew the time of day or night by the sounds made by insects and birds, and the seasons by subtle changes in the vegetation.[1] They were superb ornithologists and had an intimate sense of the habits and presence of other living creatures in the forest, an awareness that extended beyond the visible into the world of spirits. Theirs was not an Arcadian life, however. Like other human communities, Bosavis suffered their share of hard work, sorrow, ill health, dispute, and armed conflict. Nonetheless, for generations and generations from time immemorial, they lived their way of life more or less sustainably without exhausting their subsistence base or degrading their forest.

In 1968 Yabiye Sogobaye told me this Bosavi origin myth:

When Things Went Their Separate Ways

In the time when the world came into form, the land/world was entirely filled with people. There were no trees, no plants, no animals. The people were wet and cold from the rain; with no food, they were hungry. They said [to each other], 'What will we eat?' Finally one man said, 'I'll be sago.' Another said, 'I'll be bananas' [Others chimed in:] 'You be birds.' 'You be fish.' 'You be cassowaries.' 'You be wallabies.' [And so on for all the things that live in the forest.] People became the living creatures or plants they were designated, each according to their kind. The few people that remained became the ancestors of human beings today.[2]

As an anthropologist I was interested in the content and performance of the stories and in how tellers and listeners understood them. Part of this information came from asking people what they took the story to mean, part from how they referred to it in discussions about other things, part from getting to know the fauna and flora the story talked about, and part from observing how Bosavis dealt with ordinary events in everyday life.

When Yabiye first told me this story, it puzzled me. The myth was very spare. How, exactly, did Bosavis make sense of it? What did it imply for them? When I asked Yabiye and my other Bosavi friends about this, they responded that that was the way the myth was told and that was that. I was pretty certain they were not trying to hide anything. Rather, I thought, the story was in some way so self-evident to them, its significance so deep in their bones, that there was no need to unpack it.

So I considered the story itself. Its major themes clearly focus on food: most of the plants and animals mentioned in the story are eaten by Bosavis at one time or another. I began to explore the significance of food in Bosavi life for clues to its significance in the story. Here there was plenty to go on. It became clear from what I observed, from the way people acted and what they said, that food was much more for them than simply a means of sustenance. It was the major vehicle of human social connection.

In Bosavi communities the offering and accepting, giving, sharing, and exchanging of food, with their implications of nurturance and mutual dependency, were the primary means of creating, extending, and deepening all social relationships. The relations established by hospitality and the sharing of food had strong emotional resonance: they communicated affection, dependability, safety, and trust. By contrast, to be *hungry* evoked images (in the Bosavi imagination) of loneliness: the loss of human relationships, the absence of assistance, sharing, and hospitality, pointing ultimately to a condition of abandonment and profound vulnerability.[3] Poignant representation of this plight is the subject of the most moving passages in Bosavi poetry, ceremony, and song.

Given the centrality of sharing food to the making and maintaining of Bosavi social relationships, the opening scene of this origin myth presents a poignant situation. Primordial humanity stands in a barren world without food or shelter. These individuals have nothing to eat – and, what is worse, social life as Bosavis understand it is not really possible. They can neither appeal to one another for sustenance nor extend it to those they care for. It is a situation of paradox and paralysis: amidst a crowd of others, everyone is isolated and on their own. This thwarted sociality is brought to an end in the myth by the voluntary self-transformation of most of humankind into different species of animals and plants – particularly species that allow the gifting and sharing of food. At this point, when relations of (thwarted) social reciprocity (the give and take of ordinary life) become converted into (actual) relations of ecological interdependence (plants and game that can be given and shared), social life can proceed.

Among Bosavis the gifting and sharing of food was about more than the ordinary relationships between relatives and friends. It also had political importance. Large-scale ceremonial exchanges of pigs and game, reciprocal offers of hospitality, and exchanges of women in marriage formed the substance of a wider regime of formalised social reciprocation through which relationships between communities were organised and maintained. Injuries and wrongs were also righted through the retaliatory taking of 'payback' (vengeance) or the exaction of compensation. In this way the rules and practices of social reciprocity provided Bosavis with their moral sensibility. This myth is therefore not, as it might seem, only about the origins of animals and plants in the world. From a Bosavi perspective, it is even more about the origins of human society.

The way the plants and animals of the forest come about in the origin myth has further implications. If we view the myth in the light of other Bosavi cultural beliefs and practices we discover something surprising. When a person dies, Bosavis told me, their spirit goes to live in the tree-tops in the form of a bird. Older Bosavis explained that the world of the spirits is an invisible place located at the top of the forest canopy. The spirits appear as people to each other within their world, but they 'show through' to living people as birds. The calls of the birds in the canopy are what we overhear of the spirits conversing in their world. 'Do you hear that?' Yabiye once remarked in response to the plaintive call of a fruit-dove in the forest. 'It is a little child calling for its mother.'

Other wild creatures were similarly believed to appear to each other as human in their own world, though they appear as animals in ours. This had seemingly little practical consequence for Bosavis. They hunted wild game to eat, for, as several people said to me, 'after all, to us they are just animals'. But, in certain circumstances, Bosavis *behaved* towards wild animals in ways that seemed to acknowledge they possessed a hidden human nature. For example, they did not kill animals found in newly planted gardens lest those be the animal forms of beneficial garden spirits. Similarly, Bosavis never tortured, mistreated, or ridiculed wild animals, lest the animals take offence, gather allies, and emerge from the forest in a huge vengeful horde to attack the community.[4]

If we view the origin myth in the light of these beliefs, it appears that the primordial transformation of humans into animals was not straightforward. The animals retained a hidden human side which could become relevant in certain circumstances. Consequently people's relations with animals bore a residual uncertainty about whether these were simply ecological interactions (such as humans hunting animals for food), or whether, through thoughtless behaviour, humans might provoke a 'human' reciprocal response from the animals (retaliation, vengeance). Though Bosavis were keen hunters, they hunted with the awareness that they could not take the behaviour of animals towards themselves for granted. From this perspective the origin myth lays the groundwork for the Bosavi awareness that the natural world may well respond to them with an unwanted 'human' social reaction if they fail to treat it with a certain human social respect.

A second Bosavi story plays a further permutation on this theme by highlighting that productive relations with wild food resources entail properly measured reciprocal behaviour among human beings themselves.

The Mother of the Animals

One morning Dorsali tells his cross-cousin Newelesu he is going hunting. Travelling to the heights of Mt Bosavi he comes upon a strange house with lots of game on the smoking racks but no one at home. Dorsali sits and waits on the veranda. Presently an old woman carrying firewood appears. She invites Dorsali in and gives him a big meal of sago and game. In the evening she goes to the edge of the clearing as though to call her domestic pigs in for the night. When she calls, however, it is wild animals – wallabies, bandicoots, cuscus, and others – that emerge from the undergrowth and follow her into the longhouse. She feeds them, then beds down among them in the women's section of the house. Dorsali sleeps in the men's section. The next morning the old woman gives Dorsali two large bags of smoked game to take home.

When Dorsali arrives back home, Newelesu begs one of the bags for himself and then asks Dorsali how he got them. Dorsali tells him the story. The next morning Newelesu wants to try his luck. Dorsali warns him not to enter the house if no one is home, not to eat other than what he is given, and not to have sex with the old woman. Newelesu finds the house, but he goes in and eats his fill of the game from the racks. When the old woman arrives and offers him another big meal, he eats that too. After she retires to sleep, he goes into the women's section and tries to force her to have sex. The old woman beats Newelesu away with a piece of firewood. During the commotion, the animals flee the house and down the south side of the mountain. The old woman also escapes and follows down after them.

Newelesu comes home battered and bruised and empty-handed. Dorsali scolds him for not doing as he was advised. Later, hunting together on Mt Bosavi, they find the house broken-down and abandoned. The old woman never returns. And from that time on there have been more animals on the south side of the mountain than there are to the north where the Bosavi live.[5]

This is one of a series of traditional tales involving two of the Bosavis' favourite stock characters: Dorsali, the perennial straight man, and his goofy, screw-up cross-cousin Newelesu, who continually gets into trouble because he can't control his appetites. These Dorsali/Newelesu tales, though invariably told with gusto and hilarity, often, like this one, have a moral or cautionary substance.

This story seems fairly transparent in its significance for sustainability. It recounts how selfishness, greed, and lack of social restraint between human beings bring havoc to their relations with the sustaining natural environment. However, this story also holds several interesting Bosavi cultural resonances that are not immediately obvious to non-Bosavi listeners. It is a mark of Dorsali's character that he behaves with restraint towards the old woman and her offer of hospitality. What is less obvious is that the situation offers him a strong temptation to do otherwise. A strange house full of rich pickings with only an elderly woman to protect them could look like a chance for easy plunder to some opportunistic and unruly young Bosavis. Dorsali's restraint is significant, for he is sent home with a huge present of meat as though he was returning from a gifting-feast.

Newelesu, however, is the more interesting character. His stupid violation of the old woman's hospitality leads, in the story, to permanent depletion of game resources for all Bosavis. Newelesu is an amusing figure, well known for his huge capacity for food, his lustfulness, and his heedless proclivity for taking shortcuts in pursuit of easy rewards – and always coming a cropper. But though his antics and pratfalls provide great hilarity, Newelesu also embodies a darker quality. He exhibits most of the character traits of what Bosavis call a *sei*. *Sei*s are people who have an evil substance in their hearts which secretly causes them to bring illness and death to others. *Sei*s were deeply feared and loathed in Bosavi culture, and they were held accountable for their nefarious actions. If a person was identified as the *sei* responsible for a death by illness in the community, they were likely to be summarily executed.

It is this witchy aspect of Newelesu, the dark side to his hapless incompetence, that marks him as a treacherous and destructive figure. Every Bosavi listener knows this before the story begins. At the same time, Newelesu is Dorsali's cross-cousin, a close relative, and thus 'one of us' who cannot be ostracised. Bosavis regard him with bemused affection, wariness, and distaste.

Getting the original message across: incorporating ethnographic knowledge in your storytelling

These Bosavi stories can in principle be told as they stand by any teller (but see Collins, this volume) both for the entertainment they may provide and for whatever meaning or message tellers and listeners may find in them. My premise here, however, is that if we want to tell these stories with authority, and knowledgeably convey what their original tellers intended to get across, it is important to gain understanding of what significance they conveyed for those original tellers.

Direct information from indigenous storytellers about their stories is almost impossible to find. But there is plenty of material available – in libraries and online – about the cultural background, traditional knowledge, and conventional assumptions that will inform how a story was constructed and what issues it addressed. This will give a pretty good idea of how it was understood by those who heard it.

The web is a good place to begin. Googling the title of the story, or the names of one or more characters, usually brings up a number of versions plus information about the story's history and the people it came from. Track the references to the original scholarly collection of the story by an anthropologist or folklorist. It is worth trying to get hold of this version of the story, via an interlibrary loan if necessary, in order to obtain an unexpurgated text as close as possible to the original version(s) told by the indigenous tellers, rather than one rewritten for Western popular consumption.

To get an in-depth perspective on the cultural background of your story, you will need a good general ethnographic study of the culture it comes from. Ethnographies can be used in various ways. To learn about the natural setting, read up on the climate, natural environment and landscape, the seasonal cycle and modes of people's livelihood, the kinds of dwellings they live in and their settlement pattern. Read the introduction to get an overview of the author's argument and a preliminary take on the people, their character and culture. Savour any photographs of the region and the people. This will help you to visualise the story as enacted in this setting by these people and may alter the way you think about it. Informed visualisation really helps when you wish to describe the story's setting and characters.

To address deeper questions there is little alternative to reading the whole of the ethnography. But you can do so efficiently. Having identified the major themes of your story, read with questions in mind like: Do aspects of the people's way of life as described in the ethnography find expression in the story you are working with – in ways that might inform its meaning or the way you tell it? How do the people's customary practices affect the longer-term sustainability of the way they live? To what extent do such matters of sustainability play a part in the story?

For storytelling purposes, the more systematic sociological aspects of an ethnography (kinship systems, political structures) are mainly important for the way they play themselves out in the daily life of the people – and thus inform their stories. Look for *descriptions* of events in which these structures shape the complexities of people's lives on the ground. How might kinship relations be involved in the protagonist's endeavours? Are there culturally privileged relationships between certain types of kin, such as older sister and younger brother or mother's brother and sister's son, which could be important in your story? Might some aspects of the customary behaviour and obligations entailed in kinship relations illuminate what happens in the tale?

Pay attention to the spiritual and cosmological beliefs of the people – especially as they relate to birth, illness and death, morality, the causes of misfortune, the soul and the afterlife. Be alert to the ethnographic descriptions of people's actual behaviour in relation to these things as well as what they say they believe about them. People's relations with the natural world are often deeply entailed in these beliefs. Follow your nose for particular things that draw your interest.

The better your feel for the subtleties of the ethnography, the more challenging it may seem to incorporate ethnographic knowledge into your tellings. At the same time, your feel for the ethnography will help you find a way. Consider, for example, how you might depict Newelewsu in telling 'The Mother of the Animals', and put across his unsavoury and sinister edge, to give non-Bosavi listeners a whiff of the assumptions that every Bosavi brings to the story. This sort of challenge draws on the poetic ingenuity and imagination of the teller and is quite fun.

A stiffer challenge is to communicate complex configurations of social attitudes which are more often depicted in generalised ethnographic exposition than concrete description. How, for example, to suggest that the Bosavi origin myth is as much about the origin of human society, conceived in terms of reciprocal giving and sharing, as it is about the appearance of plants and animals in the world? I sometimes tell the story like this:

> In the time when the world came into form, the land was entirely filled with people. There were no trees, no plants, no animals. The people were wet and cold from the rain; with no food, they were hungry. The people said to each other, 'What will we eat?'

'I tell my older sister I am hungry, but she has no food for me.'
'My brother asks me for something to eat, but I have nothing to
share with him.' 'What shall we do?'

Finally one man said, 'I'll be sago.' Another said, 'I'll be
bananas' Others chimed in: 'You be birds.' 'You be fish.' 'You
be cassowaries.' 'You be wallabies.' And so on for all the living
things of the forest. People became the creatures or plants they
designated, each according to their kind. The few people that
remained became the ancestors of human beings today.

The addition of two lines of dialogue drawn from what we know of Bosavi
attitudes about food suggests clearly the unspoken Bosavi perspective.
This represents an informed attempt to convey a crucial indigenous im-
plication of this story to non-Bosavi listeners.

Conclusion: the broader message

From a broader sustainability perspective, our two Bosavi stories, when
viewed in their cultural context, reveal a profound and complex interconnectedness between human beings and the natural world, which is
not fully visible from the stories taken at their face value. The origin
myth, understood in the light of Bosavi food practices and spirit beliefs,
reveals that the boundaries between animals and humans are ambigu-
ous and so their ecological interdependence is not completely separable
from social reciprocity.

'The Mother of the Animals' suggests that whether or not we act
socially in a responsible manner towards other human beings automatically impacts on our relations with the natural world – and therefore implies we should take some responsibility for our own and others' actions.
How might Dorsali have better constrained his *sei* cross-cousin? How
does one deal respectfully with others who would destroy a world we love?
That is one of the most difficult tasks that the challenge of sustainability
presents us. 'Tragedy', Paul Radin once said, 'must be ascribed to that irresistible craving which exacts from man and the world more than he is
entitled to and more than his abilities and powers warrant.'[6] It was just
such uncontained endeavour that was responsible for depleting the hunt-

ing – in the story and in Bosavi perception – for all Bosavis. Non-Bosavi storytellers who want to explore the story's meaning for their listeners might focus on two critical questions: What can we learn from the relationship between Dorsali and his cross-cousin? And how can we curtail our own as well as others' tendency to behave like Newelesu, thereby to minimise the tragedy to which Radin so eloquently refers?

Notes

[1] Schieffelin, *Sorrow of the Lonely*, pp. 29–31ff; Feld, *Sound and Sentiment*.

[2] Author's field notes 1966–68. See also Schieffelin, *Sorrow of the Lonely*, p. 93, for a slightly mission-inluenced version.

[3] Schieffelin, *Sorrow of the Lonely*; Feld, *Sound and Sentiment*.

[4] See Schieffelin, 'Retaliation of the Animals'.

[5] Author's field notes, 1975–77

[6] Radin, *Primitive Man as a Philosopher*, p. xx.

CHAPTER 9

Inviting us into a scene around an open fire one stormy
night on Dartmoor, Chris explains the practice of 'feeding the
story' which he uses while working with participants on a bushcraft,
survival skills, and outdoor exploration event. As he tells a traditional
story the listeners are at specific points invited to find themselves within
the narrative and offer up a related image, memory, or association.
He examines:

the value of helping people to become more responsive listeners in a group
and how this supports the creation of a sense of community;

~

how greater responsiveness to a story encourages greater reflectivity about
one's everyday life;

~

an extended fragment of one traditional story.

The capacities for active listening and reflection engendered by this
story-based process of dialogue are important qualities to
be cultivated in members of a sustainable community.

Feeding the Story

Developing people's active listening capacity and ecological awareness by means of storywork in the outdoors

CHRIS SALISBURY

Amidst the ancient rolling hills and roaring rivers of Dartmoor, a group of adults huddle on piles of sheepskins and cushions in a room lit by the soft light of candles and lanterns. The drum calls out a hypnotic rhythm to welcome an old story. After a long day outdoors everyone is more than ready to simply lie back, relax, and listen ...

But in this chapter I'm going to discuss why, instead, I use a process of dialogue to draw the listeners into an active relationship with the story being told. It's a process I call 'feeding the story'.

In the work of the Westcountry School of Myth and Story, we encourage adults and children alike to become immersed in ancient myth, bardic tradition, and the wild land of Britain. Spending time alone in nature is as important a part of this experience as the storywork. Storytelling sessions are also part of the WildWise courses and camps I facilitate. In beautiful locations teeming with wildlife, we nurture people's knowledge of wildlife, their nature awareness, and their bushcraft skills in order to expand their understanding of the value and meaning of human beings' relationship with the natural world. One of our methods is to teach them what it means to be a story-carrier.

Shy storytellers and confident story-carriers

The term 'tradition bearer' has long been applied to performing artists who know the tales, songs, or dances of a particular tradition and feel responsible for keeping these alive through performance, teaching, recording, and sharing.[1] It is also applied to people who have a strong interest in the lore of their family or place of origin. I initially expected that the people who joined our courses would not only be interested in nature, but might already have some sense of themselves as bearers of that kind of tradition. I expected that most would be keenly interested in their family's stories and in the lore of their place of origin. I was wrong. Many participants did not consider themselves to be rooted in any kind of 'oral' tradition, and many were not even that keen on nature. They said that they joined the courses on the basis of an inarticulate longing for some kind of adventure, or connection, a longing for something 'more'. This longing came across like a shy desire to feel more at home in themselves, with strangers, in the open air, in where they came from and where they were going, and above all to be more at ease with the stories they wanted to tell about all this.

Many participants hoped that by developing a more meaningful relationship with 'nature' they would find a more comfortable relationship with themselves and with each other. Not infrequently, we found residing beneath this a deeper hope that the workshop environment might bring some relief from the burden of a troubling personal story. By telling such a story to a sympathetic 'passing' other, some participants hoped to release its curtailing grip on their everyday life. They expressed the desire to encounter a nature-inspired story that might help them to go forward in life. I sometimes wondered if such people longed in their heart of hearts to find out in the midst of nature what was special about them, to discover how best to relate to their own and other people's personal stories – in a setting that was unfamiliar, natural, and somewhere else. That's when I noticed the difference between people who were very shy about personal storytelling and those who carried their stories with a spirit of self-belief.

Like the time-honoured tradition-bearers, those who told their personal stories with joy and confidence tended to desire that other people would treasure them too. Moreover, they liked to catch the tales that other people told. They listened actively and enjoyed the way other people's stories sparked their own imagination and reinvigorated their own thoughts or feelings. It seemed clear that their capacity for active telling was linked to their ability to catch another person's story and to reflect on it, and that this reflective capacity in turn reinvigorated their relationship with themselves, with others, with the stories they knew and told, and with the places that mattered to them. After hearing or telling a personal story these participants said things like:

- Did you really like that? Would you mind repeating that? I want to savour it.
- You've made me think.
- Do you mind if I tell my wife your story?
- Are you sure you'll remember that? That's lovely.
- I'm going to have to look at *my* village inn and find out what stories it has to tell.
- I never knew that about robins. That's such a great story.
- The moors will never be the same again now I know what happened to you there.

These people, who were both active listeners and lively tellers, told and listened to personal stories with an eager anticipation of engaging in dialogue and reflection that would feed everyone's relationship with the story that had been recounted. I wondered if there was a way, appropriate to the context of a nature-exploration course, in which I might help shy storytellers or fidgety listeners to become a bit more like the confident, reflective ones.

Feeding the story

Furthermore, the ability to reflect on things is fundamental to a person's capacity to survive in the wild. The ability to reflect on things is also fundamental to our grappling with the challenge of sustainability, which can be understood as a collective expression of our capacity to survive. For this reason I feel it is important to help the participants in my storytelling and bushcraft courses to acquire a sound capacity for reflection. To do this, I developed the storytelling technique I call 'feeding the story'.

At its most straightforward, 'feeding the story' means that when I tell a traditional story I pause at particular points and invite the listeners to offer up an image or a moment within the narrative which has caught their attention. I then engage everyone in a group dialogue to explore how each chosen image or moment impacts on each person, and how this impact in turn affects the community of listeners. At its best, this can be a thoughtful, fun, deeply collaborative and dynamic way of working with a story. The technique can also be used to engage listeners with particular questions and dilemmas of contemporary living, such as issues of sustainability and community. I set up the dialogue either by a strategic choice of story or by framing the storytelling process with a range of activities, and then I choose particular moments to stop the story and ask purposeful, carefully formulated questions.

Let us return to the room I described at the beginning of this chapter: the huddle of people, the candlelight, the sheepskins and cushions, the hypnotic rhythm of the drum ... and a traditional story, potent with timeless themes, that begins like this:

The Golden Feather

Once upon a time in a land of broad woodlands and sweet meadows, a young hunter was riding his horse of power through a forest. Even though it was springtime, the birds were not singing and there was an eerie silence. Suddenly his horse stopped and the hunter saw lying on the path a huge golden feather.

The horse said, 'Leave it alone. If you pick up that feather you will know the meaning of trouble.'

The hunter dismounted and crouched before the feather. He had never seen anything like it. It lay on the path, glittering like a flame from the sun, and he knew it could only be from the Firebird. 'My horse is wise beyond wisdom and I don't want to know the meaning of trouble, but a golden feather from the burning breast of the Firebird would make a fine present for the King.'

He picked up the feather ...[2]

At this point in the story I often stop. I must now make a choice. My questions can steer the listeners in one of three main directions. They can invite:

- elaboration of the story's content ('Can you describe the horse?' 'What kind of plants grew in that forest?' 'What outfit did the rider wear?');
- personal connections with the story's content ('What kind of forest have you recently visited? What did it look like?' 'Do you remember

an occasion when you picked up something from a path? What was it and what happened?');
• a philosophical or socio-political connection to the story ('How would you define wisdom?' 'What kind of troubles might the horse be talking about?' 'What motivates people to give a present to a king?').

All questions are open-ended the way I formulate them, and this invites the specific expression of feelings, facts, ideas, knowledge, memories. I try to use some or all of these in the next part of the story. An example of this might be 'that *slightly damp* feather', or 'that *sharp wisdom passed on by his grandfather*', or 'the present *that would raise his standing in the King's eyes*'. Which 'invitation' I choose depends on the circumstance, the composition and goal of the group, and what we hope to achieve with the work. Which responses I subsequently weave into my telling of the story depend on similar considerations. In the generous and mutually attentive atmosphere that we try to establish from the beginning of a course, and which I especially try to maintain in these moments, I am inviting members of the group to share how the story's images activate their listening hearts, hands, and mind.

If a particular type of question about the story attracts a lot of interest and other types of questions are ignored, I may redirect the group's attention by presenting that same domain with a differently formulated question. Instead of asking, 'When did you last visit a forest?' I may say, 'When in your life, and why, might you have picked up such a feather?' Once someone has responded to this question, the group will soon start sharing seminal memories and perceptions in the personal domain. As they listen to each other they realise that the story's feather connects with very different things for different people. In one workshop someone said, 'For me it was when I first went on stage and realised my life had just changed.' Someone else said, 'For me it was kissing a boy for the first time.' And another, 'For me it was my first joint.'

Respectful attention to every voice

Centuries ago the Persian poet Hafiz wrote, 'How did the rose ever open its heart and give to this world all of its beauty? It felt the encouragement of light against its being; otherwise we all remain too frightened.'[3]

The light that this dialogic engagement with a story allows us to shine upon some aspect of our life experience is, by and large, gentle and warm. Nobody has to speak. Nobody has to be eloquent. To quell any lurking anxiety I often say that most of us find ourselves particularly inspired by failure and imperfection – at which a wave of relief may wash through some listeners, who now suddenly find it easier to relax into the sharing process. By staying compassionately attentive to what people say about their connection to the as yet incomplete story, I enable the group to begin to appreciate the validity of wholly different responses to just a single story event. In the present example, that event might be the finding and picking up of the golden feather, or riding in a forest, or the inexplicable silence of the birds, or the warning from the wise and trusted friend. Besides personal experiences some participants may toss into the reflective brew opinions, observations, and speculations. In terms of the story none of these is 'right', yet each is welcome.

Most listeners find the periodic sharing of responses to the unfolding story deeply enriching. In the course of the four or five periods of feeding the story, some overall pattern usually emerges. It will not be a simple pattern; it will contain contradictions, tensions, nuances of difference, and thereby reveal the complexity of what it is to be human. In the philosopher Mikhail Bakhtin's theory of 'dialogism', true understanding of something involves a recognition of competing perspectives, as expressed in a 'polyphony' of, literally, 'many voices'.[4] This is an important idea when it comes to questions of sustainability, in which many different people's interests are at stake. It is easier to become thoughtful about a passionately held point of view when we can be truly surprised by the diversity of other people's responses to the very same issue that we were responding to.

Building a community of reflective listeners

The process of feeding the story works best if, *before* telling the story, I instruct the listeners that I will stop my storytelling from time to time and ask them a specific question to invite them to expand the story in particular ways. I also say that I will weave aspects of their contributions into my storytelling, but that these will not change the story's overall structure. Such preparation of the listeners for something that is going to happen during the storytelling invites and enables them to attend to the story's landscape more wholeheartedly. Listeners have told me that their capacity to listen actively to the story increased as soon as they took this intention on board. In other words, all of us can listen at a constant, more personal pitch when we allow ourselves to enter the story in this 'curious' way. In so doing, we are more likely to catch the story and thereby become a co-carrier of it.

I also find that the storyteller's systematic support of active listening in a group helps to create a sense of community. Each time that everyone present offers their response to a question about something in the story they have just heard, they continue to build that feeling of community. The sharing makes the public space of storytelling at once more social and more personal; the geometry of sitting in a circle around the fire reinforces the sense of listening collectively while the attention paid to everyone's response grants equal dignity to each person's voice (see Metcalfe, this volume). Moreover, the anticipated return to the telling of the traditional tale, which we know will continue to its ending, grants every participant the opportunity to cloak private content, in their response to particular questions, in words or images that are neither too revealing nor too confronting. I believe that this kind of respectful, dialogic engagement with a story, and with each other, supports the skills that people need to participate in any reflective community containing many voices.

As I said earlier, most people who attend a countryside camp or workshop quietly long for a change for the better in their relationship with themselves, with each other, and with the natural world. It may be readily – perhaps too readily – assumed that those who gather to the beat of a story drum in a dim-lit room among the ancient hills and rivers of Dartmoor are a particular kind of people, unrepresentative of society as a whole: that they are predisposed to respond to stories and seek new meaning in their lives. However, I have used the same technique of feeding the story amid the hustle and bustle of a city park with a random group of park users, or with a group of distracted youngsters wobbling on broken chairs in the corridor of a bleak community centre. In these places too the lure of a storyteller who listens attentively to carefully invited responses, and ensures that everyone present has opportunity to speak of images, ideas, or memories that resonate with the story, soon proves irresistible. I therefore believe we can build a reflective community of listeners and future story-carriers wherever we are.

Why reflectivity is needed now

In recent years many participants on my courses have commented that they are not used to being invited to share their ideas or memories, or to reflect on something, let alone on their lives in the presence of truly attentive others. If they are, they say, it is generally in therapy, which is private and removed from the world of community and environment outside the door. From their perspective the process of responding to a potent story in a creative, personal way, in a social and natural context, both allows them to reflect on what is happening in their lives and between each other in the present, and also introduces them to a group culture in which it is normal to respectfully share experiences, ideas, and reflections. This accustoms them to the kind of shared reflection and 'good public conversation with true negotiation and compromise' that are necessary to bring about change in the direction of more sustainable ways of living on the earth.[5] When we feed the stories, we feed our souls, and an ancient contract between ourselves and others, and the ecosystem that contains us all, is honoured.

Notes

[1] Von Sydow, 'Geography and Folk-Tale Oicotypes'.

[2] Retelling of the start of 'The Firebird and Princess Vasilisa'. Sources: Ransome, *Old Peter's Russian Tales*; Afanas'ev, *Russian Fairy Tales,* trans. Guterman.

[3] Hafiz, 'It Felt Love', p. 121.

[4] Vice, *Introducing Bakhtin.*

[5] Sunderland, *In a Glass Darkly*, p. 159.

PART III

IN AND AROUND THE CITY

CHAPTER 10

Helen reflects on what happened when, early in her career,
she took a group of troubled urban young people to a wildish
environment that felt very alien to them but deeply familiar to her.
She presents two traditional stories and describes:

how telling stories can build bridges between people and the natural
world, however strange this world may feel at first;

~

the importance of taking time to appreciate the survival function of urban people's
behaviour when they first encounter an open, natural environment;

~

the value of story-inspired chat in promoting pro-environmental interest.

The chapter highlights the uniqueness of each person's experience
and shows how facilitators' mindfulness of behaviour they do not
yet understand can encourage mutual curiosity and
greater environmental sensitivity.

Fishing Tales and Catching Connections

The role of storytelling in establishing common 'natural' ground with troubled youngsters who feel alienated from the outdoors

HELEN EAST

When things go well in change-oriented groupwork, it's easy to talk about them. Honest talk gets harder when things are difficult. If it's a problematic single session, we may shrug our shoulders and let it go. But what if you have to facilitate a tricky group for weeks on end? In this chapter I discuss a group I worked with early in my career. I highlight how taking them to a wildish place helped me learn some enduring lessons about working with young people who have a very different attitude towards the natural environment from my own.

Talk, especially stories, has always been my primary means of connecting with and making sense of the world. When in my early twenties I moved back to England, I got a part-time job in South London as an outreach storyteller and another as playleader at a centre for young people deemed to be 'at risk'. Younger siblings often attended the centre too, especially in the holidays, when we had about twenty kids aged from seven to sixteen. Some were shy, uncertain of themselves, or withdrawn; others dominating, destructive, even aggressive. Some had difficulties at home or at school. A few were in trouble with the law. Despite plenty of boasting and pushy attitude, most lacked a sense of self-worth. They were surrounded by poverty, violence, addiction, inequity, racism, and low expectations. My job, within the framework of the centre, was to give them more options, help them become more resilient in the face of this adversity. But how?

I had hoped to use storytelling and drama, but soon found we were not expected to spend time 'sitting around and talking'. The only room available was too small and noisy, with nowhere to relax or chat while others were doing something more active. After a break-in and fire damaged the centre, the problem of lack of space got worse and I found it harder and harder to think of effective ways to channel our energies creatively. I began to feel out of my depth.

The bare essentials of a 'good enough working alliance' were in place.[1] Everyone knew how frequently we would meet, where we met, how new members were introduced, what we were supposed to do, what boundaries mattered. I got on reasonably well with everyone in the group. We just didn't have a good time together. The problem, especially with the older ones, was that we not only had different notions of 'fun' but also had very different life experiences. They couldn't believe I hadn't grown up with a TV. I couldn't believe that many of them had never seen the sea. It wasn't easy to talk about these differences in the clamour and cramped space of the centre. And you could forget about storytelling; stories were 'just for kids'.

These young people had grown up in urban, man-made surroundings, mostly indoors or in enclosed spaces, with the constant noise of TV, radio, and other people. The streets were full of traffic, litter, and fumes. I'd spent my childhood in many different countries, usually with wide open vistas and wild outdoor spaces to roam. I'd lived among communities that were close to the land and had strong storytelling traditions. Everywhere people told me stories, of many different kinds and often referring to the natural world around them. I listened to tales about a snow-bound mountain, or a terrible fishing trip, or one that explained a bird's plaintive cry; reminiscences of why someone moved away or planted a walnut tree; and threads of narrative that conveyed the name of a flower or a belief about a tree. From this I learned to observe what was around me, to recognise the sounds of my locality. I discovered what to trust, where to be wary. This was how family lore traditionally passed from one generation to the next. The stories drew me into the relationship the storytellers had with their environment: how to behave not just to other people but to the rest of nature, and the basic principles of sustainable living – 'Waste not, want not'; recycling a necessity. I grew up assuming it was normal to tell stories and that everyone knew their local natural environment as a space to go to freely and as a source of materials and food. I assumed the same was true for the young people in the centre; I just didn't know how to access their stories.

I decided to get the group away from the confinement of the centre and asked permission to take them by minibus to nearby Richmond Park. The park is a wildish place with hills, woods, copses, and grassland. Deer, woodpeckers, stag beetles, and many other creatures abound there. A colleague agreed to help but warned me that some kids 'might run off'. I was startled to see how they actually reacted. Clinging to each other and the car park, they were terrified of entering this open space where deer roamed free. They had no desire to run about and were reluctant even to walk down the sandy paths. They were equally taken aback by the way I behaved, especially when I gathered and ate some blackberries, sweet chestnuts, and beechnuts.

'Can you eat this then?' one lad asked, in all seriousness, offering me a stick. When he showed interest in tasting a nut, I warned he might find it bitter, but he persisted. There was immediately more interest from the rest of the group. But to get more nuts down they began throwing stones and whacking the tree.

'Pick up the ones on the ground,' I suggested.

'Urgh! That's dirty!'

I felt at a loss. I was only six years older than some of them but felt as though I was from a different world. I didn't yet fully understand that they'd missed out on many experiences I took for granted. I'd presumed they'd have visited this park before because it was so near where they lived. I understood now that this was their first visit. They didn't know how to enjoy the unfamiliar freedom of this unfamiliar space.

I was convinced the outing was a disaster. I was about to give up and go back home, when one boy noticed a pond.

'Can you fish there?' he asked.

I was surprised. 'Do you fish, then?'

He nodded. So did someone else.

'Where do you go?'

'Clapham Common.'

I was used to sea fishing. The pond on Clapham Common – another park – seemed to me impossibly small. 'What do you catch?'

'Fish,' said the boy.

The others laughed.

I didn't persist. Instead I followed his lead with a comeback: 'What do you call a fish with no eyes?'

No one could guess.

'Fsh.'

Everyone laughed again, this time with me.

By now we'd moved closer to the pond. I seized my chance. 'You see those trees, there?' I pointed to some willows by the water. 'Well, you know the way people like to go fishing? Even if they don't catch much?'

The Willows by the Water

There were these two friends. They'd hung around together all their lives. Grumpy old pair they were usually, but they'd cheer up a bit when they got away from work – and from home too. They'd slip off whenever they could, down to the river, or any-where they could have a bit of peace and do some fishing. One of them had a rod. The other just had a net, but he usually man-aged to get something.

This particular day they'd come here – probably that spot half hidden behind those bushes over there. It was a long time ago, but it was pretty much the same. That path up there was the main route past. The church is right over there; you can't see it, but you can hear when the bells are ringing. They were pealing out loud and clear that day because it was a Sunday. In those days nobody worked Sundays. It was considered very wicked if you did. And you weren't allowed to do lots of other things too – no dancing, or being noisy, or going out to have fun. Everybody just went to church.

Only these two, they hadn't. They were trying to keep hidden.

But the vicar happened to walk right past and he saw them there. He was angry. 'You there!' he shouted. 'What are you do-ing, fishing on a Sunday? You stop that at once and come along to church with me!'

Well, the man with a net had thought he'd caught some-thing, but when the vicar shouted he got such a shock he dropped his net, and lost it, and his temper as well. His friend was as bad. They both started swearing at the vicar and telling him to 'Be off!' in no uncertain manner.

'Very well,' said the vicar. 'I will be off. But you won't. Not ever. You'll stay where you are.'

Of course they laughed at him. The man with the net turned back to pull it up out of the water. But his fingers started getting tangled up with it. He couldn't get them loose. The more he tugged the worse it felt – as if his hands were winding themselves into the mesh. He yelled for help from his friend. But the friend discovered he couldn't move his feet, and when he looked down he saw they were sinking into the ground. He opened his mouth to shout too, but no sound came out – only a sort of creaking noise. Reaching up to his mouth, he felt his skin wrinkled and rough as bark and his mouth was grown right over. By the time the vicar returned, there was no sign of the fishermen. Only two willow trees leaning over the river. One was bent right down, one branch all bushy with twigs, trailing in the water like a hand trying to pull a fish from a net. That's why to this day willows grow as close to water as they can get. And some people say they're that bad tempered they'll trip you up if they can.

'Is that true then?'

'Don't be stupid, course it isn't.'

But they were hooked.

'Go and feel the bark,' I said. 'Look at that hole there.'

'Ooh, that's like a mouth. And all them little bits round it, that's the beard.'

Everyone was looking, touching, engaging. They were interested in the trees, imagining them as living beings. On the way back several pointed out other trees that had weird, suggestive shapes.

That was the beginning of a journey of learning, for me as well as the kids, about how to relate to each other and at the same time to a local semi-wild environment. Let me outline some of the lessons I learned from that experience, which have informed my work ever since.

Because of my own confident relationship with the outdoors, I couldn't immediately understand why the teenagers hesitated to rush into the park. Their knowledge of the great outdoors was mainly from TV and films. This hadn't prepared them for the overwhelming sensory impact of being in the park. The vast 'emptiness' of it! The intense smells of autumn! The grunts and bellows of rutting deer! Actually, the fact it was the rutting season was real reason to be wary. And there were other uncertainties: Where could they go to the toilet? What if they got lost? Were there spiders or snakes? So their behaviour in the car park was, for them, both appropriate and wise. They knew not to rush into a place so different from their familiar urban surroundings. Their hesitation and wariness were emotional assets these young people could build on, provided they could connect their caution with curiosity and not get stuck in uncertainty. And they didn't; they followed me into the park. So my first lesson was the importance of taking time to try to understand any behaviour that seems strange to me.

My second lesson arose from my picking nuts and berries. I was pleased that my behaviour awakened the teenagers' curiosity, but there were risks as well. I have always been a forager; I knew a lot about edible wild plants, but they did not. You wouldn't want kids to pick and eat any old berry. It might be harmful. Fortunately, my group showed the caution they'd learned on the streets and demonstrated in the car park: Don't eat stuff you pick off the ground or some random bush. Today I would praise their wisdom, as well as their willingness to try eating something new in the wild *after* checking it out with a knowledgeable person. My second lesson, therefore, was the importance of both respecting people's boundaries and encouraging them to stretch these where appropriate.

It was my frustration with the centre's noisy confining space that prompted me to take the teenagers to Richmond Park. It was the right thing to do. Once the kids got their bearings, and trusted me as their guide, they enjoyed the breathing space of being out in nature. Most young people enjoy challenging activities in the wild, love the fact that nature doesn't tell them to go away, and find that time outdoors inspires them to do things, especially if they can do them with a (preferably mixed-sex) group of friends.[2] The excitement of the trip and the unfamiliarity of the surroundings made it easier for the foraging and storytelling to stimulate their interest. So my third lesson was: if things aren't going right, meet the group in a new location.

The afternoon in the park also helped me to realise how my own background informed my perceptions and how that in turn affected my handling of the group. I've learned to understand how the differences and similarities between people's backgrounds affect what we do and don't do. I take time to discover how the people I'm working with experience their environment and I try not to interpret their behaviour too early, since behaviour I initially don't understand usually reflects self-protective moves that have been useful to them. First impressions shape who we understand each other to be. It takes patience, humour, and skill to out-grow their influence on our interactions and therefore on our ability to learn from and with each other. This was my fourth lesson.

It's the job of nature interpreters, playleaders, storytellers, teachers to help people bridge the gap between the familiar and the unknown. With my fishermen's tale, I responded to what I felt to be the group's intensely urban character, including the need to be 'cool'. I changed a fragment of Roman myth about Pales, the shepherds' deity,[3] into the conversational reporter style – 'It happened right here' – and the slightly nasty edge of urban myth. The teenagers could identify with grumpy fishermen and characters who break a social code. Though Sunday worship might not be part of their life, being expected to be at school at a certain time was. Like the fishermen, they played truant. Parents, social workers, and teachers disapproved of their behaviour. They got punished by exclusion from school and/or being grounded at home. These punishments made you feel stuck – like the men who'd transformed into willows. And, like the trees, they were considered weird and hard.

This approach seemed to work. Should I continue down this line of adapting my stories and style to suit my perception of my listeners? Or might that limit the range of possibilities I could offer them? As I got to know the group better, taking them outside whenever I could, I discovered how important are the threads that make up the weave of story in human interaction: the anecdotes, jokes, riddles, the story snippets like those I'd heard as a child, the reminiscences of life, and the rich complexity of talk that arises when people explore something in nature together. I realised that the main success of that first story was that it opened the door to this kind of small talk. It facilitated a dialogue that bridged our differences and allowed a meeting of hearts and minds. My fifth lesson was the importance of the story-based chat that a story can trigger. I now dedicate plenty of time to eliciting my listeners' ideas, memories, feelings after I've told a story. When this process of joint exploration becomes part of a group's social practice, the individual's motivation to change in a benign direction arises more easily and receives greater social support.

The sharing of stories and experiences with my group of teenagers inched us towards deeper imaginative and emotional waters and a playful relationship that they and I both enjoyed. Through this I gradually arrived at my sixth and final lesson: that it's possible to share stories in a deeply authentic way, true to who you are and what you've experienced, at the same time as respecting the very different background the people you're working with may come from. In this I gained much inspiration from getting to know the Scottish Traveller storyteller Duncan Williamson, who not only possessed an enormous repertoire of tales but was always authentically himself wherever he told them. His tales brought together his knowledge of the natural world, and his first-hand knowledge of farmers, fishermen, horse-dealers, wall-builders, with emotional depth and with strong magic grounded in the solidity of real life. His storytelling always felt like an intimate exchange, even when he was speaking to an audience of hundreds. Watching him tell stories to teenagers excluded from school, I saw how quickly he established himself on equal terms, without ever trying to be like them or impress them.

When I retell Duncan's stories, I remember him and try to speak, in my own way, as authentically as he did. Of all his stories, his tales of the 'selkies' – or seal people – move me the most and connect most deeply with nature and questions of sustainability. They come from a community that depended on fishing.

The Selkies and the Fishermen

Away on the west coast of Argyll, in Scotland, there was a fisherman who lived with his wife and his three sons in a croft on the shore of a sea loch. They had a bit of land, but mostly they relied on fishing. There was plenty of fish, if you knew where to look. The old man had learnt all about that from his father – the best place to set nets, how to watch the weather, or spot signs of a shoal coming in. Naturally, he'd passed everything on to his sons. But now he was getting to feel his age, so he decided it was time to hand over altogether; he wanted to take things easy. The sons were happy enough with this. They were young men, the eldest two well on in their twenties; they were eager to run things their way. And there was enough work to share between them.

But there was one problem. Way out in the middle of the loch was an island. The water round it, being a bit shallower, was warmer. And that drew the fish. You could always get a good catch there. But that island was also where the seals loved to come. You could see them in the morning and the evening, enjoying the sun, and you'd hear them grumphing and moaning and singing. They'd come there to pup – hundreds of them – and they'd cover the whole island. No one else went there, you see; they had it to themselves. But of course they'd have the fish too – all around there – and if you set your nets too close you'd get fish stolen, or find fish bitten in half, and sometimes the nets were torn too. This began to infuriate the young men, especially as the winter drew on and more and more seals came into the loch.

'Never you mind,' the father told them. 'Don't begrudge a bit of fish. There's plenty for us all. Seals have their families to feed too.'

But of course the sons did mind!

'Times have changed,' the eldest said to his brothers. 'It's hard to get a living now. And prices are going up all the time. We can't afford to lose any more nets – or the time it takes to mend them. And once the pups are born and need feeding it will be even worse.'

The second lad agreed. 'It's them or us,' he said. 'We'll have to do something about it.'

The youngest wasn't so sure, but he couldn't go against the others. And so they decided to have a cull: they would go over to the island and kill as many as they could.

They waited till late December, and then one night when the moon was full they took the boat out. Each of them had a big cudgel, with nails stuck into the end. They weren't worried about spoiling the skins; they just wanted to slaughter as many seals as they could, and maybe scare the others off.

They were very quiet as they came near the island, hardly even splashing the oars. But when they looked up at the rocks they couldn't see a single seal. It was oddly silent too. Perhaps they were on the other side.

Carefully the brothers pulled the boat up on the sand and began to work their way round the shore. There was a little cove below them and they thought they could see some movement, so they pulled out their wooden clubs and began to scramble down.

Suddenly a tall man stepped out in front of them. 'What are you doing?' he cried.

'It's none of your business!' whispered the eldest lad. 'And keep your voice down!'

'No,' said the man. 'It is my business.' And he held out his arms.

Now they could see he had a long grey coat. Sleek. Thick. Like sealskin. As he lifted his hands he signalled to the left and right. The brothers could see on either side there were more people coming. Tall. Strong. Dark-eyed. All wearing those same coats.

The lads turned to run back to the boat, but the way was blocked. A line of women this time, but just as solid. Powerful. Angry-eyed.

'Your Bible says, "Do as you would be done by,"' the seal man whispered. 'You came to kill.'

One by one, all around, clubs, sticks, and rocks were raised up high. The brothers were on their knees, begging for mercy. The youngest was crying.

Then there was a murmur as an old grey selkie man pushed his way through the crowd. 'Stop!' he said. 'Stop! You can't do this. Let these children go. Send them home to their father.'

'Children?' the seal leader cried. 'Grandfather, you don't understand. They are murderers. They wanted to destroy your children.'

The old man shook his long grey hair. 'No. It is you who don't understand.' He turned to the brothers, helped them stand up. 'Seal people,' he said, 'look at these men. If it wasn't for their father, none of you would be here. When I was young I was caught in a net. Tangled so tight I couldn't breathe. Their father found me, cut his own net to let me go free. He gave me back my life. Now give him back his sons.'

And so the brothers returned home safe. But as soon as they could the two eldest moved away, inland, to work in the town.

'There isn't enough fish for us all to make a good living,' they said.

One night the youngest son was sitting with his father, mending nets.

'Do you remember helping a seal out of your net?' he asked. 'One all tangled up, out by the island?'

His father stared at him for a long time. 'Well,' he said at last, 'I believe I did. But how did you know? I was alone, and it wasn't anything worth mentioning. Just one of those little things ... I had all but forgotten it.'[4]

Much of the authenticity of a story's telling is carried in non-verbal qualities of the teller's voice, but if you compare the text of this story with that of my earlier fishermen's tale you'll see that even my choice of language conveys a very different tone. It's a voice more truly my own and carries within it my memory of Duncan's telling and hence something of the life and environment in which the story originated. This story has sparked intelligent discussion even among tough teenage lads about real-world conflicts between wildlife and making a living, between old and new ways, between need and greed. Others have spoken of the hope the story gives, that small actions can pass unforeseen gifts to future generations. It's the authenticity with which stories are told, I believe, that enables them to have that kind of effect; that and the relationship you've built with your listeners and the conversations you allow the stories to lead into. As Duncan put it, 'Stories from tradition are magic because they are given to you as a present – you are let into the personal lives of your friends. You are accepted as one of the family.'[5]

Since that afternoon in Richmond Park in the 1970s I've shared stories with many people, young and adult, as a means to help them gain confidence in themselves and find a new relationship with their living landscape. Engaging people in the journey towards sustainability is rarely easy. The long-term uptake of new, sustainable behaviour is something that most people – and organisations – initially resist. Lack of knowledge or misunderstanding of the consequences of one's behaviour can impede people from adopting ways of living that will ultimately be better for them and for everyone else, including other creatures. So I continue to work with stories and storytelling to enable people to become imaginatively and emotionally involved with both new and familiar environments and thereby to explore their importance and the implications for sustainable behaviour.

Notes

[1] See Bordin, 'Generalizability of the Psychoanalytic Concepts of the Working Alliance'.

[2] OPENspace, 'Wild Adventure Space'.

[3] Skinner, *Myths and Legends*.

[4] Retelling by Helen East of a story told to her by Duncan Williamson with an explicit request to retell it. Duncan's version appears in Williamson, *The Broonie, Silkies and Fairies*.

[5] Williamson, *Land of the Seal People*, p. xv.

CHAPTER 11

How might long-term groupwork with residents on a
deprived urban housing estate ease their personal difficulties,
enable them to lighten their ecological footprint and improve their
surroundings? Alida introduces two groups – one for unsettled women
and one for carers and children – to illustrate how this can be achieved.
She explains:

how to approach indoor groupwork with an environmental orientation;

~

what, in the participants' words, helped them to connect with their surrounding world,
and how this resulted in a willingness to act in more sustainable ways;

~

ideas for creative story explorations with an understated sustainability focus;

~

how three traditional stories were used in the work described.

The participants' own words clarify how stories and activities that
enlivened a desolate place with 'green things' underpinned
their ability to adopt more sustainable behaviour.

Bringing Nature Home

*Story-based groupwork in a rundown neighbourhood
to encourage pro-environmental behaviour in
adults and children*

ALIDA GERSIE

In the 1970s I became the director of a new community centre in the heart of a deprived inner-city housing estate with approximately 3000 residents. Our 'sink estate' comprised several neglected blocks of flats, a few rows of densely packed houses, one grim pub, many broken lamp-posts, and a couple of bare fields of grass where the kids were not allowed to kick a ball around. Most residents struggled with unemployment, loneliness, debt, school refusal, their own or other people's criminal be-haviour, substance abuse, and above all hopelessness.[1] Our community development work soon involved numerous outdoor activities such as: narrowboat trips, farm stays, and outings to the seaside, a forest, a city farm, a park. Enjoyable times outdoors were vital to the residents' well-being. If it weren't for such trips many people might never have seen a cow, watched a sunrise, listened to birdsong, or played with shells on a beach. Upon their return from the country both kids and adults were invariably full of life. However, after a while the impact would fade. Soon a prevailing greyness re-emerged. Though rain pelted against their win-dows, spiders climbed up the wall, and food lingered on their kitchen tables, many felt that the environment was where they were not. It was as if 'nature' had forgotten their estate and that if it were to show its face this could only be in the form of a pest.[2] In this chapter I discuss how story-based groupwork with a broadly 'green' focus can enable tenants in such housing projects to 'bring nature home'.

Sunflower seeds and the planting of hope

The mental and physical benefits of living with plants are well documented. The quiet rhythm of care for garden and house plants literally and symbolically clears the air. Besides providing colour, shape, and wonderful scents, plants transform the waste carbon dioxide that people breathe out into life-giving oxygen. Being responsible for the care of just one house plant has been shown not only to make old people in a residential home more content but also to increase their health and extend their life.[3] For many of us flowers turn a house into a home and a site into a place. Inspired by my lifelong interest in the environment, love of the outdoors, and passion for stories, I have over the years gathered folktales and designed accompanying creative activities to encourage pro-environmental ways of living, especially for people who live to all intents and purpose in an urban wasteland.[4] Some of these stories came to mind when I supervised a community arts worker, Liz, who facilitated a women's personal development group in a community centre in the heart of another tough housing estate.[5] The group's 90-minute sessions followed a predictable pattern: check-in, warm-ups, an arts-based input (stories, music, poems, or pictures), followed by sharing responses to this input, creative activities, and closure (see Introduction).

Most group members felt unhappy with their lives and were 'fed up with the boredom of it all'. They longed for something 'different' and wanted to feel better. Any stories Liz told were therefore carefully chosen.[6] They needed to be relatively short, capture the group's interest, be clear and somewhat unusual, contain relevant themes, and support the creative activities. When we discussed potential stories, Liz remembered that one participant had recently noticed a tray of seedlings on the room's windowsill and commented that she used to enjoy growing things but now could not be bothered. Others had made similar comments. Because gardening is a well-known therapeutic activity and also because the centre hoped to convert a nearby derelict lawn into a community garden, Liz thought of bringing a 'gardening' focus to the next session.[7]

The session outline

We settled on two stories from the oral tradition. In both tales women are transformed into a sunflower as a result of impossible love. We then created a session outline. After some relevant warm-up activities (such as sharing a memory of a flower) Liz would tell the Peruvian folktale 'The Girl Who Married the Sun' and the Greek myth of 'Clytia and Apollo'. After discussion of the stories' core themes, Liz planned to invite the women to sow sunflower seeds. If they did not want to do this, she would suggest making a group painting or collage with a sunflower theme. As usual the session would close with time for reflection.

The Girl Who Married the Sun

Long, long ago a beautiful young maiden reached the age for marriage. Her parents introduced her to one eligible young man after another, but the girl stubbornly refused to marry any of them. She would only marry the Sun. Finally her infuriated parents cast her out of their home, shouting that she should try to marry him and take the consequences. After a long, long journey the maiden arrived at the house of the Sun's mother. Deeply touched by the girl's devotion to her only child, the Sun's mother consented to the marriage. However, the girl had to promise never to try to even look at her husband. As time went by she so badly wanted to see him. One day she filled a bowl with water in the hope of catching a reflection of her beloved's face. As soon as the Sun discovered that his wife had broken her promise he banished her for ever. Crouching on the rocky soil, she bitterly lamented the loss of her beloved spouse. She never stood up again. She changed into the very first sunflower.[8]

That South American tale has intriguing parallels with the ancient Greek myth about the nymph Clytia who loved Apollo, the Sun-God.

Clytia and Apollo

Clytia loved Apollo, but, unfortunately, Apollo did not love Clytia in return. He adored another nymph, Daphne, but she so disliked his advances that she turned herself into a laurel bush. Apollo then tried to seduce Clytia's sister Leucothoe. This really upset poor Clytia. Despite Apollo's blatant disregard for her feelings, Clytia woke early each morning to watch his golden chariot race across the sky, drawn by six dazzling horses. Each and every day she gazed at that chariot until it sank into the distant western sea. Her friends begged her to stop this foolish behaviour but Clytia would not or could not listen. She stood and stared and hoped. Despite her faithful watching and waiting Apollo did not come to her. At last, refusing all comfort, she surrendered hope. In the end the gods took pity on her. When she died they changed her into the beautiful sunflower that tracks the sun to this day.[9]

What happened next

During the following supervision session, Liz shared what happened in the group. The warm-ups and storytelling went according to plan. When the stories' final words had drifted away, a deep silence had fallen. Making eye contact with Liz, one woman quietly said, 'That was me.' Soon the women were openly talking about their struggle with intimate relationships, about 'being on your own' and unfaithfulness, about in-laws, arranged marriage, and especially about long-lost love. Gradually the conversation shifted to sunflowers. Some associated sunflowers with recovery from a broken heart, with light and summer, others with finality, a hospice, and death. Liz had brought along some pictures of sunflowers and calendulas. She explained that the sunflower in the Greek myth was probably a calendula or 'Mary's gold', since calendulas are native to the Mediterranean whereas the sunflower is native to South and Central America. Both plants, though, are heliotropic: they turn with the sun.

In response to the pictures and information, which the women really welcomed, one woman mentioned that her parents used to plant marigolds around the vegetables on the allotment. Someone else recalled eating roasted sunflower seeds. Another shared that she loved to nibble marigold petals when she was young. When Liz suggested that they could, if they wanted, sow some sunflower seeds, the group responded keenly. Some empty pots were standing by and so were grit and soil. Some women said they had not touched earth for years. A few mentioned that they had never done anything like this. Several voiced that their seeds would 'of course' not come up. However, all of them planted seeds. To finish, everyone returned to the circle of chairs and reflected on the session.

Over the following months Liz shared that the women were eagerly watching to see if their seeds would rear their green heads. When the seedlings did appear, the women asked to grow 'other stuff' and settled on growing kitchen herbs. They also wanted to hear stories that 'went with them'. From time to time, group members commented that the emerging sunflowers still reminded them of love lost and gained. Once the sunflowers were big enough they were planted out on a narrow strip of land alongside the centre. The women's adventure with the sunflowers and the herbs could easily have stopped there, but it did not. That autumn some participants proposed to Liz that they would like to show other users of the centre how to grow sunflowers, and to tell them the stories that had enabled them to get their hands dirty again. Thus the old tales and the burgeoning sunflowers not only came to symbolise their budding confidence. As Diana (57), a loyal group member, said, 'they brought nature home'.

Indirect ecological groupwork

Around the same time, I facilitated a ten-week 'carers and kids' drama group. During the third session I told an Aesop fable in which Town-mouse visits his cousin Country-mouse.

Town-Mouse and Country-Mouse

After a hearty welcome, Town-mouse is offered plentiful but very basic food: oats, an apple, and a little ham. Town-mouse feels let down. He misses the lavish larder in his rich mansion and urges his cousin to come back with him and enjoy the fine life. No sooner said than done, both mice go to town. Country-mouse marvels at the cookies, jellies, fruits, and nuts that are simply there for his cousin's taking. A bite of cheese – yummy! A crumb of cake – scrumptious! He is nibbling a lovely cookie when there's a terrifying sound. Deep, angry barks. Two dogs blast through the kitchen doors. Country-mouse escapes as fast as he can. He runs and jumps and runs and jumps. He only stops when he is safely home. 'Never again', Country-mouse cries, 'will I go to town!' He'd rather gnaw a raw bean in peace than live in terrified plenty.[10]

The group received my story with lukewarm interest. However, when asked to do so, everyone effortlessly reconstructed the fable's settings, its major and minor characters, their respective roles, the initial and developing problems, and the resolution. In terms of its mnemonic structure this fable was clearly top. However, when asked to describe the mice and the dogs, things grew complex. What did mice and dogs actually look like? Was this a story about two house mice or about a field mouse and a house mouse? Do dogs hunt mice? How do dogs and mice characteristically move? Attempts to answer these questions fired the group up. At my suggestion young and old alike began to physically explore the animals' movements. We made mouse squeaks, barked, scratched, leapt, and scurried about. 'That was great!' exclaimed Helena (32) after some gorgeous, deep-throated barks and high-pitched squeaks. The others agreed.

Next I invited them to go into pairs and each pair to choose one moment in the story. They then used their bodies to physically represent this scene as a static tableau. This was just a starting posture, which they held silently until I said, 'Go!' The pairs then used improvised gestures and sounds to connect their scene with what happened next in the story. The joy engendered by this brief embodied story exploration took many by surprise.

After this, people formed groups of three or four in which each person would share a personal memory of seeing or hearing a mouse. Before relating their memory-story each teller forewarned the listeners that he or she would, after the telling, ask each listener to offer them a possible title for it. I encouraged the tellers to use this 'response-task' because it supports the listener's attention to the story-in-the-telling, helps the teller to feel they have been heard, develops the listener's response-ability, and primes everyone to consider the story's meaning for them on that day.[11]

During subsequent talk about the entire storywork process, some core themes emerged: the complex relations between rich and poor relatives, the impact of poverty on one's social life, fear of animals, food waste, and wanting to run away from trouble. When this discussion drew to a close, I asked everyone to do three things before the next session:

• tell Aesop's fable and their own memory-story to someone outside the group;
• ask this listener to tell them a mouse-memory in return; and
• dig out some facts about mice, dogs, and/or food.

This was readily agreed. There was a buzz in the air when people left.

At the start of our fourth session the group's mood was still excited. I was delighted that everyone had shared their mouse-memory as well as Aesop's fable with someone outside the group. They were 'stunned' how much their 'listeners' had enjoyed the storytelling. Emily (11) said that her friend had been really keen to tell her own mouse-memory. Others agreed that 'telling a story evoked a story. Just like that.' After more feedback about their experiences, Aidan (10) remarked that he'd tried to find out things about the animals, and concisely informed us that 'Mice snack'. His teacher had told him that mice rarely finish what they start to eat. Others wondered whether this was true, but when Aidan asserted that his teacher was right, lively discussion ensued about mice and people leaving food on their plate. Before long the group concluded that it was 'really' wrong to waste food. At this point I asked what they now considered to be the core meaning of 'Town-Mouse and Country-Mouse'? Two adults argued that the tale 'obviously' highlighted class issues. An older child (12) said it was about conflict between town and country people. Most felt that the story was 'definitely' about eating and food.

I then requested that they form a pair or small group with others who shared a similar take on the story. Each group worked together to create a retelling of Aesop's fable in line with their agreed core meaning. The retellings were full of life. Each group's language and gestures clearly reflected their special take on the story. Some spontaneously elaborated or invented scenes. A few retold it in the role of one of the characters. When we later reflected on these retellings, Anton (13) remarked, 'I didn't know that you could do so much with a little story.' Sue (23) added, 'We've all got our opinions, don't we? It's a relief to hear them and to let them out.'

During the ninth session we used part of our time to reflect on each previous meeting. Some commented that the 'mouse' sessions had made them much more aware of what they did with food. Others said that they now felt more sympathetic towards creatures that shared their house, understanding that 'they've got to live too'. When asked why or how these changes had come about, the group weren't sure, but they thought it probably owed something to the time spent playing with that story as well as telling it to others. Doing so had made the mouse story enter their social world. It had also helped to retell the old story 'through your own lens'. This Mark (13) observed 'made you not just own the story – it made you own your ideas'.

From private to public sustainable behaviour

When the participants first joined these story-based groups most felt that their world was welded shut. In this disenfranchised state the link between doing something and anticipating its outcome is severed. Before long, effort seems futile. With the zest for life gone, warnings about environmental problems or suggestions about how to live in a 'greener' manner were, as one resident said, 'a waste of time'. Their conviction that failure was inevitable precluded even the contemplation of possible productive action. In such circumstances it is quite ineffective to organise a meeting in the tenants' hall (if there even is one) to discuss 'how to save water' or 'how to green the estate'. On such occasions the few residents who attend will likely want to talk about graffiti, anti-social behaviour, urine in stairwells, or broken streetlights. These legitimate complaints poignantly vocalise their sense of powerlessness and disappointment. In such circumstances the increasingly talkative visitor cannot persuade the ever more silent residents of the value of his or her green ideas. And thus the dismal perception of 'useless communication with outsiders who never ever listen' stands at high risk of being reinforced.

During an evaluation session that occurred some months after the 'carers and kids' drama group ended, several participants noted that not only had the work increased their self-esteem and confidence, but they now also felt that it mattered to look after themselves and others better; to have plants and trees around the place and to make sure that these stayed alive; to feed the birds; to be really careful with water, whether or not there was a drought; not to waste food, and to buy fresh, local stuff in the market. As Emily explained, 'If you can't be bothered about anything because you're miserable, you'll hardly care for some bird or about what you eat.' Sue continued, 'Trees need water when there's no rain. I needed encouragement. When I got the encouragement I could look after the trees.' When asked how, from their point of view, the effects of this groupwork differed from the effects of the trips to the countryside which most of them had also participated in, they more or less unanimously said that the trips were vital to give them some fun, a good time, contact with greenery, and above all hope; but the ongoing groups made them believe that change was possible – here and now.

Some closing thoughts

Reflecting on these groups from the perspective of the present, I am struck by the unbroken relevance of some core ideas. It remains true that sustainability issues that clearly affect people's daily life are strong motivators for pro-environmental behaviour change. It is also still true that new behaviour tried out in the presence of collaborating others is likely to stick. It is nowadays widely recognised that social and individual well-being increases when people have access to a community garden where they can touch, see, and smell flowers or vegetables. Most housing tenants welcome home insulation that reduces energy bills, marvel at a reliable local bus service, love bread that is freshly baked in a local baking club, and enjoy classes in upcycling and re-stitching skills. When such 'green initiatives' are on offer, it is not that hard to bring about elective change towards more sustainable behaviour. As John-John, a perceptive 17-year-old who volunteered in the centre's youth club, put it to me in 1978, 'All you need to do, Alida, to get just a bit of your greener world, is to make sure that you organise the right things and then you've got to stick with them. You've just got to keep at it. That's all.' Exactly.

Notes

[1] Gersie, 'Arts Therapies Practice'.

[2] Bell et al., 'Greenspace and Quality of Life'.

[3] Langer, *Counter-clockwise*, p. 9.

[4] Gersie, *Earthtales*, pp. 26–30

[5] For background ideas about short-term groupwork, see Gersie, *Dramatic Approaches to Brief Therapy*, pp. 1–25. For further information on depressive assumptions and the need to create a secure base, see Gersie, *Reflections on Therapeutic Storymaking*, pp. 154–169.

[6] Gersie & King, *Storymaking in Education and Therapy*, pp. 297–391.

[7] Simpson & Strauss, *Horticulture as Therapy*, pp. 157–197.

[8] One of my primary schoolteachers, who was a keen storyteller, told us this story. A contemporary version can be found on the Dutch website <www.beleven.org>.

[9] Versions of 'Clytia and Apollo' can be located on many websites, including <www.online-mythology.org> and <www.rickwalton.com/folktale>.

[10] Summary retelling of story from Aesop, *Complete Fables*.

[11] For in-depth discussion of response-tasks and the development of response-ability, see Gersie, *Reflections on Therapeutic Storymaking*, pp. 113–153.

CHAPTER 12

Malcolm introduces a short-term story-based project with
disadvantaged urban children and illustrates how they became
engaged with a locally nesting colony of kittiwakes that the municipality
planned to eradicate. He explains:

why he used different types of stories to give meaning to the children's
relationships with the birds – such as personal stories, the kittiwake's life-cycle
story, traditional stories, and a culminating story that combined elements of all;

~

the importance of the children's performance of this final story in a
prestigious city venue;

~

aspects of the project that enthused and empowered the children.

The chapter includes four stories of different genres and concludes on
an optimistic note: the project contributed to the local authority's
decision to drop its plan to remove the kittiwakes.

Kittiwakes on the Bridge

Storytelling and storywork in a primary school on a deprived housing estate to awaken children's curiosity about nature

MALCOLM GREEN

'Move on and take your mess with you!' someone was heard to yell at the kittiwakes trying to nest on the Tyne Bridge between Newcastle and Gateshead in northern England.[1] Not a stone's throw away, the children of a run-down primary school, knew nothing of these birds. Coming from a very poor inner city estate, they too, like the birds, were 'clinging to the edge'. The kittiwakes and children were brought together in a project run by Sage Gateshead Music Centre on the banks of the Tyne. A group of artists, with myself as the lead, worked with these children as part of the 'Voices of the River's Edge' project. What better voices to work with than those of the kittiwake and these too often silent children?

The kittiwakes

Kittiwakes are medium-sized gulls with a small yellow bill, white head, short black legs, and black-tipped grey wings. Across the UK their population has more than halved in recent decades. Bad breeding seasons, shortage of sand eels, and an increase in predators are frequently mentioned causes, as is the disappearance of breeding sites.[2] For many years a colony of these gulls, which normally occupy steep coastal cliffs, had nested on the ledges of a disused flour mill by the Tyne near Newcastle city centre. When the mill was converted into an art gallery the ledges were deliberately made inaccessible to the birds. An alternative nesting platform, locally called 'the Tower', was erected a short distance from our primary school. Miraculously, this worked and many of the kittiwakes nested there. But many others joined the small group already on the Tyne Bridge. Here they generously deposited guano on the cars and streets and woke up people in nearby hotels with their early-morning antics – kittiwakes like to announce their presence to the world. This lively colony caused fierce controversy. Some people delighted in their presence. Others insisted they were a nuisance that should be eradicated. At the time of our project there was a stand-off between the various parties about what to do. The kittiwake was thus a topical bird to study in this area, and the Tower's proximity to the school meant this species was a representative of wild nature within the children's urban neighbourhood.

The children

The pupils of the primary school lived with their families in blocks of low-rise flats less than 100 metres from a busy six-lane highway. After school hours the children spent hardly any time outdoors. They could not play outside or make dens as their grandparents or even parents had done. They could not roam freely in the countryside. Their limited knowledge of nature was gleaned at school or from television. Yet like most children their age they were fascinated at heart by life in all its forms. It was their limited access to the outdoors and to relevant knowledge that kept them from developing further interest in and caring attitudes towards nature.

The context

When the Sage Gateshead invited this school to participate in Voices of the River's Edge, it was agreed that for a whole term a class of 13 children aged seven to eight would devote one afternoon a week (plus some day-long field trips) to the study of kittiwakes on the Tyne. The artists consisted of myself – a naturalist and storyteller – plus other visual artists, movement specialists, and musicians who worked with the pupils on different occasions and for different lengths of time. (I was involved in every session.) The class teacher enthusiastically supported our plan to use the birds' life cycle to increase the children's curiosity about the natural world and their understanding of it. Using storytelling, music, and visual arts as our prime educational tools, we aimed to increase the children's observational skills and help them formulate innovative and personal responses to what they saw, discovered, or learned. The teacher harnessed this work to cover required elements of Science, English, Technology, Geography, Art, Music, and Personal, Social, and Health Education (PSHE) in the National Curriculum.

Telling their stories

The project was based from the beginning on observation, reflection, and storytelling. Firstly, the children kept a diary to record things they saw, heard, smelled, wondered about, or learned during the week, especially observations of nature. They also made drawings. We shared this diary-work during regular 'show and tell' sessions. Such 'observational storytelling' intentionally led to the pupils telling more personal stories about their lives and experiences: siblings leaving home, things to do with growing up. We used these brief personal stories to create parallels and comparisons between their lives and the life cycle of a kittiwake. Our hope that this would stimulate empathy with the bird without anthropomorphising it was later borne out in the children's writing (see below).

Sometimes the children told their observational or personal story to a partner, who then told it back to the wider group. At other times we helped them tell their story straight to the whole class. To honour these stories the artists kept a 'really big diary' in which we recorded the ideas, experiences, and observations the children had shared. This continuous 'show and tell' storytelling process prepared the ground for the later group-based storymaking.

Observing

One of the first things we did was to go and see the kittiwakes on the Tower near the school. More than 60 pairs of birds were nesting there. This outing gave the children the chance to see, hear, and smell the birds for themselves. Before walking there, we asked the children what kinds of questions they might like to ask the birds, what they might be able to discover simply by using their senses, and what they might need to research. They came up with questions such as:

- What do you look like?
- What is your home made of?
- What do you eat?
- Where have you come from?
- Do you have the same mate every year?

Because drawing supports one's capacity to look carefully at something or to record an idea or feeling, we took pencils and paper with us. We encouraged the children to add to their pictures some words that expressed things they noticed or felt. These tasks readily helped some children to observe the kittiwakes and their environment more closely. Other children, we found, learned most from just being there and thoughtfully wandering around. Back in the classroom, all the pupils were invited to tell the others what they had witnessed and experienced. We then used these experiences to create lots of individual and group poems. This three-stage process of observation, expression, and creation enabled most of the children to reflect in some depth on what they had observed, to assimilate information, and to make a personal response (see Cree & Gersie, this volume).

The following group poem was composed shortly after that first visit to the Tower:

I Wonder How Far a Kittiwake Flies?

The view of the glorious Tyne
White shining foam on the rushing waves
I saw a kittiwake, washing in water
Orange beak
Hovering
Red mouth
Shining feathers in the sky
I wonder how far a kittiwake flies?

It exquisitely illustrates the children's developing capacity to be inquisitive, to take delight, and to observe.

Curiosity and questioning

The capacity to be curious and ask questions is central to any investigation (see Salisbury; MacLellan; Cree & Gersie, this volume). It is, however, hard to ask good questions when your background knowledge is very limited. It is harder still to ask open questions. One way we enabled to children to learn to do this was by getting them to focus on an area in which they were experts. This was their own lives. We asked them to discuss which questions they thought might be important if someone wanted to find out about their life. They were quickly able to make a meaningful list of open-ended questions. We explored with them which of these questions might be relevant to asking questions about the kittiwake's life. We particularly focused on questions about the life cycle of both humans and kittiwakes. When we pulled together the questions about their life and that of the kittiwake, we took care to start with what the children knew:

- What's home to you? What is home to a bird? What is different? What is similar? Does the word 'home' have a meaning for a bird?
- Does a human have the same mate for life? Does a kittiwake?
- What happens when a young person leaves home? What would it be like to be a young bird out in the middle of the ocean?
- How do teenagers spend time together? Young kittiwakes return to the colony for the first time not to breed but to hang out in gangs. How do they behave?

The children answered these questions through book research and also by role play: I assumed the role of a kittiwake and they asked me questions about who I was and what I did. This use of role play empowered them to find out what they wanted to know instead of just sitting and listening to me telling them.

For every phase of the kittiwake's life cycle, from birth to death, we used an arts activity to consolidate what they were learning. We used storytelling, song, movement, and rap. The children also made a large learning board, a 'map of kinds' of their learning and emotional journey, on which information, thoughts, and feelings were displayed throughout the project.

Telling traditional stories

In addition to the children's observational and personal storytelling, and their growing factual knowledge about kittiwakes, we also told a traditional story on most project days. We did this for several reasons. Not only do many of these old tales succinctly articulate common human fears or aspirations, but children will readily identify with the tales' protagonists. When they then explore this identification through role play or other arts-based activities they swiftly develop insights they can integrate into their life (see Medlicott, this volume).

Traditional stories can also convey information in a memorable way. Moreover, listening to stories provides a kind of chill-out time, in which children enter another world for a few minutes, see pictures in their head, and stretch their imagination. Mythic tales can add intriguing dimensions to an animal species,[3] and I created some stories by applying mythic motifs from stories of other creatures to the kittiwake: the kittiwake as reincarnation of a drowned child; the kittiwake that transforms into a woman (see also Collins; East, this volume).

At the beginning of the project, I told this tale:

The Jackdaw's Skull

A chief of a Scottish island takes a wife from a neighbouring island. She tells him that it is her people's custom that their first-born child should be given water from a jackdaw's skull. The chief finds a skull and fills it with stream water, which his wife gives to their child, Seamus. As Seamus grows he loves to play outside. His mother tells him that her songbird is very important to her and he should never open its cage door. Sometime later she finds the cage open and the bird gone. Seamus admits to releasing it because the bird told him it wanted its freedom. The mother realises that her son can speak the language of the birds. She forgives him and thinks of the jackdaw's skull.

One day the chief hosts a banquet. According to custom, his first child Seamus kneels to feed his father the first dish. The chief points to the roof and asks Seamus to tell the assembled company what the sparrows are saying. Seamus begs him not to ask but his father insists. Seamus declares that the birds are saying that one day his father, the chief, will kneel and serve him, Seamus. The chief is furious, calls these words treachery, and banishes Seamus from the island.

Fifteen-year-old Seamus finds a merchant ship in the harbour and is taken on as crew. He travels the world as a sailor. Five years later, grown into a man, he asks to be put ashore. Finding himself in a busy city, he seeks out a quiet forest in which to relax and get in touch with himself. The forest is strangely silent. There are no birds. Seamus hears the sound of axes felling trees. Distressed, he asks a woodcutter why the forest is being felled. A woodcutter says it is by order of the King, who needs wood to build ships and a new summer palace for the Queen.

Seamus finds the existing royal palace surrounded by a black cloud of birds. The King and Queen inside do not know how to get rid of this plague of birds. For the first time in years Seamus talks to the birds. They say they will go if the King stops cutting down their forest. The King reluctantly orders the woodcutters to stop. The birds disappear in a great cloud and there is peace. Seamus is lauded as a wise man and asked to stay and rule with the King. Seamus refuses. All he wants is safe passage back to his island. He is given fine clothes and a boat in which to make the journey.

When he arrives at the island it is late evening. His father, the chief, does not recognise him and treats him as a visiting noble. He bows on one knee and offers Seamus food. Seamus asks his father to rise and look into his face. The father recognises his son, weeps in shame, and offers him his chieftain's cloak. Seamus accepts it, but, as he listens to the cries of the seabirds, he realises the burden it brings.[4]

I saw this story as both a stimulus and a metaphor for the children's work. It contains various ecological themes: communication with other species perceived as having their own consciousness and needs (see Hall, this volume); wild places as somewhere to get in touch with yourself (see Green & Hennessey, this volume); the silencing of birdsong when habitat is destroyed; nature's power to strike back when it's treated with disrespect (see Schieffelin, this volume). And just as Seamus learns the language of the birds and sets off on a long journey in which he accomplishes something of worth and develops as a person, I intended that by their telling and listening to stories throughout the project our pupils would learn a language – a sense of rhythm, images, and words – that would enable them to create their own group story towards the end of the project: a story that would bring together their lives and that of the kittiwake in both a factual and a metaphorical way.

Creating a new story

To facilitate the making of this new story I applied a basic storymaking structure devised by Alida Gersie.[5] I asked the children to answer the following key questions:

- Where does this story happen?
- Who is the main character?
- What is their problem or dilemma?
- How do they come to meet the kittiwakes?
- How do the character and the kittiwakes help each other?
- What is the positive outcome?

At each stage the whole class had to decide which answer they wanted to go with. Once we had agreed the basics (the where, who, and what), the children would at key points break into smaller groups to brainstorm the different directions in which the story could go. After these had been presented to the whole group, the class voted on the one they liked best.

The story that emerged was very rich and personal to the group. One pupil, a boy called Josh, who struggled with literacy, had throughout the project talked about a bird book his deceased father had left him. This book was clearly very important to him. The group decided to make the story's protagonist a fatherless child who found a kittiwake in his bird book. Another pupil, Sharon, had often visited Holy Island, where her grandmother lived. Her experience of these trips influenced the journey the kittiwake makes in our story.

Flying Silver [the children's story]

Billy lived with his grandfather in a big stone house not far from the Tyne. One day the developers came. They wanted to build a new estate in the area and Billy's grandfather had to move. But the old man refused, saying his family had lived there for generations and he didn't care about things like central heating. So they built the estate around him.

Billy had to go to a new school with the children of the estate. The children bullied him, saying they bet his house was dirty and full of rats. So Billy had few friends and spent a lot of time in the house on his own. One day he found a tattered bird book under the stairs. His grandfather said it was Billy's father's who had loved looking at birds. Billy said that he too would like to see some of the birds in the book. So his grandfather took him down to the Tyne at the weekend.

They went many times and saw many birds, but their favourite was a kittiwake that had a feather missing in its wing. One day they heard the bird speaking, saying she was in trouble because the little fish were disappearing from the sea and she had nothing to feed her family. Billy and his grandfather knew the problem was caused by people, so they went to the fish quay each weekend and got scraps to feed the kittiwakes. The birds became Billy's friends and he would sneak away from school to watch them on his own.

One day Billy heard his grandfather mumbling to himself that he couldn't go on, that there were too many bills and not enough money. Now it was Billy who went to his kittiwake friend to tell her that he was in trouble. The kittiwake beckoned to Billy to jump into a small boat. 'We'll do some magic,' she said – and she called all her gull tribe from the Tyne. They came with strands of seaweed that they attached to the boat and then slowly they pulled it up the Tyne. They went north up the Northumberland coast until they reached Holy Island.

There they called Billy into one of the old limekilns. One of the birds stood beside him with a silver fish in his beak. The others sang, and flew a magic dance around them. Slowly the bird in the middle began to transform into a boy – feathers to skin, beak to mouth, and the silver fish became silver coins in the boy's pocket. The birds announced that this boy was Billy's new friend.

They went back to Billy's home and there was enough silver in the boy's pocket to pay all the grandfather's bills. Billy took his new friend to school and he was so mysterious and powerful that the other children did not bully Billy any more. In fact they asked if they too could go down to the Tyne to watch the birds.

Performing the story

We planned to perform the final story to the school at the end of term and then, later, publically during the Voices of the River's Edge festival in the Sage Gateshead. The class chose four children to do the telling. Supported by the music and movement specialists, the others created songs and movement to accompany the telling. In the performance I was responsible for remembering the story's overall structure and telling its key transitions. We had to manage intense emotions during the build-up to the performances, but all went well on the day. The children performed their kittiwake story to great acclaim on both occasions, and the final presentation made everyone feel immensely proud.

Other kittiwake activities happened around about the same time. The Royal Society for the Protection of Birds (RSPB) mounted a telescope so people could watch them nest outside the Sage Gateshead's concert hall. An artist made a huge model kittiwake in the entrance. The children were thrilled that their story was part of this collective celebration of the kittiwake. They were even more delighted when the council dropped its plans to eradicate the kittiwakes from the Tyne Bridge.

Evaluation

A project like this involves constant readjustments to the pupils' needs. Sometimes I questioned the relevance of our work, given the harsh reality of many of the children's lives. Such worries were banished by their enthusiasm. All the artists were touched by the warmth and generosity with which we were received each week. And why shouldn't these children want to engage with nature, if only they were given chance to do so? The teacher told us, 'One of the major reasons for the children becoming so interested is that they felt a personal link to the kittiwake through the visits, *stories*, and taking on the role of the bird [in their imagination and the role play]. I have noticed so many times in primary teaching that if you give the children personal ownership they feel more involved and it becomes relevant to them. This combined with the cross-curricular nature of the project was the key to its success ... If we are to enthuse our pupils once more [about nature] in our increasingly industrial age we must make it relevant to them and use as many areas of the curriculum as possible to teach it.'

It is hard to know what long-term impact the project will have on the children's interest in nature. But let me finish with an anecdotal story from the teacher. On a trip a couple of months later, he and the children were passing a pool. The great edifice of a football ground towered behind it. The children immediately noticed the gulls on the pool. A new child in the class said, 'They must be kittiwakes,' to which another replied, 'Don't be silly. They won't have come back from the sea yet.' At the start of the project I doubt they would even have noticed the gulls.

Notes

[1] See <www.bbc.co.uk/tyne/features/kittiwake>.

[2] See <rspb.org.uk/kittiwake>.

[3] For example see 'The Story of a Bird Woman' in Carter, *Second Virago Book of Fairy Tales*.

[4] Summary of oral retelling. Source: Sleigh, *Winged Magic*.

[5] See Gersie & King, *Storymaking in Education and Therapy*, pp. 98, 152, 178, 202.

CHAPTER 13

The Bath Storytelling Circle is a community storytelling club
that has met monthly for the past 14 years.
This chapter describes:

the practical mechanics of running a storytelling circle;

~

how the circle raises (and resolves) some issues that arise in the maintenance
of sustainable communities;

~

why the Circle's non-alignment with any overt ideological stance allows a
meeting of voices from diverse backgrounds of thought, and thereby permits
the sharing of stories containing themes of ecology or sustainability with listeners
who might not attend an overtly green event.

David shows how, thanks to these characteristics, the Circle helps to
foster both an experience of community and ideas of sustainability.

Voices in the City

*How a monthly storytelling circle can become a forum
for pro-environmental ideas and contribute to informal
community-building*

DAVID METCALFE

The Bath Storytelling Circle has met monthly for more than a decade
to promote the tradition and practice of storytelling in the English
city of Bath.[1] This chapter discusses the Circle not only as a space in
which stories dealing with social responsibility and environmental sustainability may reach a broad public, but also as embodying a framework
of principles for living in more mutually respectful and interdependent
ways in the wider community.

The Circle's genesis

The first meeting of the Circle took place on a suitably dark and stormy
night in December 1999. Two dozen strangers met in the back room of a
pub at the instigation of Anthony Nanson, a storyteller who had recently
arrived in Bath and previously been involved with a storytelling club in
Oxford. Few people knew each other. What drew them together was the
opportunity to tell and listen to stories, in prose, verse, or song, and delivered from memory or extempore. The Circle's 'one rule' – no reading
from text or notes – immediately distinguished it from other literary and
spoken-word events in the city and continues to do so. Since then the
Circle has carried on attracting twenty to forty people each month. As one
of numerous storytelling groups that thrive in Britain today, it actively
contributes to the storytelling 'revival' of recent decades.

Unlike many storytelling clubs our Circle does not feature guest storytellers who are paid to perform.[2] All the tellers, singers, and reciters come from the floor. Their contribution is a gift. And we use a free room in a pub rather than a hired space. Consequently the event can be open to all and free entry, though people are expected to buy a drink as you usually would in a pub. In keeping with this do-it-yourself ethos, we use home computer technology to maintain webpages and print posters, and leaflets to promote our sessions. Our venue also kindly advertises the Circle on its website.

The fact that the Circle designates itself a 'circle', and not a 'club' or 'group', testifies to the 'in-the-round' style of the meetings. Achieving a perfectly seated circle for our meetings has proved somewhat elusive in practice, given the geometry of the different spaces in which the Circle has convened. But the core concept of gathering in a circle, rather than sitting in rows or cabaret style at tables, underpins our democratic dynamic by blurring the distinction between performers and audience. That's something we see as intrinsic to the folk nature of storytelling in general. Physically the circle reinforces the principle that each teller has an equal right to a hearing and that the listeners have a responsibility to actively listen. In some places the facilitators of 'storytelling circles' prioritise the telling of individuals' personal stories. Our Circle does not prioritise any particular type of story. Rather, it represents an expression of our folk ethos: 'the peasants entertaining themselves instead of paying to be entertained'.[3]

A master of ceremonies

Each session's entertainment lasts about two hours, plus time before and afterwards, and during an interval, for conversation and refreshment. Although the Circle has never had any formal organising structure, three primary MCs have successively guided its proceedings to date: Anthony, Kevan Manwaring, and now myself. Guest MCs periodically take the floor to provide variety of voice, celebrate a special occasion, or cover for absence.

Before the event starts we put some leaflets around the room that request a protocol of mutual respect – of performers towards listeners and of listeners towards performers. People who are there for the first time find this especially helpful. Meanwhile the MC works their way round the room, greeting people and inviting them, if they wish, to put their name on the list to perform. Newcomers may have to be reassured at this point that performance is not compulsory!

The MC then calls the meeting to order, welcomes everyone, and typically anchors the occasion in time and place by referring to some calendar or seasonal marker (such as a solstice or saint's day), the anniversary of a historical event, or some topical news item. By ringing a bell, or beating a drum, the MC signals the crossing of the threshold into the performance world. Everyone's attention now being focused, the first performer is invited to begin. Throughout the evening the MC acts as caller, connector, and timekeeper. He or she selects the order of performers and tries to balance the varied nature, pace, and intensity of contributions. It can be good, for example, to alternate between storytelling and song or poetry, and between male and female voices. At the end the MC thanks everyone for being there, invites them to stay to chat, and then closes the meeting with another ring of the bell.

Propagation of environmental themes

Among the wide, open-ended range of topics broached by each evening's stories, songs, and poems, questions of ecology or sustainability often arise. It's not part of the Circle's advertised mission that they should; nor are they engineered into its proceedings. But it happens that the primary MCs and many regular contributors have felt engaged with such issues and motivated to tell tales that reflect humankind's impact on the natural world or man's inhumanity to man in pursuit of land and resources.

Kevan, for example, gave the Irish legend of 'The Yew of the Disputing Sons' a contemporary environmental twist. This tale is a revenge story in which the fairy folk create a beautiful yew tree to stir conflict among the race of men as punishment for past abuse of their kind. In Kevan's retelling the yew tree with its black fountain of branches became a metaphor for oil and the discord and slaughter that often follow once oil is found.

Another night, Verona Bass tackled the issue of resource scarcity by retelling the well-known folktale 'Stone Soup'. Instead of highlighting how starving mendicants trick villagers into feeding them, she put the focus on a community's willingness to cooperate to resolve their common hunger: all the characters eventually agree to contribute something to the soup and they finally partake in a delicious feast. After telling the story Verona explicitly linked it to the cooperative qualities promoted in the Transition movement. She said, 'We can celebrate the austerity we might face because sharing puts us in touch with the community behaviour we've lost.'

On another memorable evening Anthony Nanson shared the sad story of the golden toad, a tiny amphibian that was known to science for only 25 years before it became officially extinct. The golden toad disappeared from its cloud forest home in Costa Rica owing to a complex combination of reasons driven by climate change (see Nanson, this volume). The story's poignant focus on a particular place and short space of time conveyed the toad's tragic vulnerability and elicited a wave of sympathy at its demise.

On a more positive note, Kirsty Hartsiotis's moving true story of 'The Ghost Shirt' concerned the growth of intercultural understanding and respect. It revolved around a protective sacred shirt supposedly worn by a Lakota warrior at the massacre at Wounded Knee in 1890 and put on display in a Glasgow museum for the next hundred years. Kirsty recounted that when the people of Glasgow finally learnt the shirt's history and the Lakota people's ongoing lament for their dead warrior, they took the story to their hearts and supported its return to the Lakota in 1999. Her story about these events also exemplified the power of 'story' to inspire community action.

The evidence of conversations among listeners after the telling of stories like these at the Circle bears out the principle that once you truly hear someone's story you cannot help but understand them better – whether that 'someone' be a person, a community, a creature, an object, an environment, or a place – and that such understanding can lead to greater respect for the other, to improved relationships, and to the possibility of more ethical solutions to problems.[4]

A genuine community gathering

People who have attended an evening at the Circle often give voice to a revived sense of well-being and optimism. They say not only that it has been good to be part of the Circle, but also that they would like to transfer some of the qualities of the experience to their everyday life: 'If only I could listen so carefully most of the time.' 'It's so good to feel respected when I speak.' 'I feel that people really care about things here.' 'It's great that people can speak uninterrupted for a little while.' Since the beginning we have aimed to promote this quality of experience. The Circle is a genuine community gathering, a space where all kinds of people can perform all kinds of material in all kinds of ways (provided it be from memory or extempore and not too long). I believe that a vigorous, mutually respectful sense of community is fundamental to the endeavour of living sustainably and all the challenges that it entails. I'd like to suggest that three interdependent principles that underpin the interpersonal experience we hope to achieve at the Circle have application to the community at large and thereby to the aim of sustainability.

1. Inclusiveness

The Circle is a showcase and meeting-place for an ever-changing mix of amateur and professional storytellers and poets, raconteurs and jokers, ballad singers and rappers. They and their listeners come from all walks of life: teachers, students, artists, accountants, care workers, the unemployed, naval engineers, and students of creative writing and performing arts from local universities. Many of us live in or near Bath. Others are tourists or visitors, some from distant countries. Because there are no tickets or door charge, anyone can walk in from the street. Anyone's voice can be heard. We take the risk that anything may be spoken. Quite a number of people who are just sitting in the pub, unaware – in spite of the posters – that the Circle is about to happen, get drawn into the session. Sometimes they even end up telling a story.

The range of content and style of contributions is as varied as the people who perform. The inclusion of poets and singers as well as storytellers makes for a more richly entertaining evening. Unsurprisingly, the quality of performances varies greatly too. The Circle deliberately blurs distinctions between amateur and professional, beginner and expert. The accepting, nurturing environment helps both inexperienced and experienced performers to learn by watching and listening as well as by taking a turn on the floor. It provides a congenial arena for the more experienced in which to try out a new approach or take a performance risk. And it is a safe space in which people who have never told a story in public before can have a go. Because we encourage them to do so, everyone is reminded that we can do things that initially frighten us and that every journey starts with a first step – whether that journey be telling a story or taking steps to live more sustainably – and that courage and confidence walk together, hand in hand.

The meetings' prevailing climate of mutual respect is embodied primarily in the quality of listening. Month after month, people listen to one another with intense concentration. The silence is broken only by laughter and occasional exchanges of banter, and the background sounds of the living city around us, and the applause that follows every contribution.

The diversity of contributions includes also the diversity of beliefs and values inherent in what is shared. The Circle brings together atheists, agnostics, Christians, Jews, Buddhists, Pagans, and other spiritual seekers. The articulation and sharing, through stories, of such different worldviews cultivates a climate of respect, which people can take away with them into the larger community. Ecological values are part of this. If the Circle included only 'green' storytellers whose stories have an explicit ecological focus, it would risk becoming a narrow clique, preaching only to the converted. The Circle's openness to all kinds of stories gives it a broader appeal to the wider community, including people who may not yet be very environmentally aware or committed to living more sustainably. Because ecological stories are part and parcel of the evening's usual diversity, they have the scope to make a more powerful impact.

2. Connectivity

In some storytelling situations, especially with more serious stories, listeners may tend to 'lean back' and experience the story in a largely inward way.[5] People who have never before encountered live storytelling sometimes do not immediately understand its relational dynamic, being used to forms of entertainment that one experiences in a more passive way. The convivial pub atmosphere of the Circle makes for a particularly interactive dynamic among tellers and listeners. The sheer physical proximity of everyone, the brightly lit room, the fact that everyone can see all the other listeners as well as the performer – these things tend to pull the listeners out of themselves and into active participation in the performance process and the co-creation of the story. Some tellers direct semi-rhetorical questions to the listeners or repeatedly turn to a particular member of the audience as if to identify that person with a particular character in the story. The interaction intensifies yet further in the conversations about the stories that ensue during the interval and after the formal proceedings have ended. Regular attenders have said that once their capacity for active listening and creative involvement has been revived in these ways, they take this new vivacity back to their family and to other groups, where their increasing ability to listen and to speak has been appreciated.

Because stories, poems, and songs that are told, recited, or sung are by their nature portable, repeatable, and transferable, they are also an excellent means of distributing ideas simply, cheaply, and effectively. Many people who hear a new story in the Circle tell it to other people elsewhere. In accordance with storytelling's folk ethos and the wider spirit of a 'gift economy',[6] most of the tellers are happy for them to do so. Standard etiquette is to credit the source you heard the story from. However, if the story is plainly not a folktale but rather a story devised from scratch by the teller, you would ask explicit permission to retell it. Note that the ethics of folk transmission are not entirely congruent with modern copyright laws that were formulated to protect authors' commercial stake in the publication and performance of written texts. Storytellers need to be aware of this when they perform professionally; it's less of an issue in a non-commercial context like the Circle.

It is intriguing to think of the Circle's announcement slot as a flurry of stories-in-the-making. People take the opportunity to advertise all kinds of forthcoming events in Bath and further afield: performances, workshops, courses, readings, conferences, ceremonies, bardic contests, even political demonstrations. Not uncommonly someone turns up for the evening solely to make an announcement; such is the Circle's reputation as a place to spread the word into the wider community. Many of these events are 'countercultural' in that they lack the publicity resources of the mainstream entertainment and leisure industries, and so greatly depend on networking within the community to attract an audience. Many individuals who attend the Circle are involved in other components of Bath's cultural ecosystem, and the Circle has formally collaborated with larger cultural entities such as Bath Literature Festival, Bath Fringe Festival, Bath Folk Festival, and Bath Spa University. By these means the Circle contributes to the weave of connectivity through the life of the city.

3. A sense of time and place

A sense of time and place can help each of us triangulate the trajectory of our lives: to know where we've come from, where we are now, and where we are going – in other words, to know our own story.[7] A sense of time and place also helps us connect with the community and environment around us. Communities too need a sense of time and place, to appreciate and sustain their uniqueness while recognising their commonality and connectedness with others, and to help them respond to change, chance, and challenge.

The Circle helps to cultivate this sense of time and place through its rhythm of meetings that bring people back *every* month – even in the summer holidays – to the same pub room in Bath's city centre; through the MC's reference to some marker in time; through the announcements that invoke the wider life of the city; through the acknowledgement of far-flung places from which stories and visitors have come; through the ringing of bells and the circle of chairs which delineate the space and time within which performers and listeners will be intensely present to each other.

Why do people keep coming to the Circle? For a host of reasons: curiosity, habit, friendship, the opportunity to perform, the delight of being entertained, to discover new stories, to publicise one's activities. The Circle goes on because, in the words of its founder, 'it's become part of Bath's civil society'.[8] It is a public space for sharing stories, poems, and songs that reflect the human condition and the diverse interests and concerns of those who come to tell and to listen. But there is more to it than this: there is also something in the social ritual of sharing stories that draws people together and holds them in a common bond of belonging.

Conclusion

To live together in more sustainable ways, people need to recognise lessons from the past, respect others' circumstances and views in the present, and take personal responsibility for making decisions today that affect tomorrow's world. For me, storytelling is about connecting people – with each other, with their past, and with their own potential. Over time the Bath Storytelling Circle has become a place where people feel they can belong. This happens partly because we are a 'circle' and partly thanks to the stories we tell.

Notes

1. See <http://www.bathstorytellingcircle.btck.co.uk/>.
2. See Factsheet No. 8, 'Organising a Storytelling Club: A Beginner's Guide', for advice on how to set up such a club. Published by the Society for Storytelling, <www.sfs.org.uk>.
3. Nanson, *Words of Re-enchantment*, p. 69.
4. See Nanson, *Words of Re-enchantment*, pp. 122–137.
5. See Lipman, *Improving Your Storytelling*.
6. See Hyde, *The Gift*.
7. See Fire Springs, *Ecobardic Manifesto*.
8. Nanson, *Words of Re-enchantment*, p. 69.

PART IV

IN THE GREAT OUTDOORS

CHAPTER 14

In this one-day workshop the participants hear and make up
stories and explore, through play with clay figures and model
building, practical issues of sustainability and regenerative culture –
such as being part of nature, climate change, ecological footprint,
and sustainable building. Chris describes:

a one-day programme for adults or children in the outdoors;

~

story-based activities using clay and found natural objects;

~

an understanding of how these activities enable participants to grasp that
human dwellings can be a complementary part of the ecological make-up of
an area rather than disrupting or devastating it;

~

two stories: one traditional, one fictional.

We learn also how these stories and techniques can be extended
to explore other ecological and environmental issues.

Stories, Houses, and Dens

*Using stories and creative activities to raise practical
awareness about sustainable building*

CHRIS HOLLAND

Q uite recently in the history of life on our planet, humans learnt to use fire to keep themselves warm and safe and to cook up a fine meal from the land's resources. The scattered human populations increased in size, at first gradually, then rapidly. Simple dwellings or storehouses built with local stone, clay, grasses, and wood developed into homes and workplaces made of bricks, marble, concrete, metal, and glass. It's easy to see that vast amounts of energy are used in a building's construction, inhabitation, maintenance, renovation, and demolition. Each building's life cycle has innumerable, interconnected impacts on the habitats of non-human life-forms as well as on human health. In this chapter I discuss how I use storywork to encourage groups of children to consider this impact. Listening to stories, playing with clay, and making mini-dens and a micro-village can generate their lively involvement with topics such as: feeling part of nature, ecological footprint, climate change, and what 'sustainable building' means.

Sustainable building

The terms 'sustainable', 'natural', and 'green building' all refer, with slightly different nuances of meaning, to the creation, use, and demolition of buildings in an environmentally responsible and resource-efficient way.[1] This is a very wide-ranging subject. So, which topics come to the fore in my story-based workshops?

- Site location and how a building affects the surrounding landscape.
- Site maintenance and working with nature to inspire and direct design.
- Using local, recycled, and renewable materials for the buildings.
- Energy efficiency, including transport of materials, and passive solar design (the use of the sun's energy to heat and cool a building).
- Efficient water use, rainwater harvesting, and toilets.
- Composting.
- Impact of house design and internal decoration on the health of humans and other living beings.
- Making a home a habitat for other organisms, e.g. turf roofs, built-in bat boxes, pots on terraces.
- Where will food come from?
- What can we learn from the past and other cultures?

I've designed the following one-day event for groups of children aged 8–11 years. It is suitable for school classes or summer camp groups of about 30 children (and also works for smaller groups). The morning and afternoon sessions include storytelling and creative-expressive activities in the outdoors, such as making miniature figures and dens with clay and found natural objects.

The children are always accompanied by two or three adults (usually their teachers) who often assist me in a mentoring role during the workshop. We ask the kids prompting questions about their constructions to get them to think more deeply about what they are doing: 'Do you think that stick is big enough to hold up the roof?' 'What about those leaf walls if the wind comes up?' and so on.

By the end of the day the children will have a better understanding of:

- the multiple links between homes for humans and the dwellings of wild creatures;
- the fact that human dwellings can contribute to the ecology of an area rather than disrupt it.

I suggest that you first try these ideas out with some colleagues or friends, and then find a way to lead the sessions that best suits you and your group's needs.

The tales and the telling

The two stories around which I have structured the workshop are ones I chose because I enjoy telling them, because they raise important issues, and also because I like to hear the images that the listeners tell me these stories evoke in their minds. If the children are very young I sometimes tell the 'The Three Little Pigs' instead of the first story.

Each of us has a unique style of storytelling, which may vary from story to story. Mine is generally quite animated. I use musical instruments and different character voices to engage the listener with the story's content. I hope you will be inspired to tell the stories in your own way. Whatever telling style you use, the purpose of telling the tales in this workshop is to get the children outside and connecting with nature.

With the group sitting in a circle, I begin the morning session by introducing the workshop goals and any important practical matters. Then I tell this story I heard from the American storyteller Odds Bodkin.[2] The tale is set in a North European country.

The Elf and the Farmers

There was a time when most people believed that every farm had its own elf, who looked after its inhabitants, creatures, and plants. However, not everyone believed in the elves. In that land there was one farm where, for the last hundred years, every farmer had died of starvation. At last a farmer who did believe in the elves came to the farm. He immediately went outside to speak to the invisible elf and invite him to a feast the following spring. His crops grew well. The family could store food, sell some of it, and even had enough money to buy a few presents at Christmas. When spring arrived they prepared the promised feast. As soon as the elf knocked on the farmhouse door he was warmly welcomed and allowed to eat almost everything on the table. The elf then invited the farmer to visit him in his dwelling beneath the cowshed. The farmer didn't hesitate. He slipped down a mouse hole to the elf's house. Here the elf sat him down and gave him a bowl of porridge. When the farmer began to eat he saw there was cow poo dripping down into his porridge from the ceiling. The elf explained that this indignity had gone on for a hundred years. That's why the farm had failed and the farmers starved. As soon as he could, the farmer moved the cowshed. The elf's home was safe again and they all lived happily ever after.

The moral of the story, as I see it, is to be sure to check in with the spirits of the land before you do any building. 'Spirits of the land' or 'nature spirits' is the language I use, derived from animist understandings of the world, to refer to the forces that animate nature. You may have your own preferred language to refer to these forces.

Making blobsters and blobster dens

To introduce the next part of the session I say, 'We're now going to make our own nature spirits, or "blobsters", from clay and found natural objects. I will then ask you to make a den for your blobster. At the end of the day you can take your blobster home with you, but we will take the dens apart before you leave. The blobsters can be any shape and can have as many eyes, arms, legs, hair, spines, wings, teeth, heads as you like.' The scope for blobster design varies with the environment and the seasons. With a blob of clay, I now make a blobster. I usually start by finding something to be the eyes, and then some legs, and so on. I remember to respect and give audible 'thanks' for everything I use or pick. I explain this by saying, 'There are nature spirits in everything. Let's say "thank you" to them before we pick something from nature to stick into our bit of clay.'

When my blobster is finished, and everyone has had a good look, I may give it a name. '"Hi!" This is Archie. And now I'm going to make a den for him to live in. In fact, when we create our blobster dens we might actually create a village. Let's remember to think about the spirits of the land before we put a den on it, for almost everywhere is a home for some kind of creature and we don't want to upset them.' So saying, I delineate a small area where the group will place their blobster dens to form a village. It's then time to hand out blobs of clay and let everyone get on with making their blobster, its home, and the village. It doesn't take long before people of all ages are engrossed in the activity.

If you are new to working with clay, I can give you a few tips. To make a blobster you need a blob of clay or sticky mud (from a riverbank, a hole in the garden, or a bag of clay from a pottery supplier). If you plan to in-corporate soft-stemmed flowers, such as daisies for the eyes, first make a hole with a little twig in the blob, then poke in the flower stem and secure it tight. You can also use hidden sticks to pin blobs of clay together. If you wrap clay around twigs, you can make a snake or some other kind of long thin blobster that won't break when it's dry. I make sure that the only wild flowers that are picked are very common ones like daisies and that we pick no more even of these than we actually need.

If someone looks a bit stuck with the den-making, I help them by asking things like:

- Does your blobster live on the ground or beneath it?
- How can you work with what is here to make a nice den?
- What kinds of materials look like they would be good?
- Would you use earth or wood or stone to make a den?
- Would your blobster like to live near some friends?

Sometimes I introduce books with photos of hand-built houses. *Shelter* by Lloyd Khan is a classic. As the den construction goes on, I ask questions such as:

- How are you going to heat your blobster's home?
- How will they get water?
- Would it make a difference if the den faced the sun?
- How far did you walk to collect those sticks?

Depending on the group, different things happen. Be open to a whole village taking shape, or a street, or a tribe, but insist that each person makes their own home for their blobster – no matter how close it is to their best friend's!

Visiting the blobster dens

When construction time is up, we all gather to visit each den. I ask people to offer comments on what they like about each other's den, what they think were good ideas, and how well the dens may fit in with the spirits of the land. I then say that the blobsters must now move out of the dens and that each person must say goodbye to their den but without taking it apart. We put the blobsters in a special safe place and cover them with leaves to stop them drying out. We then have 'circle time' – sitting in a circle again – where everyone is encouraged to say something. I tell the group that we will return to the dens after lunch but that while we are away it is likely that the dens will become homes for actual living creatures. I also pose the question, 'What would it be like if your blobster had to move into someone else's den?'

Eco-renovation

When the group has gathered again after lunch I ask each of them to imagine what it would be like if they were given a small bit of land with an old building on it. I invite them to imagine they are Bob the Builder and they can renovate this home in any way they like provided that what they do is as friendly as possible to the earth and the creatures and plants that live around the building. I tell them that this process is often called 'eco-renovation', and point out the huge environmental costs of producing cement (which produces more carbon dioxide globally than air travel), bricks, and metal. Inevitably a few hands will go up with children burning to tell you their ideas. Ask if they can hold on to their ideas for a while, because you would like to tell another story.

This second story is inspired by a gorgeously illustrated children's book by Benedict Blathwayt.[3] It describes how a man finds and buys a tumbledown house by the sea.

The Little House by the Sea

The house looks derelict, has no windows, and the roof has fallen in. It has become home to lots of other creatures, and plants grow everywhere. But as soon as the man starts to renovate it the creatures and plants get cleared out. When everything is done up, the man moves in. The house looks beautiful but the man feels really lonely. Before long he knows that he has to change things. He wants the creatures and the plants to come back and share his home. He does everything he can to make them want to do so. And they do.

When I've finished the story, we have some circle time to share ideas about eco-renovation that feature in the story and to invite further ideas from the children.

Eco-renovating the blobster dens

When I've closed the discussion, I ask the children to go into pairs, and tell them that each person will now eco-renovate their partner's blobster den. I ask them first to show their partner where their den is, and I remind them that some creatures may have moved in since the blobster moved out, and so they will need to be careful and respectful. Each participant will also collect their blobster to install in its new home once it has been eco-renovated. Before the group starts work, it is helpful to remind them quickly of some of the ideas about eco-renovation that arose from the discussion. It is good to have more clay available in case the blobsters need repair. For the eco-renovation work you may want to provide some recycled materials such as cut-up bits of drinks cartons for roofs, solar panels, or insulation; cardboard or wooden shapes for moulding earth bricks in; that sort of thing. Can they fix it? Yes, they can!

With older groups further scenarios can be introduced: from imagining a New Town for blobsters – to reconstruction of the entire community after a disaster. Planning officers can be sent round to make sure all buildings are up to the latest building regulations. Try to invent some strange regulations for a bit of fun. Bring in modern building materials to discuss their relative merits and environmental impact. You might also limit the supply of resources in various ways:

- A quarry can be opened (a bag of stones), or you can pretend some old industrial buildings have been knocked down and stones are there to be reused.
- Introduce some cement (more clay), but restrict how much each person gets and explain why cement is so costly to produce.
- Pretend a port closes down and many metal containers are available

(200 ml juice cartons work well and can be cut with scissors).

- Community design can be experimented with as small groups (not pairs) work together to renovate a set of dwellings.
- Mark out an area as a National Park and give that area extra building restrictions.
- Provide some hollow-stemmed plants to serve as pipes for collecting water from the roofs.
- Cut up some sticks with secateurs to be logs for basic wood-support construction or to build log houses.
- Insist that every extension to existing structures must have a green or living roof, or some green walls.
- Limit the number of steps they can walk to gather resources.
- Provide a miniature bat or bird box for everybody to fit on to their dwelling.
- Have periods of siesta time to stop rushing about and to think about earth time instead of deadlines.
- The creative possibilities are only limited by the imagination. One group of blobster-den-makers explored the concept of climate change, carbon footprints, and permits for carbon production by giving each builder a set number of acorns to trade with.

Visiting the renovated dens

The pairs then show each other how their original den has been eco-renovated. Then we have a building inspection tour in which the whole group visits each renovated building and sees what has been dreamt up and created. We marvel at the ways the builders have done things and feedback is invited about how earth-friendly the renovations are. In a further period of circle time the group discusses how it felt to be renovating your partner's old blobster den and to have your own den changed and developed by your partner. I ask them if there is anything they would like to do, if they could, in the houses they actually live in to eco-renovate them. I might share an example of something I have done in my own home to make my life more earth-friendly.

Closure

Now I tell the group that we have arrived at the end of the day and there are four things we need to do: make a decision about what to do with your blobster – either take it home or disassemble it; undo the blobster dens and pack away materials that we brought in from outside; restore the den and village sites to how they were before the construction work started; clear up anything else and then come back into a circle to reflect on the day as a whole. I normally close the day's work with a song and some friendly leave-taking.

Further inspiration

I hope these stories and activities will help workshop participants see the positive contribution that green building techniques can bring to our future. Related aspects of sustainable living may be illuminated during the day and focused upon in further workshops: things like woodland management, energy efficiency in the home, organic gardening, eco-sanitation, renewable energy, food miles, community regeneration. The focus you choose will depend on the stories you tell. The stories are like seeds for the mind. As the Italian proverb says: 'All the flowers of tomorrow are in the seeds of yesterday.'[4]

Notes

[1] Hopkins, 'A Natural Way of Building'.

[2] Retold with permission from Odds Bodkin. The original version of the story is possibly the Danish folktale of 'Raginal'. See Thiele, *Danmarks Folkesagn*, Vol. 2, p. 242.

[3] Blathwayt, *The Little House by the Sea*.

[4] No. 218 in 'List of 2053 Italian Proverbs', <http://www.special-dictionary.com/proverbs/source/i/italian_proverb/22.htm>.

CHAPTER 15

During this nine-month environmental project, adults
and children from isolated, mixed-heritage families met at five
locations along the course of the river Exe. The chapter describes:

what was done to encourage the parents and children to join the project;

~

why 'shared attention' increases people's intimacy with each other and with the
natural landscape, its ecology and history, and helps them to feel more at home;

~

two story-based creative activities that are particularly effective in
generating such intimacy;

~

three story prompts based on fragments of traditional/historical stories.

According to the participants, the project generated a lasting sense of
connection with themselves, each other, and their environment.
This in turn motivated them to engage in more
sustainable ways of living.

A Riverside Journey

An innovative 'three seasons' project with isolated mixed-heritage families to nurture their sense of identity and desire for more sustainable ways of being

SARA HURLEY AND ALIDA GERSIE

B lazing Tales is a combined arts company that facilitates creative outcomes for difficult situations. A major focus of our work is deepening people's connection to 'place', including their environment and heritage.[1] The company is particularly interested in enlivening local 'places' for people. As part of this work we facilitated an environmental project for mixed-heritage families who live in the rural English county of Devon, with its patchwork of villages, market towns, and one city. The families came from varied circumstances, brought together through their experience of being mixed-heritage in a rural region. They said they frequently felt isolated, being a tiny, often misunderstood, minority. Few of the families went out into the countryside or had much knowledge about the area they lived in. Lack of transport, low income and a prevailing social shyness prevented this, they said.

Between February and November, Blazing Tales held five weekend events at different locations along the river Exe. This lively river begins high on open moor, drops down through wooded valleys, meanders through villages and mixed farmland, and then passes the quay in Exeter before arriving at the estuary and open sea. Since time immemorial, people have tried to manage its dynamism by building weirs and bridges, straightening its curves, and, more recently, by cleaning it up and preserving habitats for plants, fish, birds, insects, and mammals. The river bears lively witness to its long history as a source of sustenance and locus of exchange between people, creatures, water, and land. It therefore seemed, in its infinite variety, an apt environment for our mixed-heritage families to get to know.

Being in a mixed-heritage family is culturally complex. Our project sought to ask how these children and adults could make, and maintain, a relationship with their environment when they have 'not from here' etched on their skin.[2] Feeling a sense of belonging can support self-esteem and identity. Our families began the project with a compromised sense of belonging because their 'mixedness' positioned them as outsiders. Devon was their 'home', but they faced a challenge in trying to build up their unique relationship to where they lived and to claim their right to belong there.

Little research has been published to date about the experience of mixed-heritage families or individuals who live rurally, unlike that of their urban counterparts. Prejudice and discrimination affect members of all minority groups.[3] In addition to the complexity of mixed heritage, some of the children and adults who took part in the project were also treated unfairly due to age, disability, or gender. While the project did not explicitly aim to deal with these issues, we did inform participants about appropriate agencies or authorities with responsibility for sorting out 'stuff like that'.[4] Persistent exposure to wrongful, ignorant, or unkind behaviour damages one's sense of self-worth and inner dignity. Many manage the feelings this induces by adopting a single identity, like their 'mono-identified' peers, or by shifting their identity allegiance across contexts.[5] However, neither of these moves solves the daily reality of their mixed-heritage situation.[6] Because the complexities and disadvantages of a mixed-heritage background are so often to the fore, few mixed-heritage people realise that their ability to belong on their own terms to various social groups tends to make them more tolerant of 'the otherness of others' than their mono-identified peers. They more readily accept out-group members and show a relatively low rate of inter-group bias. These are great social traits and delightful human values. In addition, many mixed-heritage children and adults are more capable of complex thinking about groups than their single-identity peers. These are extremely valuable capacities and attitudes to have in our rapidly changing and increasingly global world.

Right from the start the project aimed to help mixed-heritage families to find and to recognise these strengths and to overcome their tendency towards undeserved self-criticism. We did so by bringing them together in unfamiliar, inviting places, by focusing on creative explorations of the river, its ecology and history, including the history of black people in Devon, and through the celebration of life in all its diversity.[7] The families shared these workshops together, and children relaxed into a feeling of 'us', a kind of cultural validation. The participants' experiences outdoors were made more memorable because they were shared. They felt they had permission to bond with the physical landscape; in so far as all of us are people of place, a mixed-heritage person is literally and metaphorically someone of many places. In their memories and embodiment are traces of a multiplicity of landscapes. How do we negotiate such multiplicity of place to become present in the immediate environment?

The project's criteria for workshop sites built on these ideas. How close were they to the river? Were they safe for our families? What was special about the landscape? How accessible were they by public transport? Was there a play and picnic area? This being Britain, were there any nearby 'wet weather' options? We organised five unique events. The first was a residential weekend at a youth hostel close to the river. The second was a camping weekend on a nearby farm; the third a day on the riverbank not far from Exeter; the fourth a day in Exeter; and the fifth a day by the sea. A total of 104 people attended. Ten families did so on a regular basis, others occasionally. The project's aims were finalised as follows:

- introduce people to unfamiliar places and increase their confidence in being outdoors so that they will revisit the area;
- develop their knowledge of the river's ecology, history, and stories to strengthen a sense of belonging to the region;
- enable everyone to play, learn, and find inspiration in the outdoors;
- reduce social isolation and strengthen the participants' network of mixed-heritage families.

Next came recruitment. The hoped-for families did not usually attend workshops. Consequently the publicity material had to be immediately appealing. After consultation with some keen families (marketing people might call this a focus group), it was decided that the advertising would emphasise 'doing something new in the outdoors' and that the posters would imply, rather than explain, the environmental and sustainability themes. These latter had to be in the background. First and foremost the families needed to have fun, get to know each other, and learn to care for themselves (see Cree & Gersie, this volume). In the end, most recruitment happened through a regional organisation for mixed-heritage families as well as local radio, print, and web media. Some families heard about the project by word of mouth.

At the start of each event the facilitators checked why people joined. By and large they said they had come in order to make friends with others in a similar situation, to be in a new place where their children could play together creatively, and to do 'arty' things in the outdoors. The project's other goals, such as enabling people to get to know more about local history, flora and fauna, the river, and the countryside, gathered momentum as the events unfolded and we travelled along the river's course.

Each event had a different theme. Continuity resided in the staff, a core group of attendees, the kind of things that were done, a recognisable session pattern, and a steady style of facilitation. Some activities were repeated, which deepened the participants' experience of the activity (see Collins, this volume) and taught them experientially that it is possible to transfer creative learning from one event or situation to another. Below are two techniques that were especially successful in engaging our families with each other and with the natural world.

Technique 1. Accompanied exploration

This exercise can be done as a whole group, in small groups, or in pairs. For clarity's sake it is here outlined for pairs. The implementation of it is open to exciting different interpretations, depending on the age and ability of the group.

One participant adopts the role of 'explorer'. She or he is instructed to go on a time-limited walkabout with a companion. Whenever something grabs the explorer's attention the pair stops to focus on what the explorer notices. The companion then selects some of the explorer's words or images to record 'what's noticed' in the explorer's notebook. Throughout this, the companion strictly follows the explorer's lead. She or he picks up on any signs of interest by attending to the explorer's direction of gaze, casual comments, and body language.[8]

The presence of an attentive companion quickly helps the explorer to deepen their observations. This happens especially when the companion expresses excitement at the explorer's findings, or gathers others around to draw attention to something the explorer has noticed, such as a delicate lichen, a footprint in mud, some shifting shadows, a shapely stick, a leaf with holes, an unfamiliar sound, or a smell. The companion's heightened interest strengthens the explorer's capacity to perceive things in the outdoors. It also helps the explorer to formulate some basic ideas or questions about their findings. This in turn generates a culture of curiosity, as well as joy in precise articulation.[9] In order to scribe effectively, the companion must attend really well to what the explorer says or detects, especially because the exploring speaker is often unaware of the gold that comes from their lips. When someone else catches their language and, by scribing, makes it available for the explorer's subsequent use or development, the explorer's confidence in their observational and expressive abilities quickly grows. The team discovered that as soon as an explorer became involved with something in the environment that had attracted their curiosity and another person showed a lively interest in what this was or what they imagined it to be, the explorer felt more at ease and more connected with the place.[10]

After these explorations, there was circle time to share experiences (see Cree & Gersie, this volume). One participant, aged ten, recited a scribed poem that she created at the first workshop, near the river's source:

Like a river I meet different people
Like a sea I go to different places
Like the water-cycle we sometimes have to start all over again
Like a tributary we see each other in all sorts of different places
Like a stream we have to say our goodbyes.

This exploring process can stand alone or be followed by other activities, such as leading others on a focused walk, or making a new poem, song, or drawing. Occasionally the explorations were developed into full-scale storymaking, but this was not necessary for the process to work. In general, 'accompanied exploration' is an accessible tool that, once experienced, can be repeated many times.

Technique 2. Story-starters

During one event we told several 'story-starters'. A 'story-starter' is just the beginning of a story. After hearing the story-starter, the participants

– alone, in pairs, or in small groups – are invited to investigate the immediate surroundings and look for any lingering traces of what happened
next. Initially, people had about 10 minutes for this; when they became
more experienced the exercise took about 15–20 minutes. The facilitators emphasised that, using clues in nature, everyone would develop their
own hypothesis or story about what happened next, just like a detective or
tracker would do. We used the story-starters to awaken people's historical imagination and combine this with their ability to create meaningful
connections with the natural environment.[11]

Here are some examples of riverside story-starters:

1. Devon is part of a peninsula with sea to both the north and the south.
In the old days sailors walked the 'Mariner's Way' across the county's
moors in search of work. Some were local people; others were sailors
from around the world. Women sometimes disguised themselves as sailors. There was a sailor (a man or a woman) who walked in this area with
some other sailors on the way to north Devon in search of work. An incident by the river slowed their journey. What was this incident, what
happened, and how did they continue their journey?

*Find the clues to what happened in the landscape and make up a story that
uses these clues.*

2. In 1796 a slave ship called the *London* was shipwrecked on the north
Devon coast. The ship had left St Lucia in the West Indies. Even though
they were near to land, Captain Robertson refused to bring the boat into
the 'wrong' harbour to shelter from the storm. Everybody drowned. Bodies, coins, and shackles were washed up on the shore. One person survived the shipwreck. He or she hid in these woods but knew nothing
about this place. What did they do next? Why did this work out?

*Find the clues to what happened in the landscape and make up a story that
uses these clues.*

3. A string of fascinating outsiders lived in the region. *Tom Faggus* was
an Exmoor highwayman whose dwelling was never known. He shod his
horses' shoes backwards so it looked like he was coming when he was going. *Princess Caraboo* was a local village girl, Mary Wilcox, who for many

years successfully passed herself off as an exotic princess from 'Javasu' Island. *Bampfylde Moore Carew*, the son of a vicar, claimed in his later years to have been elected 'King of the Gypsies', having run away at 12 and spent his life as a traveller. He was born and buried by the river.

Choose one of these people. What brought him or her to this place by the river? Who did they meet here – a friend, enemy, landowner, weaver, another disguised person? What happened in these woods and what was the outcome of what happened?

Find the clues to these events in the landscape and make up a story that uses these clues.

Before the participants set out they received a 'detective bag'. It contained a mini-clipboard, paper, another bag to collect small 'loose' things (nothing was to be picked or broken off), and some pens, pencils, and pastels. Then their hunt for story clues began. Note that these hunts were unlike traditional treasure hunts in which the organisers have placed artificial clues in the landscape. The clues that our participants found, or imagined, were already present in the place where we were. Once everyone had listed, drawn, or gathered their clues the team helped them to structure their findings into a rough story outline. With their outline in hand, each person then illustrated their story, created a memorable object from clay or dyed cloth, developed their story into a song, enacted it, or simply told it to other participants. The search for clues taught them to observe their surroundings in a playful, sharp-eyed way and bonded them with the site. It vivified the wondrous fact that landscapes are keepers of history. This embodied awareness fed their curiosity about 'natural' features or phenomena. Their searching also clarified experientially that actual and imagined events from long ago do have an impact in the present – for worse and for better, just like the diverse cultural influences in their own lives.

Reflection on the techniques

The team were aware that every technique needed to appeal to the families at multiple levels and resonate with the fact that they were constant negotiators of the complexity of mixed heritage. It was also important to ensure that their discoveries nurtured their ability to be curious about things. Without such a capacity to question and reflect on things we may not understand that our current environmental behaviour urgently needs to change (see Cree & Gersie, this volume). Before the project began, most families had to a significant extent withdrawn from engagement with their physical environment. At the end everyone said that they felt more connected to Devon and knew more about its environment and history.[12] They expressed how important they felt it was to spend time outside together with other mixed-heritage families for the sake of their own and their children's well-being and confidence. They had gone to new places that they would visit again and had learned new ways to look at the world and express themselves. New relationships had been made with each other and also with the place where they lived.

Few people thrive in isolation. The project's suggestion that the participants could and would find interesting things where they were, and that 'what they found interesting' would in turn interest other people, created helpful scaffolding for a potentially intimidating open-ended time outdoors. The expectation that they would selectively attend to one thing amidst a myriad of other noticeable things not only opened up the place for them; it opened up their minds. The invitation to communicate their findings to interested others (in the form of an observation, a song, a poem, an object, or a story) further increased their capacity to select something and to prepare this for creative communication to others in a lively, concise, and creative manner. This too built their confidence that they had something to say. By using others' ideas and perceptions to advance their own, they expanded their social understanding of events that anchored individual as well as social memory in fun, celebratory ways. We confidently believe that this pattern of activities and the ideas behind it not only increased the participants' personal well-being, but also informed their ability and willingness to engage with their surroundings in a thoughtful and thereby more sustainable manner.

Notes

[1] In this chapter the authors use 'we' and 'our' primarily to refer to the staff and project-workers of Blazing Tales. For more details about the project and the independent evaluation, see Hurley, *Blazing Tales*.

[2] Parker, *Salt, Sweat and Tears*.

[3] McKeith, *Local Black History*.

[4] Caballero, *Mixed Families*.

[5] D. Lincoln, <http://www.mix-d.org>.

[6] Rocas & Brewer, 'Social Identity Complexity'.

[7] Gray, *Black History Report*.

[8] See Moore & Dunham, *Joint Attention*.

[9] Gersie, *Earthtales*.

[10] Lupton, *Dreaming of Place*.

[11] Gersie, *Storytelling, Stories and Place*.

[12] See Hurley, *Blazing Tales*.

CHAPTER 16

This chapter argues for the value of repetition: repeating the
same stories and activities periodically to build a sense of shared
community founded on the sense of belonging to a place.
Fiona presents:

a one-day programme for children and adults in the outdoors;

~

practical ideas about how to engage a mixed-age group with stories
linked to an adventure activity;

~

issues to consider when adapting a traditional story to the particular
needs of a group;

~

reasons why such storywork nurtures people's feeling of being part of a place;

~

two traditional stories she uses in this programme.

She describes an annual expedition to a 'cave' with
children and adults of a community who are
deeply committed to re-wilding a valley.

'I Saw the Heart of the World'

*The joy of repeating stories and activities to strengthen a
sense of community among children and adults who are
committed to rewilding a valley*

FIONA COLLINS[1]

The Spirit Horse Foundation is located in the beautiful Pennant Valley in Wales. Those of us who take part in the Foundation's many
events have over time become an informal, non-resident community of
about 200 adults, many with children. Our gatherings draw on stories
and ceremonies from various cultural traditions and engage people in
manual work to rewild the Pennant Valley for the benefit of future generations.[2] Our work is therefore directed both inwards and outwards. This
chapter focuses on one of my contributions to the Foundation's work: a
one-day expedition undertaken as part of the Children's Circle I take care
of during 'The Cauldron of Plenty', our annual four-day summer camp.
In the course of describing this expedition, which involves the children in
a playful but challenging experience of the outdoor world, I shall explore
how repeating stories and activities that have been done before supports
the building of community and helps foster a sensibility of living lightly
on the earth. In this context I will also discuss the adapting of traditional
stories to serve contemporary purposes.

The Children's Circle

The Children's Circle is open to all babies, children, and teenagers. We
welcome back youngsters who have regularly come to the valley since
birth, and honour new children, whether last year's babies tasting inde-

pendence for the first time, or newcomers of any age. Each morning and afternoon for two hours, the Circle offers a space for children to be together without their parents – though adults are welcome by invitation. It is not a crèche. It exists to benefit the children rather than parents. We have four guiding principles:

- we trust each child to know their own limits;
- the valley is our play-space;
- we respect at all times the well-being of other living beings as much as we expect this for ourselves; and
- 'there shall be stories', some told by me or other adults, some by the children.

I tell traditional tales of all kinds, especially Welsh ones to introduce the children to the mythology and geography of their surroundings. To spark their interest in getting to know their environment, I like stories whose main character is a youngster who sets out into the world to deal with a threat, or in search of adventure. I also tell animal tales to encourage the children to think about the other beings with whom we share the earth, and stories of gods and goddesses from other times and cultures, so that they encounter different ways of understanding the world. Often nature herself contributes to the telling – such as when a flock of ravens flew over while I was telling the story of 'The Seven Ravens'.[3] And also I ask the children to tell stories about their own experiences or the adventures of imagined characters. Storytelling is a fundamental feature not only of the Children's Circle but of the whole camp: we tell stories in mixed-age talking circles, during evening gatherings, and sprinkled through our conversations.

The Children's Circle meets at various sites in the valley. This grounds the storytelling in the natural environment and allows us to explore aspects of a story in this other-than-human world. We can find the monster's face in a stone, create the marks of the hero's struggle with the dragon in our forest, or dance the elves' dance in a clearing. We may use river clay to model something from the story or how we feel about it. If it links with the story, some adults or older children may show the younger ones how to safely make a fire or use a knife to shape a stick. Sometimes we collect twigs, feathers, leaves, or common meadow flowers to make a doll, a weaving, or a prayer bundle to remind us of the story we've heard.

Repetition and storytelling

Many of the stories I tell, together with the activities that accompany them, are deliberately repeated from previous years. This repetition creates a structure of familiarity in a world where many things rapidly change. Repetition is also the mother of learning. The first time you do something you want to do, it is a novelty. The second time, you grasp it better. Doing it again and again allows the experience to deepen, to become part of who you are. Over time, variations creep in or are tried out. The adaptive process of rehearsal, repetition, and adaptation is set in motion. The capacity for repetitive and thereby for adaptive practice becomes part of our repertoire of life skills and even of our identity.

Storytelling and repetition go together like bread and butter. When stories are told, words and phrases are repeated for emphasis, to build dramatic tension, to link separate incidents, images, or ideas, and/or to involve the audience. 'He searched the undergrowth, he searched the riverbed, he searched the treetops, and found her not.' Or: 'He looked at that dragon. That dragon looked back at him.' Repetition brings poetic intensity, rhythmicity, and juxtaposition into the texture of both the content of the story and the way it is told. Many traditional stories recycle and reuse ideas and motives, characters and actions – even whole plots – from other stories as well as from common human experience.[4]

Part of the power of repetition in storytelling comes, I believe, from the fact that such repetitions are akin to the larger rhythms of repetition that regulate our lives and govern the natural world: the physical cycles of day and night, the tides, the seasons, the biological cycle of love, birth, life, and death, and the ecological cycles that bind us to the rest of nature – the repetitions of decay, recovery, recycling, and reuse that reclaim the detritus of life, transform waste into nourishment, prepare it for renewed use, and thereby sustain their own continuance.

The living practice of storytelling similarly reclaims many of its ideas and motives, plots and characters, etc. from other stories, as well as from common experience, and reuses them to enliven or enhance the further telling of familiar stories and to create new ones. The retelling of familiar stories is itself a sustainable activity, since it feeds off the accumulated remains in memory of previous tellings while providing sustenance for future ones. It is linked to the ecological cycles to the extent that the joy of storytelling aligns our will to the ecological sustaining of our existence and that, in turn, our sustained existence enables us to continue telling stories.[5]

For these reasons, in my work, I have tried to let go of the restless search for new stories to tell the children, and instead rely on retelling tales I have told them before and on repeating familiar activities. Far from this boring the children, I have found that many like to hear stories they have heard before. 'Can you tell that one again?' they say. 'Please, tell it again!'

The Expedition to the Cave

One of the Children's Circle's most beloved activities is our 'Expedition to the Cave'. Repeated every year, this is an important emerging tradition in our summer camps. Its destination is in reality a disused slate mine, a man-made tunnel into the hillside, but for the expedition we call it, and imagine it to be, a mysterious cave. We take every child who wants to go: usually 12–15 young adventurers, plus six or more adults and teenagers as helpers. Safety is important. As for any story-walk, the most essential preparation is to walk the route in advance on the same day that you will take your group. Weather can transform paths overnight: what was easy going yesterday may be slippery, or even impassable, today. We support small or timid explorers one to one, carry babies and toddlers, and have other helpers on hand throughout.

The Origin of a Story

Before we set out, I tell the children a story to invite them to step into the shoes of a young hunter who enjoys direct communion with wild nature. My story is one I first heard told by June Peters, who in turn had heard it from Aury Shoa. However, the chain of retelling by successive storytellers had transformed the story a long way from the original tale. The original, as further research revealed, was a foundation myth of the Seneca Indians about how the First People obtained the stories of their traditions and history. In 1883 a Seneca elder named Solomon O'Beale told this myth to Jeremiah Curtin, a philologist who had learned the Seneca language. Another Seneca elder, Two Guns, passionately objected to the sharing of sacred stories with Curtin. He feared that people in the future would treat the written-down stories as mere curiosities. O'Beale argued that recording the stories was the only way to save the Seneca's wisdom and knowledge for future generations. The community supported O'Beale and the stories were recorded.[6]

Issues raised in this disagreement continue to be debated by the storytelling community today, since they deal with the ethics of adapting a people's sacred myths for use in different contexts and for different purposes – and subjecting them to the natural mutability of oral tradition. To acknowledge the complexity of this debate and say something about the retelling of traditional stories I will share in this chapter summarised versions of both the original Seneca myth and my own version of it as told in the Children's Circle.

The Origin of Stories

The story provided by O'Beale begins with an orphaned village-boy turning old enough to start hunting. The first day, he kills a good string of birds. The next days even more. On the tenth day the sinew holding the feathers to his arrows loosens. Seeking a place to sit down and repair it, he notices a big, flat-topped stone. When he has jumped on top of it and laid down the birds, he hears a voice nearby, which asks him, 'Shall I tell you stories?'

The boy can't see anyone. He replies, 'What are stories?'

The stone responds, 'It is telling what happened long ago. If you give me the birds, I'll tell you stories.'

The boy gave the birds and the Storystone began. Until dusk it told story after story. Then it said, 'Rest now. Come back tomorrow. And bring me birds to repay me for my storytelling.'

Day after day the boy returned. Soon he was followed by another boy and then by two men. They wanted to know why he failed to bring back the game he had hunted. They too were entranced by the Storystone and paid it for the stories. After many days the Storystone asked them to invite the whole village and tell them to bring meat and bread. All came. This time the Storystone said that some would remember every word that it spoke and become the carriers of its stories. Others would remember only a few stories or just fragments. A few would merely remember having been there, and that was fine. But all of them should remember that when the Storystone had finished telling stories they should give something to the new story-bearers whenever they told a story.[7]

The folklorist Stith Thompson explains that folktales and myths normally have variations and that 'creating variations' is what storytellers do.[8] They forget or add details, swop characters' roles, alter or repeat incidents, allow the tale into a new environment, replace an obsolete trait with a modern one. So oral tales continually and inevitably change, just as living things do. Contemporary ecologists recognise that at the same time as the cycles of nature keep renewing themselves the ecosystem is always incrementally evolving and things are never quite the same as before.[9] So human culture, being interdependent with nature, will always need to change as well as sustain. There is a creative tension here. At the same time as we repeat old stories to carry forward wisdom from the past, we also adapt them to the circumstances we face. In this spirit and tradition, having received 'The Origin of Stories' through oral transmission, I structure the story as follows:

The Storystone

Long ago, there was a girl who had made a bow and arrows to hunt birds to feed her family. One day, while hunting, she sat on a large stone to rest. It asked her whether she wanted to hear a story. The girl answered, 'Yes!' The stone asked for a gift in return. Having nothing else, she offered the birds she had shot. The birds then came back to life and flew away. The stone told her stories until it grew late, then she ran home, hunting as she went, but could find only two birds to replace her rich pickings earlier. In the morning the girl went hunting again, and returned to the stone. Again it asked if she wanted to hear a story, and for something in exchange.

At this point I often pause to ask the children what might be a good gift for a storytelling stone. I receive replies such as 'a ball', 'a mirror', 'another stone to be its friend', 'a blanket of moss to keep it warm'. The story continues:

The girl had only her birds to offer. Once the stone accepted her gift, the birds came back to life and flew away. Once more the stone told the girl stories until it was late. She ran home, but found only one bird on the way. The next day, her mother – worried because they were short of food – sent her little son to track his sister. So it came about that sister and brother sat together on the stone, listening to stories. The day after, the mother sent their cousin after them ... and all three sat and listened to the stone. Next day, more people came; the day after, more again ... until the whole community was there, every day, listening to stories. Then one day the stone said, 'I've told you all my stories. Now *you* must tell them.' The stone cracked and fell into pieces. Everyone took a piece to remember the stone that told stories. And they remembered the stories, and told them as best they could.

In my telling, I preserve some core features of the original – a young hunter who encounters a storystone and gives it something in return for being given his people's stories – but reshape other elements to fit the purposes of the Children's Circle and our expedition. My hunter is not an orphan boy, but a girl who lives with her mother and brother. The dead birds come back to life and fly away. I have the stone crack to pieces at the end and the people each take away a piece. The story has changed from the original myth, so its meaning has changed too. My aims are to make the story easier for my audience to identify with, to express my belief in the healing power of giving (as in the birds' return to life), to emphasise the importance of receiving stories, and to proclaim that we are all storytellers (as in everyone taking away a piece of the stone).

When I have finished telling the story, we talk for a while about it, about where the children think stories come from, and about how stories can change as they are passed on. We each then search for a special stone, which we either put in a safe place or carry with us on our journey to the Cave. The story and the stone set up an unspoken anticipation that on our adventure into the wild we may each, like the young hunter, receive some unexpected blessing, which will be remembered as a story and symbolised by the stone.

Inside the Cave

The route begins with a challenging climb up the hillside above the camp. It then descends into a steep-sided river gorge below a waterfall. We cross the river on stepping stones or by wading, then scramble up to the cave entrance two metres above the river. The climb is a real physical and psychological test for the children. Little ones can only reach the cave mouth with help, and the walk into darkness challenges us all. The tunnel leads horizontally into the hillside for about ninety metres. It is high enough inside for an adult to walk upright, brushing the arching sides with outstretched hands, but in darkness it may seem awesomely large to a child. The tunnel curves slightly, so that after a certain distance no natural light enters and we have to use torches.

When we arrive at the end of the tunnel I invite the children to turn off their torches, if they dare, to experience the dark, the mountain, and the underground sound of the waterfall outside. In this darkness I share a story I have woven together from threads of Egyptian mythology and adapted for my young listeners:

The Boat of a Thousand Years

In the old times there was nothing but darkness, until the Creator made a woman. Her body formed an arch, arms stretched downwards. Her name was Nut, the Sky. She wore the moon in her hair and the stars on her shoulders. Then a man was made, lying on his back, leaning on his elbow, one knee raised. This was Geb, the Earth. Between Nut and Geb the Creator placed Shu, the Air, so all things could live. But everything remained dark, until Ra, the Sun, set sail across the sky in his Boat of a Thousand Years. In the morning, Ra is a baby with golden curls. At midday, when the Boat reaches the highest part of the sky, Ra is a young warrior with long bright hair and beard. By the evening, Ra has grown old and his hair and beard are white. Then Nut opens her mouth to swallow the Boat of a Thousand Years, and darkness falls again. All night long, Ra travels through Nut's body, and in the morning he is born again. Every day, Ra sails the Boat of a Thousand Years out into the morning, and brings light. [10]

The children are vividly present to their experience as they undertake their adventure into the Cave; I tell the Egyptian story to offer a mythic framework for their experience, one that conflates the cycles of sun and earth, dark and light, with the human life cycle. In the darkness and stillness of the Cave after the story has finished, the demands on the children's courage made by the process of growing up are brought to a symbolic focus together with the images of the myth and the challenges of participating in the expedition. When the words of the myth have died away, we switch on our torches one by one. The light returns. The cycle of life is renewed.

To mark our participation in this climax of the journey, each of us makes an offering. This might be something material, such as some water or food from our own provisions which we offer back to nature, or an object that symbolises something important to us. (If material offerings are made, someone will probably need to go back afterwards to clear them up so they don't become a mess.) Alternatively, one can make an ephemeral offering of words or gestures, which will leave no impact on the environment but may express some intention or promise.

Returning with stories

We then turn to retrace our steps towards the daylight. We cross the river and climb back up to the lip of the gorge. In a clearing we make a circle to drink water or juice and eat snacks we have brought with us. We share something we appreciate about each person on the journey, talk about the adventure, and listen to someone other than me tell a story. This story is a wildcard amidst the familiar repeated elements of the expedition; it often illuminates our shared experience in an unexpected way.

Upon returning to the camp, we collect any storystones that were left there and dig the other ones from our bags. We decorate the stones with indelible pens to make each stone unique and to help us each remember something special about the journey or the stories we heard. We finish by showing the decorated stones to the group and inviting each child and helper to speak whatever is on their mind. Thus the stones represent in our lived experience the same role as the pieces of the Storystone in my telling of 'The Origin of Stories'.

Talk about the day's events often spreads into the camp's wider life. I remember one four-year-old boy, Brychan, whose family know and love the valley, who decided to join our expedition by himself, stalwart in wel-lies and shorts, a big torch at the ready. He was thrilled to relate his experiences to his parents when he got back. That evening in a talking circle, his parents told the whole community that he had said, 'I saw the heart of the world. It was pink, and the shape of a human heart, but a lot bigger.' Whatever this little lad had experienced, it clearly had a powerful effect which he still remembered years later. Other children have different experiences, and these too are memorable enough to impel them to return to the Cave another year on another expedition. The annual expedition thereby becomes part of their deepening relationship with the valley. It is also a reference experience for the community, something that eases conversations among the families. But it is more than that. Doing or having done the expedition contributes a mark to our group identity and helps the children become alert to the natural world. During the trip they are physically challenged in a demanding environment while surrounded by peers and adults who give them the confidence to be courageous and make it safe to be so. We think this generates crucial psycho-social learning for the children and encourages among everyone an attitude of looking out for each other and the natural world in which we live.

In conclusion

The return to the Cave has become an emerging tradition for our community. Many children and adults remember it fondly and look forward to repeating the experience. But away from the Spirit Horse gathering the remembered journey also provides an intimate template with which to meet real-life challenges. It reminds us that these can be dealt with in a way that strengthens community and also respects the natural world within which human community exists.

I have tried to show that in storytelling work that aims to promote values such as these, it is as important to repeat activities or stories used previously as it is to introduce new ones. I believe that such repetition provides the participants with a structure of familiarity which allows a deepening of their experience and steeps them in the atmosphere of shared expectation that underpins emerging community traditions. Such acts of repetition provide a vital counterweight to the prevailing cultural tendency, driven by the exploitative logic of our economic system,[11] to privilege that which is new over that which is traditional and proven to be sustainable. Moreover, the re-immersion in shared experiences in nature with others re-grounds us in our individual relationship with the natural world. At the same time, tradition and stories do evolve, just as the ecosystem evolves. To this end, I have also explained why I make my own versions of stories I hear or read. I have tried to address this much-debated matter openly and respectfully. Doing so strengthens my ability to deal resiliently with other touchy subjects, such as those that will inevitably accompany us as we move together towards a more sustainable way of living.

Notes

[1] The opinions expressed in this paper are my own and are not necessarily shared by, nor do they necessarily reflect, any opinions held by anyone in the Spirit Horse Community.

[2] <www.spirithorse.co.uk>.

[3] See Hall, this volume.

[4] See, for example, Propp, *Morphology of the Folktale* and Ranelagh, *The Past We Share*.

[5] This idea draws on Goodchild, *Capitalism and Religion* and Gersie, *Earthtales*.

[6] Curtin, *Seneca Fiction, Legends and Myths*.

[7] Summary of story from Curtin, *Seneca Fiction, Legends, and Myths*.

[8] Thompson, *The Folktale*, p. 436.

[9] Botkin, *Discordant Harmonies*.

[10] Summary of oral retelling. Sources: Barnett, *Gods and Myths of Ancient Egypt*; Green, *Tales of Ancient Egypt*; Sproul, *Primal Myths*.

[11] Edgerton, *Shock of the Old*.

CHAPTER 17

Traditional stories, such as local legends that are strongly
connected to particular places, have a unique potential for
capturing the interest of people who hear them. Mary presents two
stories (one traditional, one made up using a character from the
traditional story) and describes:

ways of bringing local legends to life in their home landscape;

~

how such stories can become a basis for activities and discussion that lead
naturally into questions about the ethics and sustainability of human activity
in the area;

~

the use of these legends during a teacher-training programme to encourage
storytelling in schools.

Mary shows how the legends' connection to specific features in the
environment catalysed emotional engagement with place and
thereby a greater openness in the participants to
environmental issues.

'Miss, *Is* Skomar Oddy Extinct?'

Training teachers in skills to bring local legends to life and thereby engage children and adults to enjoy their local landscape and care for it

MARY MEDLICOTT

The king who sleeps beneath the mountain is a subject of stories in many lands. Ever potent in his recumbent majesty, he sleeps until he is once again needed to restore his people and their lands to their rightful power. For Alan Garner as a boy, the mountain was Alderley Edge, the wooded Cheshire prominence near which he lived, and it was his grandfather who made sure he knew about it.[1] In Wales there is more than one peak that holds the sleeping king in a cave, and it is usually Arthur, jewelled crown on his head and his knights with their swords at the ready around him.

Another kind of being, not a king but equally potent, lies somewhere beneath the Preselis, the magical range of hills in the Welsh county of Pembrokeshire from which on a clear day you can see almost all the county spread out before you. He is a giant called Skomar Oddy. To judge by my experience of the appeal of his story to those who hear and think about it, he could be resurrected as a symbol of another sort of restoration, namely our awareness of the land where we live as one of our most vital resources – a kind of awareness that is crucial to our learning to care for the land and to work to restore its health where it has suffered damage.

Traditional stories – like 'Skomar Oddy' – about a specific place in the landscape are known as 'local legends'. In the British Isles, as elsewhere, they are very numerous. Traditionally they were often believed to be true; sometimes they still are.[2] A local legend 'means a great deal to those living in a particular area, or visiting or exploring it, but in most cases has not become widely known outside its own community'.[3] In this chapter I shall describe some of my work with local legends with primary-school children and teachers in Pembrokeshire, where I grew up, and highlight how this work can help to stimulate environmental awareness.

Legend of Skomar Oddy

In the legend of Skomar Oddy, two sea monsters begin to fight in the ocean at the entrance to Milford Haven, the beautiful sound that in my lifetime has been built over by massive oil and gas terminals which, while causing devastating change to the landscape, have also brought much-needed employment to this comparatively impoverished part of Britain. As the vicious sea monsters dive-bomb each other, they create great waves in the ocean, and as the waves break over the land, they deposit enormous splodges of salty mud that the fighting has stirred up from the seabed. As the mud begins to cover the land, it starts to fester and stink. The mud is full of sea creatures that have been displaced from their natural homes. What is going to happen? An ancient sea horse remembers that beneath the Preseli Hills lives a kindly giant who has been there since time immemorial. If the sea creatures seek him out, he will surely help them. Advice is followed by action. In one of those wonderfully unlikely scenes that spring into believable life when visualised, the sea creatures begin a long procession into the Preselis, which even today are sparsely inhabited and little visited by the tourists who descend on Pembrokeshire at holiday times. In the hills, they meet mountain creatures – elves and dwarves who are part of the land – who guide them to the underground cave where Skomar Oddy sleeps. Normally he awakens only once in every hundred years. Even before they reach his refuge they hear him snoring. It's like hundreds of underground turbines revolving. At last, they see him asleep in the shadows, his legs as massive as tree trunks, the muscles of his arms like ropes of steel, his whiskery beard like vines before pruning. How will the sea creatures wake him?

That's a very good question and it can be used to encourage children – of any age from five to eleven – not only to think but to respond. There have been other points in the story which invite such a response: for example, what the giant's snoring sounds like or the problem of envisaging how enormous he is. Storytelling, in my view, is essentially a matter of awakening the listener's imagination, first in a sensory way, and then to perceive consequences and connections. This does not require role play or physically moving about. With the group sitting comfortably around the storyteller, there are ample opportunities for sounds and actions to be added to words to conjure the scenes of the story into life.

At this point in 'Skomar Oddy' the children who are listening can be encouraged by my pauses, facial expressions, and actions to think of ways to awaken the giant. After all the expectable ploys have been raised – jumping on him, pulling his whiskers, blowing into his ears, shouting at him – the children may well hit on the idea of singing to him. If not, I will suggest it. It's a very Welsh thing to do. But when I was preparing my telling of 'Skomar Oddy' I settled on an English tune, 'London's Burning', as one I could more or less guarantee that everyone present would know. I also decided on a set of words for the song which would make sense in Pembrokeshire and elsewhere too. To make them easy for children to remember, these are accompanied by actions: flung-out arms for the big head and big body, imploring hands to beseech the giant's help.

Skomar Oddy, Skomar Oddy
Big head and big body
Help us, help us
Help us, help us
Get the mud back in the ocean.

Repeated several times, each time louder, the song finally wakens the giant. As he sits up, listens, and agrees to help, my voice describing the scene may become quite hushed, so awesomely vast is this creature. And now another chance for participation arises as, kindly giant that he is, Skomar Oddy tells the sea creatures he will take them back to the sea and, picking them up one by one, disposes them in different places around his body. Where, we wonder, will he put them?

Next, so I say, he picks up the mountain creatures – he will take them as well to give them a nice day out – and when he is ready he leaves the cave. Outside, seven magical steps is all he need take before he reaches the start of the mud and begins shovelling it up from the land with his hands and throwing it back in the sea. Even today, according to the legend, his route downriver retains the footprints he left, his toe-prints becoming the little coves visible on any map of the Haven. When the job is done, and the land restored, Skomar Oddy returns to the hills. The sea monsters meantime have either burst from terror at seeing the giant or dived down to the seabed and fled.

'Skomar Oddy' is a great story for adults to share with children in an educational or even a family context. I first came across it in one of Brian John's anthologies of Pembrokeshire folktales, which quote the stories from original sources.[4] In such sources, local legends are often little more than tantalising snippets of story. For the purposes of telling, they need expansion and then preparation. In the case of 'Skomar Oddy', besides looking for opportunities for participation, and making a song, I also worked on the wealth of detail that could be brought in. Names of sea creatures, types of fairy-tale creatures, metaphors or similes for describing the giant – all these could fill out the story and be elaborated further as listeners contributed their own suggestions.

I considered, too, the opportunities for follow-up work. Because it actively involves the children on an individual or small-group basis, following the story with other creative activities can embed it more deeply in their imagination. After the telling (or, indeed, during it) they can be asked, eyes closed, to visualise scenes. Then pairs or groups can be invited to use their visualisations to make drawings and captions to story-board the tale. A large group or whole class can collaborate to make, for instance, a 3-D giant out of found materials such as stones, dead wood, twigs, leaves, seed cases, shells, and feathers.

There can also be opportunities for discussion. Especially when a local story is told to local children, significant issues may emerge, either spontaneously or prompted by the storyteller. Thus, Pembrokeshire children who have listened to 'Skomar Oddy' might use their local knowledge to consider what has happened to the part of the county where the story takes place. Is it right for an area of great natural beauty to be permanently changed by the need to supply the fuel needs of the nation? What will happen when the oil runs out? Will there be wind farms instead? What about the need for employment? How can people in an outlying area like Pembrokeshire manage to earn a living? Introducing such questions is one way to encourage environmental thinking.

Local legends are not only valuable for children. I have made them a focus of a number of storytelling courses for Pembrokeshire teachers which I have helped to design and run. From previous experience in various parts of Britain, I had discovered the strong capacity of local legends to engage children's interest. Although any particular local legend is likely to be most effective in the areas where it is 'local', my experience is that the apparent reality of such tales, especially when the story is well shaped, can make them almost equally powerful for people elsewhere. I had come to feel that the immediacy of local legends' appeal and the interest they arouse in children could help to increase the confidence of teachers in their own potential as storytellers and also introduce them to the wide range of creative possibilities afforded by storytelling.

Seen in this light, working with local legends may have far-reaching implications. In my view, a real and urgent problem is how to make storytelling itself sustainable as an integral part of people's lives. Storytelling in the modern world is too often regarded as an occasional activity – a special treat for children in schools, an additional entertainment available to adults. When it *is* provided as an extended project in primary schools (secondary schools don't usually get a look-in), this too is treated as a one-off. Courses and workshops are sometimes provided for teachers, parents, community leaders. These at least ensure that people other than professional storytellers are learning the skills and value of storytelling. But people's lives move on. Teachers change schools. Parents get busy. Community leaders retire. We need to be far more ambitious. Stories, storytelling, and related activities offer an important way of helping us to create that new literacy of sustainability that is so needed today (see Introduction, this volume). That's why I would like to see storytelling training and practice built systematically into the educational system and the life of local communities on an ongoing basis.

The storytelling courses I ran for Pembrokeshire teachers were unusual in their length, the complexity of organisation they involved, and the back-up they received. They were set up by the county's Literacy Adviser and devised by the two of us working together. Each course was conducted over a ten-week period with gaps of a fortnight between sessions. Each was located in a primary school where two classes of different ages (Early Years, Key Stage 1, or Key Stage 2)[5] had been selected. One class would receive a morning group of visiting teachers from other primary schools in the county, the other an afternoon group. The visiting teachers (between five and seven per group) were joined by the class-teacher, and before each session they met with me in a quiet place to discuss the plan for that session. In the classroom the teachers would observe me telling stories, join in where appropriate, and work with small groups of children in the follow-up work. After this, we would meet again to discuss what had taken place and their reactions, before they returned to their own schools where, over the next fortnight, they would try out what we had done.

One aim of these courses was to assess improvements in the speaking and listening of the children who took part. Another was to create a long-term increase in storytelling in the county by training teachers to tell stories themselves. Overall, I worked with quite a large number of teachers, since every time I ran a course in one school I was also running a parallel course in another school on another day of the week. Since the whole enterprise was repeated three times over a couple of years, it gave me an excellent opportunity to judge what kinds of stories worked best. Teacher feedback was crucial. An invigorating part of our fortnightly meetings was when the teachers shared how they'd got on, passing on ideas of fresh ways they'd found to follow up stories and also reporting on children's reactions and the work they'd done.

Among the different kinds of stories I told on these courses, the Pembrokeshire legends went down especially well. After the sessions that focused on Skomar Oddy, I heard excited reports from teachers of how children had responded. News came in of maps of the Preselis being consulted, portraits of Skomar being painted, illustrated books being made of the story. In one school a huge 3-D model was created of the giant festooned with sea creatures. From several schools came reports that pupils had been taking their parents on weekend expeditions to explore the beaches along the Haven. In these various ways 'Skomar Oddy' had travelled far beyond the occasion of my telling. It was particularly pleasing that children had gone exploring as a result of the story. Anything that gets children outside, making a physical relationship with nature, seems a good thing to me. But, since my larger hope is that local stories may do more than this – that they may stimulate an imaginative connection with the land, perhaps thereby awakening questions and feelings about the way the land is used[6] – I was especially delighted by an invitation that came after one of the courses had ended. An invitation, inspired by 'Skomar Oddy', that led to a very special day out.

An Iron Age fort caps the stony summit of Foel Drygarn in the Preseli Hills. At the start of that special day out, when the hired bus drew to a halt, there was a palpable air of excitement as we caught our first sight of the mountain. Would the sun emerge from the clouds? What would we do when we got to the mountain? The children with whom I'd travelled were six or seven years of age and numbered about forty. They got out of the bus with raincoats and kitbags, with assorted teachers, mothers, and carers, and we all trooped through the puddles towards the base of the mountain, there to be met by another whole group of teachers and children from another school that had been involved in my course. Waiting for us too was a wonderfully weathered-looking National Park warden who'd agreed to lead groups to the top of the mountain to explore the fort. As the first group for the ascent was assembling, preparations also began to be made for a kite-making workshop at the base of the mountain. Nearby a flapping tarpaulin was slowly pegged down as the place for me and my storytelling.

For the teacher who'd initiated the idea of the trip, this day out was a validation of her own development in storywork. From the start of the course that she'd attended and the first of the stories she'd told to her Year 2 class,[7] the reactions of her pupils had exceeded her expectations. She'd been pleased at her own increase in confidence and the new approaches to teaching that storytelling had brought her. 'Skomar Oddy' had been a particular success. After she'd first told the story back at her school following the training session where she'd observed me telling it, her class had asked for it again and again. Then, while making books of the story, a deputation of girls had come to her with two questions. The first was, 'Miss, is Skomar Oddy extinct?' The second was, 'Miss, can we go up the Preseli mountains to look for Skomar Oddy?' Taking these questions to heart, the teacher had started exploring the possibilities. And now here we were on Foel Drygarn.

Just as storytelling had given rise to the trip, so it was to provide fresh stimulus in the course of the day. I'd been invited by that teacher to create a new Skomar Oddy story to celebrate the expedition. In creating this new adventure, I drew on my knowledge of the Preselis. I knew that the slopes of Foel Drygarn are heavily strewn with rocks. This unusual terrain inspired me to centre the story on an ancient conflict (I made this up) between the giants of the Preselis and some North Wales counterparts. From Brian John's books,[8] I knew that Skomar Oddy was not the only giant to have inhabited Preseli folklore and I could imagine that North Wales, which has much bigger mountains, might hold some long-forgotten relatives of Skomar, including perhaps a cousin called Gog. 'Gogs' are what we South Walians call the people in the North. A conflict could provide an explanation for the rocks on Foel Drygarn, since the rivalry between North and South Wales is a long-standing feature of Welsh tradition and, in story at least, the resolution of conflict may involve some good learning.

Skomar and Gog

In my new story, 'Skomar and Gog', Gog Oddy is a stone-throwing boy-giant whose laddish behaviour finally proves too much for the mountain dwarves of the Preselis. Night after night, their homes on Foel Drygarn have been shaken to their foundations by the impact of the rocks that Gog Oddy has thrown from the mountains of Snowdonia. They decide to go and consult Skomar Oddy, who is known from the past to be helpful. When they finally succeed in waking him up, with an appropriately adapted song, he listens to their complaint with concern and at once sets off northwards. After only ten steps, he sees Gog Oddy sitting on a slope in Snowdonia, piling up rocks for the night's throwing. Confronting the boy-giant, he quickly makes him realise that they are cousins. What is the point of this useless conflict when they can have more fun visiting each other? Peace breaks out and is soon consolidated when Gog Oddy brings his family down to Foel Drygarn, which is a beautiful place for a day out.

Making up new stories based on local legends is a nice challenge. A good way to start is to survey your main ingredients – in this case, a mountain littered with rocks plus a kindly giant who normally sleeps but has previously helped solve a problem that arose because of a conflict. In this case, too, we know that on Skomar Oddy's mountain there also live some mountain dwarves. New scenarios do not come from nowhere: the patterns of old ones are always there. It occurred to me that, if I were a mountain dwarf, I would be very upset if my home were regularly shaken by the pounding of rocks. Other details followed from there, plus the fact that from Foel Drygarn you can see North Wales and South Pembrokeshire.

On the day of the trip, my new story was just one element in the host of excitements on offer. The teacher who'd asked me to provide it had wanted it as a way to set the scene, reminding the children of why they were there and their original excitement at the idea of the giant in the mountain. I began my storytelling with each group of children by retelling 'Skomar Oddy'. Since they knew it so well by now, there was a great deal of participation. Then I went on to 'Skomar and Gog'.

No sooner had I finished telling the new story to my first group of children than they spontaneously decided to get up and run across the lower slopes of Foel Drygarn to search out evidence of where mountain dwarves lived. Everywhere on the rough sides of the mountain they found signs of the dwarves' lives. Small pools of rainwater were where the little creatures bathed. Straggles of sheep's wool caught on thorn branches were their towels hung out to be aired. Berries formed part of their diet. Tiny holes in the mountain were ways into their houses. Neither these children nor the subsequent groups needed any directing. Their engagement and delight were visible in their joy in running about, their care and patience in discovering the tiniest signs of occupation, and their fun in gathering what would surely become enduring memories of their day out. None of them, I was told, had ever been to the Preselis before. I hoped that, later, some of them might drag their parents there to share what they'd learned that day and the views and fresh mountain air. Afterwards I heard that some had done just that. I also hoped that this joyful experience might help foster the awareness that would fuel future ideals.

My contribution to the Foel Drygarn trip pleased me for two main reasons. Not only were the children engaged by the day and by my new story; the day also justified one of my basic hopes in using local legends on my training courses – that telling these stories can help to engage children with the world about them.

The landscapes of most countries are bristling with local legends.[9] Wherever you are, you should be able to find some stories to work with in your own area, though they may need a bit of elaboration before you tell them. The term 're-storying' is being used in both clinical psychology and ecological thinking to urge that we regain knowledge of imaginative ideas and stories from the past so that they can reawaken our creativity in the present. Local legends are particularly well adapted for such a task. For one thing, they're already there, storying the land, and some of them have been there for centuries, even if lately they've become forgotten. 'Re-storying' means reminding local communities about them and developing them to resonate with today's needs. Because they concern specific features of the landscape, and because they've often been regarded as true, they have an immediacy that can catalyse an emotional engagement with a place and at the same time challenge what we think and believe.

Notes

[1] Garner, *Book of British Fairy Tales*.

[2] Briggs, *Dictionary of British Folk-Tales*.

[3] Westwood & Simpson, *Lore of the Land*, p. vii.

[4] John, *Fireside Tales from Pembrokeshire*; Jones, *Giant Tales from Wales*.

[5] In the state education system of England and Wales, Key Stage 1 is the prescribed curriculum for pupils aged five to seven, Key Stage 2 covers pupils aged seven to eleven, and the Early Years Foundations Stage regulates childcare for children under five.

[6] See also MacLellan in this volume.

[7] Year 2 is the second year of Key Stage 1: pupils aged six to seven.

[8] John, *Fireside Tales from Pembrokeshire*; idem, *The Last Dragon*.

[9] See, for example, Westwood & Simpson, *Lore of the Land* (for England); Westwood & Kingshill, *Lore of Scotland*; and de Blécourt et al., *Verhalen van Stad en Streek* (for the Netherlands).

PART V

ENGAGING THE WIDER COMMUNITY

CHAPTER 18

It can be difficult to communicate to others the impact of
a powerful experience in the outdoors and the consequent decision
to live in a more sustainable way. Here Martin explores:

why it matters to be able to convey one's experience when one returns
from a wilderness rite of passage;

~

how participation in the telling of traditional and other stories before and after
such a rite enables the person to integrate their newly gained insights and
ideas into their community of belonging;

~

story-based techniques, including voicework and 'radius walks', that safeguard
the integrity of the person's new understanding and create a positive
trajectory towards more sustainable ways of living.

Though the return from a wilderness experience will always be
complex, such storywork can support people's commitment to
a more sustainable way of living.

Beyond the Crisis of Return

*How storytelling can help participants in a wilderness rite
of passage to keep their new-found insights alive and
communicate them effectively to their community of belonging*

MARTIN SHAW

This chapter addresses the relationship between wilderness rites of passage, 'myth-telling', and the development of living in a sustainable way. At the rite's core is a man's or a woman's solitary fast for four days and nights in a wild place, watched over by an experienced guide. After focusing on the crisis I perceive in the rite's current practice, I shall describe what myth-telling is and explain how participation in myth-telling before and after the experience can help the 'initiate' successfully through it and facilitate their reintegration into their home community. I also indicate how this work can help catalyse change towards living in ways more sensitive to the earth.

The crisis of return

In the 1970s Steven Foster, Meredith Little, and others brought wilderness rites of passage to the consciousness of the industrialised West.[1] The wilderness rite contains five stages – preparation, severance, threshold, return, and implementation. It is based on the three-stage rites of passage that many boys and girls in traditional societies undergo to achieve a change of status in their community, such as being treated as an adult, gaining permission to marry, or becoming an elder.[2] In contemporary Western society, ritualised events that mark a person's transition from one status to another – such as baptism, confirmation, graduation, marriage, or retirement – are familiar equivalents.

In almost twenty years of working as a wilderness guide and helping people from many walks of life undergo a fast, I have learned that many initiates meet considerable difficulties when re-entering their community. Many first-time fasters say they felt unable to tell the story of what had happened to them. Others say they could not translate their hard-won insights into a workable new blueprint for life. Here is the rub. Of the five phases of the wilderness rite – preparation for the fast, severance from the familiar, exposure to the intensities of the natural world during the fast, return to one's community, and implementation of the positive effects of the experience – initiates sometimes fail to achieve the final two phases. I believe this matters, in fact is crucial. Most initiates hope their fasting experience will bring them closer to themselves and to those they have left behind. When they cannot communicate their experience to others or integrate it into a more conscious way of living for themselves, then the most profound element – to be of service – is lost.

The fast offers a crossroads between the story of an individual's life, and the larger, primordial emerging story of the land itself. It engenders a deep sense of connection, but in certain cases the initiate is unable to join these motifs into a story that can take them forward as they negotiate the difficulties of re-entering their community. Yet, as I have said, most initiates hope that their fasting experience will bring them closer to themselves and to those they left behind. They look to it to advance them further towards the capacity of being an 'elder' for their community – someone who knows how to craft an insightful story from the difficult walk of their life. This carries hope with it, especially for younger people.

Most wilderness guide training programmes emphasise the importance of ensuring the initiate can accomplish their desired transformation through fasting and solitude. Having observed that a successful fast does not necessarily lead to successful return and implementation, I wanted to see what I could do to increase the chances of a productive re-entry. I thought an important catalyst of return could be the ability to convey something about what one had gleaned during one's fast, and that having crafted a powerful, eloquent expression of the experience could help the initiate to implement the benefits of the wilderness immersion in their ongoing life.

On this basis I developed a myth-telling programme that I invited first-time and returning initiates to attend before and after their fast. The programme consists of long weekends gathered under canvas and in re-mote retreat centres, to focus on the preparation and ritualised retelling of myths, folktales, and personal stories. The stories and techniques I use familiarise the participants with tales that are pertinent to the fasting experience and link their own 'story-memories' of the land, in both the wilderness and their home area, to poetic inspiration (see also MacLellan, this volume).

The Norwegian story of 'Valemon and the Wild Third Daughter' is an example of a woman breaking with the comfort of her life as a princess, venturing into the complexities of the forest and relationship, encountering her frailties and strengths, and returning deepened by the experience. Contained in this 'big story' is a myriad of subtle links to the personal stories of the students. This myth-telling process is a lively form of philosophical enquiry to be engaged in before and after the transformative fast on the mountain. I shall now outline four key facets of this work.

Myth-telling

During my own fasts and years living outdoors and guiding groups, I have grown to value the mythic images that shape my relationship to the wild. The metaphor at their core has wide associations – it makes them generous.[3] This 'multivalency' ensures myths are fluid and prevents them descending into the merely didactic (see also Salisbury, this volume). As we change and grow, the myth grows with us. Images such as 'the room of crow feathers', 'a white bear holding a wreath', 'the witches' glass mountain' have a mutable power.

How might the earth speak to the initiate in mythopoetic language? Three examples:

* The patterning of crows over a winter field could be seen as an oracular thought expressed by mud, sky, and birds.
* The elegant procession of reindeer across a spring meadow may be perceived as part of an epic train of imagination that has been run-ning for tens of thousands of years.
* The swift dive of the killer whale might express a new vision from an ancient sea.

For the one fasting, the peregrine's wing cuts a new story into the jaunty touch of the breeze. The leisurely bellow of longhorn cattle reorients a calf on its way to the watering hole.

The telling of myth-imbued stories requires a robust and grounded constitution in both teller and listener. The complex adaptation of sensory impressions and primal intelligence into speech that communicates meaning demands this. This style of myth-telling is an intricate form of dancing with words, of listening, of wild thought. You learn that stories like these cannot be entirely scripted, because then the wild becomes a garden on the tongue, elegant though that may be. Sharing these earth-resonant stories not only nourishes the initiate with the legacy of time bent open to the archaic hymns of the land; it also equips them with words and voice that others may recognise, appreciate, and validate.

Meetings with traditional stories

In the myth-telling weekends, the initiates explore particular myths or folk-tales that draw them. They discover that their chosen stories are like spirit-beings, by which I mean they are not merely part of a repertoire, or allegories, or a form of psychology; rather that they have an agency of their own. Once a tale has 'called' someone to tell it, I invite the person to treat it with respect, to study it, to engage with as many versions of the story as they can find. If the story talks about a whale-road or a sword fight I urge them go to the ocean or take up fencing – to follow their story's lead. I see this pursuit as an enactment of taking the story seriously. I urge people not to mistake lines on paper for where the story really lives. If the story really wants to be told by them they should explore whether and how they can inhabit every character in it, especially the animals. If they can't, it may be a clue to wait a while. Telling stories is not a lightning-quick process: I cooked in one tale for 15 years before I considered uttering a word of it.

Respecting an ancient story involves recognising that its impact changes not just through history but every time people gather to hear it told. In the myth-telling weekends the initiates learn that background knowledge about the story is crucial, even though it may seem secondary to the living event of the story's impact here and now.

I also urge them to get to know their inner weather. If you are generally a placid, loving sort, then leaving a mug of red beer out for the spirit of Beowulf may be a tricky fit – but then again it could bring out depths unimagined. Remember that listeners will sense in a split second any disconnect between the teller and the textures of the narrative, rather like a lump like me trying to wade through the *Bhagavad Gita*. It's reckless to presume that stories are simply 'at our disposal'. So the initiates learn that getting to know a story takes time and effort. They also discover that this deep process of familiarisation with a traditional story can be applied to any story, including their own stories of fasting on the mountain.

Attending to one's voice

Recently the storyteller Robin Williamson – Chief Bard of the Order of Bards, Ovates and Druids – sat in my house with his harp and talked for six hours straight about the Four Branches of the Mabinogion. How inadequate was the word 'voice' for what came out of his mouth! After almost seventy years on the planet and most of that singing and telling stories, it is at turns raspy, angelic, guttural, crackly, and melodic. It makes jumpy turns at unusual moments. It is a gravel creek bed that the salmon of insight lays its eggs in. Older storytellers I have met say that the more time you spend in the otherworld, the stronger your voice is. By the 'otherworld' I mean time away from the societal obligations we tend to get overloaded with (see also Hennessey & Green, this volume). So attention to dreams, time by deep lakes and in high desert, brooding over the failure and occasional brilliance of our life, is all useful for deepening the practice of the myth-teller.

I help them to get to know the voices of the otherworld in themselves – their cadence, their accents and vocal dance. Is their storytelling voice lyrical like the willow or resolute like the oak? Is it a generous gurgle or thin and sharp like a buzzard's beak? I tell them, too, to follow the energies of their body. Do they pace like a low-slung jackal or keep very still like a cat in a suntrap? I tell them to stay authentic. If they're young, I ask them not to fret about their voice being unlived in. That has its charm. There's no need to hurry. But certainly myth-telling points towards the vitality of the elders. Keen as the young may be, something unfurls with age that we can't ignore. Our voice is part of our personal ecosystem. Contained within it are the cadences of family and region, inflections introduced by television, and words shaped by workmates, travel, or education. Within just one person's voice is a convergence of ancestral, regional, and enforced influences. Let us savour the deliciousness of someone's local dialect, its burrs and rasps, its turns of phrase.

Walking within a five-mile radius

Finally, I teach the initiates, before and after their journey up the mountain, why it matters to continuously enter the immediacy of where they live, to consecrate a storied relationship to the living landscape. I encourage each of them to give their home place some distinct boundaries. Say five miles' radius. Anyone can find wild nature within five miles of their door if they are prepared to go small as well as big. You can begin with five metres. Just as they may walk the immediate locality on the mountain as they prepare to fast, I urge them to walk parts of this home area at least once a day and open themselves up, in body and imagination, to its stories.

As a wide-eyed kid, I liked nothing more than to follow my dad on one of his walks. In a way we were beating the boundaries, establishing that five-mile radius. My father would show me an old stone archway, or a stretch of lonely beech trees, or occasionally, with a long finger, point at far-off Dartmoor. To this day I could walk you the same route down tiny Devonshire lanes and point out haunted Victorian lamp posts, old tribal settlements beneath car parks, hidden trails down to the sea, and the very bench on which he proposed to my mother.

So the initiate begins to discover a tapestry of local folklore woven through their daily journeys. Those treetops are women riding in bone carriages. See those snowy hoofprints way up the church roof? And do you remember the elves who scared away that property developer? Thereby the initiate becomes intimately familiar with the sodden ewes on the lower hills beneath charcoal clouds, the honeysuckle on the banks of the summering lanes, the tractor sweating hard and pulling a trailer mad with hay, the flies sucking life from the crescent wound on a felled rabbit's hind leg, the fist-freezing snow caking a corrugated iron shelter filled with rusting bikes. Underneath it all, they now know that the great land dreams and sends them its muscled stories.

In myth-telling gatherings before the wilderness fast I tell the initiates, 'As you absorb these images, these miniature stories of the land, don't write them down. If you need to remember them, walk them into your body, chant them in, dance them in. If a pencil hits paper, use it to draw the story, not to write it. At small gatherings tell these stories, and remember, those gatherings don't have to be for humans. Some of the most joyous telling can be for granite, wind, or swamp.' When they return for another weekend I invite them to share stories of their 'radius walks' with each other.

This experience of finding, knowing, and telling the stories of one's daily walks, practised both before and after the fast, is an echo of the initiates' deeper experience of being within the environs of their fast. They learn how to become familiar with the particularity of place in such a deeply embodied way as will enable them to speak about their experiences in a place, whether the wilderness or their home neighbourhood, with an authenticity that others can recognise.

A productive re-entry: the swan-feather cloak

The work described above enhances the initiates' experience of the wilderness rite of passage because it enables them not only to better encapsulate the epiphanies of their fast, but also to transform these murmurings of the owl and stream into stories they can share with their community. Our community is not just human. The development of a strong myth-telling capacity before the fast helps the initiate to protect the intimacy of their experience on the mountain and to communicate something about that experience to others back home if they so desire. Moreover, their intense involvement in the myth-telling practice grounds them in an authentic set of values and ways of being which support their sense of identity. This prepares them for the transformation of the heart which awaits them on the mountain, and makes them aware that it takes commitment and practice to have a devotional, playful relationship to place, wherever we are.

The practice of daily radius walks shows the initiates that the earth and its beings constantly relay information and that not all of it is accessible to observation, logic, and statistics. Fasting intensifies this awareness.[4] Because they have already learned to tell stories about their everyday experiences of communicating with the living earth, it is not too big a step for them to speak about their transformative learning during the fast. Because one's sensitivity to information from the earth is greatly increased during a fast, the fast exercises a profound call to the 'prophetic' upon the initiate. I don't mean prophetic in a divinatory sense, but in the way of feeling viscerally connected to the living world – that rather than the psyche existing within us, we exist *within* a wider, tangled psyche that includes badger scat and waterfalls.

'Prophetic' is a big word. Let me put it like this: I believe that in order to function in our deepest vocation we should stand in the soil of prophetic images, be a scarecrow of words pushed by invisible winds. There is problematic grandeur in this statement but I'm sticking with it. Without the push to the edge of understanding which is part of the wilderness fast, the returnee from the wilderness may merely recite a pastoral tale, polished up to reassure themselves and their community. Such stories lack the Blakean edge of the truly visionary. Pastoral tales offer a salve, an affirmation of old shared values, a reiteration of the power of the herd and the elite.[5] The prophetic almost always brings some tension. It disarms, awakens, challenges, deepens. It has less to do with 'enchantment' and more to do with 'waking up'. If the initiates' experience during the fast may awaken them to another way of living, and give them the motivation and inner resources to pursue it, it's the prophetic edge of their stories that may challenge their community to consider the potential of other ways of organising themselves. The initiates may then quietly decide, as Gary Snyder suggests, that it suffices to be famous for five miles.[6] Famous to the thin stretches of grass between abandoned buildings, and famous too to that nest of starlings just over the hill.

The initiate's re-entry into their home community will always be challenging. The evangelical espouser of the fast's benefits will probably receive indifference or active hostility. Studying Trickster stories can reveal ways of entering communities in a more subtle manner. Coyote's power lives in his nose and tail, rather than in the centre of the body. You don't have to shout. Poetry, story, and art protect the intimacy of your personal story, but also celebrate it in this wider context. This has been a traditional way of expressing the wilderness fast for thousands of years.

The issue of home arises too. A home now exists within the stories, a den of image, as well as the wild places beyond the city limits. Despite initial vulnerability, the initiate has a broader, more sophisticated perception of what home could mean. It is impossible to return in the shape you left – or what would be the point of the journey? If we are lucky, home becomes a place with an address – with soil and plants and birds' nests and friends – but for some it is more nomadic than that. It is a place we carry within us. We are also not the only ones on a journey: on our return we find that life did not stay still; those who remained have their story too.

The Gaelic image of myth is of a swan-feathered cloak that keeps us warm during the inevitable disappointments that life provides, a cloak that also continually provides a deeper context. I believe that all initiates should be honoured with such a cloak. At the Westcountry School of Myth and Story that is what we attempt to do.

Notes

[1] Foster and Little, *The Book of the Vision Quest.*

[2] Van Gennep, *Rites of Passage.* The three stages are: separation, transition, and reincorporation.

[3] Segal, *Joseph Campbell.*

[4] Brown, *The Sacred Pipe.*

[5] Gifford, *Pastoral.*

[6] Snyder, *Gary Snyder Reader.*

CHAPTER 19

Drawing on his experience with horses, Kelvin explores
how storytelling in the acknowledged company of animals
awakens listeners to the manifest co-presence of other living
creatures in our world. He provides:

insight into the intimate connections between people and
the living environment;

~

ideas about how to increase the listener's awareness of the finely nuanced
non-verbal communication between animals and people;

~

an understanding of what happens in the language beyond words between
humans and animals;

~

summaries of two traditional stories.

Kelvin argues that storytelling in the conscious presence
of animals deepens and enlivens both tellers' and
listeners' sense of the presence and sentience of
other creatures who share our world and of
our responsibilities in relation to them.

The Forgotten Tongue

An experimental story-based approach to enhance our awareness of human–animal co-presence and communication

KELVIN HALL

> Thinking in terms of stories does not isolate human beings as something separate from the starfish and the sea anemones, the coconut palms and the primroses ... *thinking in terms of stories must be shared by all mind or minds*, whether ours or those of redwood forests and sea anemones.
>
> Gregory Bateson[1]

The photographer who spends six hours sitting beside an adder in the woods, the researcher who is accepted as a member of a wolf pack, the woman in whose hands bats nestle unafraid – these are contemporary examples of humans who know the craft of commingling with wild creatures. This craft expands upon the communicative relationships that countless people have with pets such as dogs, cats, hamsters, even fish, or with companions or working animals such as horses, elephants, or oxen. Commingling relationships between humans and animals involve deep emotional attachments as well as precise and intimate communicative skills. I believe that environmentalists and storytellers can call on this deep, but often ignored, knowledge of human–animal connectivity to strengthen people's motivations for sustainable living.

The 'commingling' way of being involves the capacity to grasp nuanced communication and transactions between humans and animals. It is portrayed in many traditional stories and also in contemporary fiction, films, and computer games. In some tales the hero or heroine seems to possess this ability innately: Little Red Riding Hood and the Wolf; Odin and his ravens. In others the character receives their gift from someone else – such as Sigurd, who understands the language of birds after tasting a dragon's heart, or Melampus, who acquires the same ability after a snake licks his ears clean. Often the animals are wiser than humans. They offer help or grant the hero or heroine powers they would not otherwise have, though some also are seductive and dangerous. The protagonist's knowledge of animals' language may enable them to survive an ordeal, get out of trouble, complete impossible tasks, cure the sick, or find treasure.

Though in part vocalised, communication between people and animals is primarily embodied in non-verbal cues. Taken together these cues constitute a web of signals that all living beings participate in and respond to, even though in modern society we rarely fully realise when we are using it. I therefore call it the 'forgotten tongue'. It has been described in the writings of David Abram, Derrick Jensen, Christian de Quincey, and Jerome Bernstein,[2] all of whom note that awareness of it is pivotal to the culture and well-being of tribal peoples but is undervalued in the West. People like Shaun Ellis, who discovered his life's purpose studying wild wolves' behaviour (living in the pack for more than two years),[3] represent a re-emergence of Western attention to commingling with wild animals. People who treat pets as full members of their family are at the other end of the same spectrum. This forgotten tongue involves sophisticated processes of interspecies communication. Living creatures ceaselessly convey and interpret attitudes and intentions through the quality or intensity of each other's vocalisations, gestures, posture, breathing, smell, movement, and body tension. Although the ways in which these signals are interpreted vary between species, this web of signals provides innumerable channels for sharing and interpreting information between species to their mutual benefit. Like face-to-face verbal communication between humans, the forgotten tongue also transmits unconscious emotions and attitudes. It therefore requires of us candid self-knowledge and self-management when we interact with animals.

When animal characters in traditional stories talk to humans or to each other in spoken language, it is easy to think of this as a fancy of the imagination, or the attribution of human characteristics to animals as actors in stories. I propose instead that this communication represents a verbal simulation of what actually happens when people interact with non-human species. Such tales are most often told at the fireside of hunters, farming folk, and fishermen: people who live in close contact with animals or rely on them as a vital resource. They know in their bones that communication with animals is dialogic, sinuous, necessary, and normal. In their fireside storytelling traditions nobody needs to have it explained that people and animals communicate constantly with intense mutual attentiveness. They know from experience how important this is. If they fail to attend to what animals communicate to them, misfortune ensues: crops are destroyed, livestock attacked, or catch wasted.

In traditional stories the animal guide, helper, bride, or groom primarily requires that humans respect certain boundaries. When these boundaries are ignored, or promises are broken, the punishment is swift; any gift bestowed by the animal disappears, usually for ever. A deep intimacy between people and animals is commonplace in countless traditional stories, such as in this Russian wonder tale:

Marya Morevna

Three birds – a falcon, an eagle, and a raven – come to wed the sisters of Ivan, the hero. The birds can change into men, and change back again. After his sisters are wed, Ivan sets out into the world and meets Marya Morevna, whom he marries. Not long after, Marya Morevna is abducted by Koschei the Deathless. When Ivan goes after them, Koschei kills and dismembers him, but a man-bird brings potions that revive him. To continue the search for his beloved, Ivan needs a horse as clever as that of Koschei. He can only get it from Baba Yaga. On his way to her lair, Ivan meets another bird, a lion, and a bee who offer to help him provided he leaves their young in safety. He promises to do so. When Baba Yaga tells Ivan to watch over her horse herd for three days without losing any of them, the birds, lions, and bees each help Ivan to accomplish this task. After many adventures, which include the rescue of Marya Morevna, the horse that Ivan won from Baba Yaga strikes the blow that flattens Koschei.[4]

Throughout this story, birds change shape and become men; humans and birds marry and live together; and birds, horses, lions, and bees converse with humans, exchange favours with them, and bond with them. Only because these things are possible can Ivan survive and triumph.

I think that some of this tale's extraordinary images are close to experiences that people have in real life. Consider Jensen's pivotal moment of encounter with coyotes, in which he struck a bargain with them: he would leave them food if they would spare his chickens. As he vividly recounts, they did.[5] I have also witnessed people achieve high levels of response and cooperation from loose horses by 'becoming' a horse in attitude, gesture, timing, and spatial awareness when working with them. A friend recently confided an instance when, looking through the window at a crow, he suddenly, for a few moments, 'saw the world through the crow's eyes'. Such moments of mirror-neuron empathy and identification[6] point towards the territory of the shamanic shapeshifting well known in many tribal cultures, in which the individual's identification with a particular species reaches the furthest limit. Most of these exchanges are deeply satisfying for the people who experience them, as though for a moment they have come home to a lost part of their own nature. I believe that folktales such as 'Marya Morevna' hold some of our waning knowledge of that interspecies web of connection, and that hearing or telling such tales can reawaken our awareness of it. This reawakened capacity has a part to play, as we shall see, in motivating sustainable ways of being.

I would now like to turn from the forgotten tongue as it is embodied in story content to how it can emerge in the storytelling situation. Most storytellers are familiar with occasions when animals make a spontaneous intervention in the middle of a story. A dog may bark, a cat sneak into the room, or a bird flit by the window. Outdoors, wild creatures may unexpectedly appear or call out, and nature at large also makes its presence known in rain, thunderclaps, or rays of sunshine breaking through the clouds at opportune moments. Canny tellers pick up on these events and weave them into their telling to add liveliness, depth, and meaning to the story. By doing so they alert their audience's awareness to the forgotten tongue.

But we can go further. We can tell stories that try to engage the forgotten tongue *intentionally*. I took my first step in this direction when I spontaneously decided to tell a story from horseback. The camp at which I was telling stories was close enough to my home that I could ride there each day on my horse. Because an animal was my companion and because of the ancient rhythm of travelling in this way, I felt more linked to the roots of story than I would if I'd driven by motorcar. I arrived at the venue deep in a mood of story preparation closely attuned to the presence and rhythm of my horse – and then, on the spur of the moment, decided to continue the process, including the ongoing 'dialogue' with my horse during the journey, by telling my story from horseback.

The story did not involve horses – it focused on a boy's kinship with bears – but it was a story that spoke to interspecies partnership, and it was this which was flowing between myself and my horse. While telling I was simultaneously immersed in a stream of non-verbal dialogue with my horse. He sometimes grazed and occasionally began to move away from the human group. I would then request, in the other language, that he stay with us and aware of us. The gesture carried in my body was one of partnership. Our contact remained light and fluid, likewise my connection with tale and audience. There was something freeing about this fluidity not only for my telling but also for the listeners' responsiveness. Something was happening. The children seemed unusually rapt. Afterwards several adults urged me to do more storytelling on horseback because they felt this animal presence and partnership were like an extra part of the story.

This experience encouraged me towards my next step, which was to tell a story (to humans) not from horseback but in the presence of a horse herd. I decided to use a quite different tale – one that involves horses and has stirred powerful emotions for me about the loss of our partnership with the natural world. The story was that of the clash between the Amazons, the warrior horsewomen of antiquity, and the Athenians of King Theseus.[7] The Greeks represented the Amazons in their art as imbued with agility, grace, and skill. For me there is something haunting, carrying echoes from a far distant time, about this Amazon culture pictured as both fiercely female and based on symbiosis with another creature.[8]

Athens, on the other hand, was a city founded on male authority and advancing technology and now becoming mercantile and expansionist. On this foundation the Athenians were later to make great contributions through science, philosophy, and political governance to humankind's increasing 'mastery' of the earth. In the Bronze Age legend, Theseus and the Amazon Queen, Hippolyta, stand symbolically at a particular juncture in human experience. The Greeks are poised to overcome the constraints and uncertainties of climate and terrain by means of trade, deforestation, agriculture, and their crafts and technology. The two monarchs are irresistibly drawn to each other. Hippolyta sees the allure of the coming era. Theseus perceives the grace and integrity of the one passing. There is sorrow at this passing, yet also a mighty momentum forward.

When I tell the story, I portray the mixture of magnetism and antipathy between the two communities. I depict one as immersed in the splendour we perceive in wide landscapes and wild animals, the other as restless, expansive, possessing the ingenuity and guile of civilisation. The Athenians admire the Amazons; they envy their horsemanship and lands, yet find them a threat. The Amazons are intrigued by the Athenians' enterprise and their goods, yet vow to destroy Athens when they realise that its existence endangers all they hold dear. When Theseus abducts Hippolyta to Athens, where she bears him a child, the Amazons retaliate. The battle is decided by a tragic irony and act of sacrifice. Hippolyta renounces the ways of the past and takes to the field on the Athenian side in defence of her new husband and baby. In combat she demonstrates the poise and skill that are the glory of her people and gives up her own life in fighting against them.

The grief this story stirs in me, at the destruction of an ancient culture's splendour and easy intimacy with other creatures, also kindles a yearning that such qualities might eventually be regained. It is ever more apparent that civilisation's endless effort to master the earth – symbolised by the Athenians' defeat of the Amazons – is approaching its limits. We are near a turning point where we must decide if we will cease trying to master nature and instead exercise restraint and seek partnership with it. This may require us to forgo some human interests in favour of other-than-human life. Hopefully, the wisdom we as a species have gained from the journey we have travelled so far will enable us to make the choice – while we still have time to choose.

I first told this tale in the presence of horses to celebrate the launch of a team of equestrian specialists whose mission is to teach a deeply relational approach to being with horses. We assembled one evening as rain clouds rolled across the sky, at a spot where a line of trees met open meadows near a paddock where a herd of eight horses were interacting in their varied ways: vying with each other, protecting, bonding; responding with alarm, curiosity, or humour to minute changes in the world around them. My human audience was made up of horse enthusiasts and lovers of story: young people, artists, folklorists, musicians, friends – about forty in all. A member of the equestrian team spoke about their ideals, which embrace the principles of the 'forgotten tongue': clarity of intention, empathy for the other creatures' perspective, engagement with their communicative conventions. While the horse herd stood by, we gathered in a circle and I began my tale.

I set the scene in verbal language – of that other plain long ago, where a horse herd grazed beside a cluster of human shelters; of a way of life lived vigorously and prized by those who followed it; and of the change that came to it unbidden. So the lament was unleashed, the grandeur exalted. The story flowed as the wind ruffled the horses' tails. They pricked up their ears at the songs, sung by my wife Barbara and drawn from cultures around the Black Sea, that were interwoven with the telling. At times the horses were placid, at times alert. Someone said afterwards that the pregnant mare seemed to pay close attention to the lullaby. The horses were a presence throughout: as the words flowed, so also the forgotten tongue moved between the people and horses, marked by a twitch, a sudden stillness, a glance in each other's direction. The horses' mood informed ours, and ours theirs. The whole was imbued with the kind of mutual awareness that sometimes leads a horse to accept a human invitation to run together.

These two experimental experiences of knowingly telling a story in the presence of animals have given me much to think about. During most storytelling the story mediates a strong two-way relationship between teller and listeners. Here three parties were involved: a teller and two species of listeners. What exactly changes during such triangulation? Moreover, in most storytelling situations the eye contact between listeners and teller is more or less level, but when I spoke from horseback I was looking down at my listeners while they looked up at me; I'm not yet sure what effect this had. And what would happen, I wonder, if I worked with a trained falcon while telling 'Marya Morevna'?

It is easy to assume that the reactions of animals in the presence of storytelling are responses, in some way, to the story – to the subject we are talking about. You may have seen a family dog perk up when conversation turns to discussing its behaviour, or simply to the topic of dogs. But what are we really conveying to our animals in the forgotten tongue while we are speaking to each other in human language? Which spoken words may our animal companions actually understand? What do they pick up from our intonation and body language? In short, what in our storytelling as a *total* communicative process are they actually responding to? Ought this to make a difference for the kind of story we tell? Is it okay to tell a story about foxes eating rabbits in the presence of a pet rabbit? What about telling the same story in a quiet versus an animated way? The only way to find out is to experiment and observe carefully what happens.

What difference does telling stories in the presence of acknowledged or invited animals make to human listeners? To me the issue isn't whether or not the animal present actually understands something of the content of the story (at this point, I have no way of knowing). What is crucial, rather, is my listeners' awareness of the animals' presence – and the animals' awareness of us – and the establishment of that link between us via the forgotten tongue. And it is the human acceptance of that link – no less than that between characters and events in the story – that matters.

While I was telling stories from horseback or near the horse herd, I and my listeners also became more aware of *other* creatures that were present, such as insects, birds, a passing dog. If nothing else, the presence of invited animals enhances the liveliness not only of the story, especially if that kind of animal features in the story, but also of our general awareness of other creatures with whom we share the world – of their lives and their relationships to us. Telling in the presence of horses made me more attuned to the sounds of other living beings and the sounds of the physical world: wind, rain, mud: the 'biophony' and 'geophony' of the world, as Bernie Krause so beautifully puts it.[9]

I believe that the capacity for communication between people and animals, and the old stories that encapsulate this capacity, can be a key resource for the mission of sustainability. I think this is so because many people find in their interaction with domesticated and wild animals a profound sense of fulfilment which counteracts the restless quest to acquire material goods. Piers Moore Ede has described how his pursuit of 'the distractions of city life', as a member of a generation 'sated by more material wealth than any before us in history', resulted in plummeting depression. Only learning how to keep bees enabled him to fall 'in love with life again'.[10] When our yearning for connection with other living beings is satisfied, the hunger to consume is lessened and we gain a deep, bodily sense of belonging and attunement to the natural world. And that is one of the conditions, as well as a goal, of sustainability.

Notes

1 Bateson, *Mind and Nature*, p. 23

2 Ede, *All Kinds of Magic*; Abram, *The Spell of the Sensuous*; Jensen, *Language Older than Words*; de Quincey, *Radical Knowing*; Bernstein, *Living in the Borderland*.

3 Ellis, *Wolf Within*, pp. 96–128.

4 Source: Afanas'ev, *Russian Fairy Tales*, trans. Wheeler, pp. 192–204; Lang, *Red Fairy Book*, pp. 14–26.

5 Jensen, *Language Older than Words*, pp. 18–30.

6 See Keysers, *The Empathic Brain*.

7 Sources and influences: Renault, *The Bull from the Sea*, pp. 233–235; Plutarch, *Rise and Fall of Athens*, pp. 32–34; Shakespeare, *A Midsummer Night's Dream*; Walton, *The Sword Is Forged*; Pressfield, *Last of the Amazons*; Rolle, *World of the Scythians*, pp. 86–91.

8 On the connection between women's experience and the treatment of nature, see Plumwood, *Feminism and the Mastery of Nature*.

9 See Krause, *Great Animal Orchestra*.

10 Ede, *All Kinds of Magic*, pp. 4–6.

Chapter 20

Kevan addresses the question of how we can develop
inspiring story-based visions of a low-carbon world.
He focuses on the following issues:

the process of creating, from a basic story structure, a fictional story
to foster a positive vision of the future;

~

how to adapt such a story to different circumstances in order to take the listeners
in their mind's eye to the imagined world while making connections with their
actual environment;

~

the evocation of 'awen', described as a particular state of inspiration
and connectedness between teller and listener which is sought during
a storytelling performance.

The chapter includes the complete story of 'The Gate',
which Kevan created for an event in a Transition Town
and later adapted for use at a major green gathering.

Stepping through the Gate

*Using stories and storytelling to foster positive visions of
an ecologically sustainable future*

KEVAN MANWARING

Not long ago I took part in a discussion, under the auspices of Transition Bath, about the role of the arts in facing the challenges of climate change and peak oil. The Transition movement is preparing for these challenges by developing modes of living based on lower energy use, lower carbon emissions, and greater use of renewable resources. Because the consequences of the 'energy descent' transition are far-reaching, it is difficult for most people to imagine what a powered-down culture would look like. Many fear it will mean hardship and deprivation. Rob Hopkins, co-founder of the Transition Movement, says, 'We have a paucity of stories that articulate what a lower energy world might sound like, smell like, feel like and look like. What is hard, but important, is to be able to articulate a vision of a post-carbon world so enticing that people leap out of bed every morning and put their shoulders to the wheel making it happen.'[1]

That call to story came at a perfect time. I had just been invited to perform a story at a spoken-word and music event, called *Heaven's Gate*, in the town of Stroud in the English Cotswolds, to celebrate the birthday of the visionary poet William Blake (1757–1827). I decided to use this opportunity to create a story presenting a tantalising glimpse of a low-carbon world that would be easily adaptable to telling in other locations. Most of all, I wanted the story to convey that the gateway to imagining a powered-down future lies within us. Blake famously said, 'If the doors of perception were cleansed every thing would appear to man as it is, infinite.'[2] I therefore arranged my story around the folkloric trope of a magic portal – an opening into another world, through which a character goes to visit another place and time. I would come to my audience with the fool's cloak of a tale and the hope that 'Encouraging positive visions of the future may actually help us to move in a more positive direction'.[3]

But with one caveat.

It is tempting to think that stories automatically involve the listeners in a pleasant, collective process of imagining. The situation is more complex than this. Listeners' attention to a story is often divided. While listening we may also make sense of other physical experiences (a sudden draught, someone's cough) or start thinking about other things (mum's health, doing the shopping). We also use some attentive capacity to deal with memories or longings evoked by the story (that holiday, conflict, or starry night). And what's an inviting story image for one person may be repugnant to another. A storyteller therefore has to work hard to engage their listeners' attention. When they do gain everyone's total attention, something special happens. A hushed concentration falls and everyone can experience the flow of inspiration and insight that I call 'awen' (Welsh: inspiration). In this chapter I'll discuss how my story 'The Gate' responds to these ideas.

The Gate

Part 1

'What's that for?' Becky looked at the old wooden gate placed in the middle of the High Street, looking sad on its rusty hinges, its wood warped and weathered with age.

'Try it. You'll find out,' said the old man, a twinkle in his eye, a strange lilt in his voice.

The gate had appeared a couple of days ago – she'd heard about it from a schoolmate. Everyone was laughing about the old man who had appeared with it, set it up next to the café off the back of his ancient bicycle with its little makeshift trailer, and sat nearby on a bench with his thermos.

An unlikely way to make money! 'You're hoping, granddad!' the schoolchildren had mocked. Many of them had tried the gate, to shrieks of laughter, insolently ignoring the old man and his dish on the pavement, with its poor scattering of coppers. 'You should be paying us! It's in the way!'

The joke about how many could fit through had soon worn off when it elicited no response from the old man, who just looked on and smiled as the pack wandered on their noisy way. After two days the 'running of the gate' was part of their post-school mischief.

Becky avoided the pack when she could – finding their loud antics tiresome. She always preferred to go off on her own, day-dream, imagine strange lands.

'It's silly.' She wrinkled her nose and frowned, pushing back a cowlick of dark hair.

'Why?' said the old man, his voice smoky, warm.

Becky walked around the gate sceptically. 'It doesn't do any-thing.'

'Should it?'

'There's no wall preventing me from going past, so it's, well, useless.'

'Oh, there's plenty of walls here,' the old man said, 'but you just can't see them.'

'What d'you mean?'

The old man smiled and poured himself some thick soup from his flask. His hair was a cloud of white, escaping from his woolly hat like steam from a tea cosy. He was wrapped in several layers of clothing, a thick scarf, mittens, a patched pair of trousers, and a pair of boots that had seen better days. It was summer and everyone was walking by in T-shirts and light dresses.

'You're a bit mad, aren't you?' said Becky.

'Of course,' agreed the old man, beaming a gap-toothed smile, toasting her with his tin mug.

Becky saw the 'pack' approach and decided it was wisest not to be seen talking to a nutty tramp, and so she walked briskly away. The old man watched her go.

Becky had strange dreams that night – of a golden land just beyond a veil. She glimpsed through it a landscape of mountains and glittering rivers, castles and fairy villages, frustrated that she could not enter. If only there was a way. But the veil stretched on for ever.

The next day, she was passing the old man again, a little relieved to see him and his gate still there – though she could not explain why. He didn't seem surprised to see her. All he said was, 'So, are you ready now?'

Becky pretended to not know what he meant, but she looked hard at the gate. It seemed a little lonely, all on its own in the middle of the High Street, with everyone rushing past it. It creaked a little in the breeze, the latch rattling, as though wanting to be released.

'Okay.' She stepped up to the gate, lifted the latch, and opened it. The High Street was still there. A little disappointed, she looked over to the old man, who nodded to her to continue. 'A gate only works if you go through it.'

And so she did.

Passage between two worlds

When telling this first part of the story at the *Heaven's Gate* event, I equated the story's High Street with Stroud's actual High Street. I also referred to the building we were in. I wanted to connect Becky's vision through the gate with the very place where we were. Such site-specific story customisation can help the listeners feel that they live somewhere special: a place of latent qualities and nascent possibilities. Stroud already possesses a Transition network, farmer's market, organic cafes, community farm, conservation project, local currency, and other building blocks of a sustainable society. I hoped that my storied allusion to such achievements would help the listeners to appreciate these things and encourage them to continue on the path of sustainability.

Because it was his birthday, and the event's name was a quote from his poetry, I based the 'old man' upon Blake himself, who offers the curious a golden thread of imaginative possibility:

I give you the end of a golden string,
Only wind it into a ball,
It will lead in at Heaven's gate,
Built in Jerusalem's wall.[4]

The trope of a gate as a passage between the 'ordinary world' and the 'special world' crops up in many works of fiction. Famous examples include the wardrobe in C.S. Lewis's *The Lion, the Witch and the Wardrobe*, the tree in Enid Blyton's *The Magic Faraway Tree*, the rabbit hole in Lewis Carroll's *Alice's Adventures in Wonderland*, and the door in the hedge in Francis Hodgson Burnett's *The Secret Garden*. Each of these acts as both an entrance to the chancy realms of the Otherworld and as an interface between the conscious and subconscious, the contemporary and ancestral, the human and other-than-human, the living and dead. Bridges, crossroads, caves, shorelines, dark woods, lonely moors – such borderlands and crossing points – are places to avoid, especially at liminal times such as dawn, dusk, midnight, May Eve, or Halloween, if you don't want to be carried off to Faerie; or places to frequent if you do. Such imaginative stories, says Tolkien, 'open a door to Other Time, and if we pass through, though only for a moment, we stand outside our own time, outside Time itself, maybe'.[5]

Let's see where Becky went.

The Gate

Part 2

The world seemed to turn inside out. The familiar layers – the High Street, the buildings, the town she had grown up in – peeled back. She was standing on a road of glittering quartz that snaked over a landscape of richly wooded hills and valleys, flower-starred meadows, waterfalls and lazy rivers. The road dwindled to a faint line in the distant foothills, dwarfed by mountains of ever-increasing splendour. Birds of many colours sang songs of crystal clarity and enchanting beauty. Becky took a couple of tentative steps into this magical landscape under boughs heavy with ripe fruit – that looked too delicious, too tempting.

But most dramatic was the change in noise, in the quality of the air. At first she couldn't work out what it was – it was so alien from her everyday experience. And then the penny finally dropped. There was no traffic. The continual drone that had been the white noise of her whole life – when had she not been within earshot of traffic? – was no longer there. It felt strange at first. A sonic hole in the world. But as she slowly explored the richly coloured landscape she began to notice sounds that would have normally been drowned out – the chirrup of insects, the gurgle of a stream, the gentle rustling of leaves in the trees, the flapping of a bird brushing by. And the air – the air smelt clean, fresh.

Delighting in this world – her daydreams come true – Becky whooped with delight and ran down the hill, tumbled until she rolled to a stop, and lay back in the lush grass and felt the warm sun on her face, the heady scent of a summer meadow filling her nostrils. The largest butterfly she had ever seen came and landed on her nose. She looked through its stained-glass wings at the sky, until the tickling made her sneeze. It took off and she chased after it, laughing, until she came to the edge of the village.

At first she was shy, but when she saw how people were merrily going about their business – hoeing the garden, milking a cow, churning butter, baking bread, sewing and spinning, mending and making – she ventured closer. No one seemed to lack a useful task; all seemed content in doing it. She explored with increasing curiosity. The village seemed to run smoothly and successfully by cooperation. The land bloomed about them, the result of good stewardship. Nothing seemed excessive or out of place. Everyone seemed to have enough, and any surplus was shared. All had a meaningful role within the community, utilising their skills or sharing them. Everywhere she was met with smiles. Children played without fear on the green, laughing in the sunlight. The only traffic was the odd horse and cart going by, laden with the fat of the land. It seemed to be a vision of how things could be.

She felt she had seen enough for one day. Her tummy was starting to rumble. It was nearly teatime. In the middle of the village green there was a rickety wooden gate. She smiled as she recognised it. For a moment, Becky considered whether to stay there. Why go back to the smelly world of cars and litter and bullies? Her folks would be worried – for them at least she had to return, and with a sigh she walked up to the gate.

The wood felt familiar to her touch and reminded her of the old man – whose wrinkly face had the same look about it as many of the villagers, a merry twinkle ... A thought popped into her head. Did he come from here? Why would he choose to live in Becky's world, the world of homework and silly brothers, noisy neighbours and dog-poo, politics and war?

The butterfly landed on one post of the gate and seemed to be waiting, gently folding and unfolding its rainbow wings. Maybe someone needed to show the way. Becky looked around at the people going about their contented lives. Had they once lived in her world? Had they gone through the gate? The butterfly opened and shut itself like a book.

'Okay, I know.' She felt she had to go back, to tell everyone about this vision of how things could be. And if no one believed her word, she would write it, paint it, dance it, sing it – make it good enough so all would stand and stare. All would notice. And so, taking one last look around, and a deep breath of the sweet air, she stepped back through the gate.

Awen and attention

When I'm storytelling I can feel, from the quality of silence between my words, from the subtle feedback of my listeners' body language, whether the audience are 'with me'. I wanted them to accompany Becky through the gate in their mind's eye. To help them do so, I changed the energy of my speech at this point in the story and tried to draw the listeners in with a softer, slower voice. I also made the images of the land evocative rather than prescriptive. As the listeners and I co-created this vision, I felt the awen flowing. 'Awen' is the Welsh term for the bard's poetic inspiration, sometimes translated as 'flowing spirit'. It flows through the teller, the listeners, the story, and the whole space around them. When it does, there is a spine-tingling frisson of magic in the air. It feels as though something might break through 'a veil between worlds' at any moment.[6]

Yet the magic can go as mysteriously as it comes. It is important to accept this. The teller is only in control to a certain extent. Telling stories to a live audience, you have to accept the unexpected – to dance with it and not be derailed by it. I see the interface between the world of the story and the world in which teller and listeners are physically present as a semi-permeable membrane that allows distractions, interruptions, and also comic digressions and site-specific references. When I told 'The

Gate' at the *Resurgence* Readers Summer Weekend,[7] held in a 'tented conference centre' with a green countercultural ambience, I gestured – as Becky enters the village – to the yurts, solar panels, wind turbine, compost loos, permaculture plots, and inspiring eco-art that surrounded us. I thereby implied that some of the story's utopian vision was already manifest around us and that it was our call to adventure to take this vision back to the world at large in order to implement it. Although such gestures momentarily divert the listeners' attention out of the story, if the awen is with us I will be able to carry their attention smoothly back into it, so allowing a weaving of engagement between the two worlds.

How do you develop the facility to do this? On one hand, it's about intention. Immediately before a storytelling session, I will in private invite the awen to flow. I visualise it as a white ray of light streaming into and through my mind, my heart, and my body from above, intensifying my energy and attention. I not only appeal to the presence of awen before a session; I also habitually invite this 'centred flow of inspiration' to permeate my daily life, and seek out opportunities to receive it – whether by attending performances by other artists or by spending time in inspiring places, especially outdoors in nature (see Hennessey & Green, this volume). On the other hand, the development of intention involves thorough preparation of one's material. I use techniques of wordplay, physical embodiment, and especially visualisation to make sure I know a story well – in a fully imagined way, not just as a sequence of events or words. Only then do I have freedom in the telling to fluidly manage my listeners' attention.[8]

W.B. Yeats is widely thought to have said, 'Education is not filling a bucket, but lighting a fire.' I think of my storytelling in a similar way. Once the candle has been lit, much can come from it. By now you may be wondering what happened to Becky after her candle had been lit and she began the return from her adventure.

The Gate

Part 3

The old man was waiting. 'Well?'

'It – it was amazing!' Becky's eyes sparkled. It was as if no time had passed. It was still the middle of the day – the sun was in the same place – and she stood in the middle of the busy High Street as though she had unpaused a DVD. Shoppers swarmed about her, oblivious. She wanted to shout out to them all to stop, to enter the gate.

She was bursting with questions. She was just about to ask one of the old man, and his eyes were twinkling with knowledge that now she shared, when a voice broke the spell: 'Sorry, sir, you cannot have that gate obstructing a public thoroughfare. If you could move along, please.'

A policeman towered above Becky, blocking out the sun. Without protest the old man started packing up the gate and put it back on his trolley.

'Who are you? Where are you going next?'

'Oh, it doesn't matter who I am. It's the gate that's important, not me. I'll go where I'm needed, leave when I'm not. Cheerio, Becky.'

Becky started to cry. 'I won't forget you! Thank you! Thank you for showing me.'

The old man turned to her one last time, as he went to cycle off, and said with a wink, 'And now it's your turn.'

Future primitive

My story ends with a weepy but grateful Becky standing alone in the High Street. This may be a bit of shock to some listeners, who may, like Becky, be reluctant to let go of their imagined world, especially if it has given them delight. But all stories end. When the story is over, we must return to the ordinary world, taking with us any wisdom or ideas gleaned from the tale and letting go of the rest. Caspar Walsh precisely encapsulates this process:

> The more beautiful and affecting a story, the deeper it will travel into our conscious and unconscious being. The more beautifully crafted, heart-felt and wise, the more power a story has to inspire and energise us to believe that change is possible, that we can build and sustain hope in the darkest times.[9]

My vision of the land and village that Becky left behind may seem to some implausibly archaic. However, it is not so different from some green festivals I've attended. These events inhabit forward-thinking territory – demonstrating cutting-edge green technologies such as solar panels, pedal-powered PA systems, alternative currencies, alongside the revival of craft skills, community agriculture, and organic produce. They offer a glimpse of what Kim Stanley Robinson calls the 'future primitive', which, Janus-like, looks both ways, to past and future, 'to imagine sophisticated new technologies combined with habits saved or reinvented from our deep past'.[10] Around the world many such sustainable communities already exist, whether permanent or in the temporary form of festivals and camps, and the rudiments of them subversively permeate many towns and cities.

Storytelling too may seem a wilfully archaic activity. But it is low-tech, empowering, and sustainable. At the *Resurgence* Weekend the circumstances of telling stories in the round – by a fire, outdoors, without PA or electric lighting – not only enhanced the storytelling experience but embodied, in the real world, some aspects of the imagined world in 'The Gate'. Ultimately, the threshold is inside each listener – and the change must come from within.

Notes

1 Hopkins, 'Resilience Thinking', p. 14.

2 William Blake, *The Marriage of Heaven and Hell*, plate 14.

3 Russell, *Awakening Earth*, p.201

4 William Blake, *Jerusalem: The Emanation of the Giant Albion*, plate 77.

5 Tolkien, 'On Fairy Stories', p. 129.

6 Manwaring, *Bardic Handbook*. p. 21.

7 *Resurgence* is a British magazine dedicated to earth, spirit, and sustainability.

8 See, for example, Manwaring, *Bardic Handbook*; Lipman, *Improving Your Storytelling*.

9 Walsh, 'Mythology for Our Time', pp. 44–46.

10 Robinson, *Future Primitive*, p. 11.

CHAPTER 21

Individuals, communities, and organisations often find it
easier to choose more sustainable ways of living when they can
look ahead to the future in a positive way. Charlene offers:

a three-hour workshop for adults that fosters the participants'
capacity for sustainable futures thinking;

~

ideas about the application of similar techniques in a Transition Town project that
resulted in the implementation of some projects to promote sustainability;

~

insights into how this future-oriented practice enables participants
to begin to 'be the change'.

We learn how newly made stories of the future can be joined up
and lead to a programme of 'action for change' to enhance
sustainable behaviour both among individuals and across
different sectors of community life.

Envisioning the Future

*Developing specific pathways towards more sustainable
ways of living by means of storywork*

CHARLENE COLLISON

You must give birth to your images. They are the future waiting
to be born. Fear not the strangeness you feel. The future must
enter you long before it happens. Just wait for the birth, for the
hour of new clarity.

Rainer Maria Rilke

A skill we need to develop if we are to live sustainably is the ability to
think across long time horizons. Some indigenous cultures speak of
examining the consequences of an action through seven generations, but
in modern societies we seldom do so through as much as one. Though
some organisations do consider the longer term, most private companies
operate on strategic plans of only 5–10 years. The financial system favours short-term gains over long-term viability,[1] and the decision-making
of elected government officials is constrained by their constant awareness
that the next election is just a few years away. Economic, political, and
other systems are biased towards short-term thinking, which makes it
difficult for any individual or organisation dependent on them to attend
to the long-term future. 'The short-term achievement of economic goals
generally trumps the long-term consideration of our human needs (including our relationship with the other-than-human world).'[2]

Another reason it's hard to maintain a long-term perspective is that
the conditions of the world are changing so fast. Our time is one of ex-
ponential change, especially technical, social, and, increasingly, environmental change. But this is the very reason it's so important that we do

think long term. Humanity's current use of resources and the impact of our activities on the environment point to unsustainability at most levels. If these trends are projected into the not-very-distant future, they converge in a 'perfect storm' of multiple crises on the scale of a nightmare.[3] Such a disaster scenario offers plenty of scope for conflict and sensation that lend themselves to exploitation in commercial fiction and film. The prevalence of grim visions of the future in recent science fiction seems to marginalise even the possibility of hope.[4]

Positive visions of the future offer less conflict to feed exciting stories. They're also more difficult to create than disaster scenarios. That's the law of entropy: 'it's easier to smash a cup into pieces than to make one'.[5] But in our rapidly changing world it's essential that we do create them. Our old visions no longer serve us. Western society is between visions, without a new one that's clear enough, simple enough, and widely enough understood to serve a new community of thought.[6] To redesign our lives on a more sustainable basis we need to imagine positive, plausible visions of sustainable ways of living. Such an envisioned future can act as a powerful magnet drawing our behaviour towards its realisation.[7]

Futures thinking, to construct desirable yet plausible future 'scenarios' and the trajectories to bring them into being,[8] tends to be carried out at high levels in government and big companies. When society is faced with the need for widespread change, there's a risk that strategies for change will be imposed rather than co-created. If a strategy is imposed, it is likely to be resisted. A happier alternative is the widespread engagement of communities of all kinds in collective ecological re-imaginings of how to live. William Morris, in *News from Nowhere*, envisaged such a preferred future: 'He realised that the manner of life of a community cannot be artificially arranged in the mind of an individual, but must be spontaneously created by all members of that community.'[9]

Futures studies does not attempt to predict the future, but rather explores ideas about it, the 'images of the future' which form the basis of people's actions in the present.[10] It examines possible alternative futures and envisions preferred ones – and ideally links up with strategic planning to realise them. Evidence on which to base these futures comes from trends people can observe happening now and also from their informed intuition about what's emerging.[11]

How then to enable processes within communities to give birth to images that can shape an ecologically sustainable future? To create significant change for the future, people need to connect with what matters to them, and to act together with others (see Introduction, this volume). 'Real change begins with the simple act of people talking about what they care about.'[12] This chapter offers a collaborative process of imagining a positive future, rooted in the places where people live and work, so that they have a personal investment in the process and will take ownership of it; so that the visioning is compelling and will bring about the first steps of transformation in the direction of the vision. Below I outline the storymaking process I use to facilitate this kind of visioning among groups of well-motivated, self-selected adults, and then discuss an application of this process in my own local community.

The vision-building process

The process uses storymaking because stories help people to imagine other worlds (see Green, this volume), and can challenge people's assumptions, which is a prerequisite for change (see Cree & Gersie, this volume). Stories can also help people to deepen their sense of relationship, and responsibility, to those who will come after them.[13] And, as we'll see, if a vision is to begin to become reality then a narrative is implied in the journey through time from now to the future.

With a motivated group familiar with the key challenges to sustainability, the following sequence of exercises can be carried out as a oneday workshop. With a group of people newer to sustainability work, they might better be spaced out over a longer period. The sequence of exercises can also be expanded as *stages* of a longer process, involving more extended work at each stage, as in the community application discussed later.

1. Outline the current global trends and challenges
Brainstorm with the group some of the major trends – social, technical, economic, environmental, political – that can be observed today and seem likely to shape the future. Write each one on a post-it note and cluster these to find themes among the trends. Identify through discussion which of these look likely to have most impact, and those whose effects seem most uncertain. Examples might include mass migration to cities, the increasing connectedness of people through technology, the rise of

green values in society. The emergent themes should also reveal major challenges that will impact on future generations.

Invite people to add anything they think essential that's missing. Then make a list of those trends that the group regards as the most crucial global challenges. For example:

- Global population is booming.
- Demand for energy, food, and other resources is rising.
- The climate is changing: global warming threatens health, life, and security.
- Finite oil and gas supplies are peaking.
- Fresh water is increasingly a scarce resource.
- Biodiversity is decreasing as species become extinct (see Nanson, this volume).
- The centres of global economic and political power are shifting.

Discuss with the group what the effects of these trends might be, each trend on its own and in conjunction with the others.

Trends like these, projected into the future, are sobering and alarming. It's important to confront them because if people try to dream up solutions for the future without having done so they'll probably be working on flawed assumptions and so come up with flawed solutions. If the group's members haven't confronted these challenges before, they'll need some time to process them before proceeding to the next stages of the process. It's important to contemplate *together*, rather than alone, this perspective on the world. So that all members of the group get a chance to voice their thoughts, you might conduct some of the ensuing discussion in pairs or trios and then invite each of these subgroups to contribute an observation or two to the whole group.

2. Look back and think what has changed in 20 years

It's time now to shift the group's energy into a more empowered vein. Refer back to the other global trends they've identified and invite them to reflect on some that could contribute to positive change. Convey to them that change is possible; give some examples of successful initiatives in the field of sustainability. Then, to explore the potential pace and scope of change, ask everyone to look back and remember what was happening 20 years ago and some of the changes that have happened since. Remember shoulder pads and giant mobile phones? Wars, earthquakes, governments, the collapse of the Soviet bloc? Some things have changed so little, such as the importance of friends and family; others have changed so much. Few of us 20 years ago had any inkling what changes the internet would set in motion or what prominence global warming would gain in public life.

3. Remember a place that matters to you

Form pairs and ask each person to think about a place they know well. To allow some emotional distance, ask them to choose a place that's in their local area, but not their workplace, their own home, or the home of someone dear to them. What matters is that they feel a connection with the place and what happens there. While they think about this place I prompt them to remember sensory details – sights, sounds, smells, textures.

Then ask each person to describe their chosen place to their partner, speaking in the present tense. Soon the rise and fall of conversation, the expansive gestures, the engagement on the faces of both speakers and listeners testify to the beloved landscapes and townscapes that are emerging. As the mood shifts in this way, people's descriptive words bring into play some of the language they'll use in storymaking later.

4. Step 20 years into the future in that place

Everyone now pictures their chosen place about 20 years in the future, when – we imagine – the sustainability challenges we've identified are being met. This doesn't mean, I emphasise, that the problems have been overcome, or that life is ideal; it means that changes to shift society's course towards sustainability have been and are being made. Don't preempt the details of this future, as the aim is that these details will emerge from the imaginative and collaborative process.

Invite the participants to close their eyes and in their imagination step into the chosen place, move around, and observe what they find there. Ask them: What has changed there? What can they see, hear, smell, feel, taste, and find there now? What is still happening to it? Then ask each person to describe to their partner, again in the present tense, 'what my place in 20 years time is like'. They might say things like:

> It's strangely quiet – hardly any traffic noises, just the occasional hiss of an electric motor. I just avoided being spun round by something that looked half bike, half car.

People are stopping and talking to one another. There's an older person sitting with some younger ones. People seem calm, not rushed. There are herbs and vegetables growing on windowsills.

Buildings look much like they did at the beginning of the century, on the outside – but something quite different seems to be happening on the inside.

5. Create a fictional character

Ask everyone to invite a fictional human character into this future setting. The character can be of any age or background, but must be fictional, i.e. not the participant or anybody they know, and must belong in this future world. After a few minutes in which everyone silently pictures their character in their setting, ask them to describe the character to their partner. What do they look like? Where do they live? What do they need or desire? Immediately after each character has been presented, the listener asks questions about them to bring out greater depth and description. Encourage the speakers to dig into their imagination, right here and now, to answer these questions even if they ask for details the speaker hasn't yet thought about. Each pair briefly reviews their time together. Then ask them to split up and form new groups of three or four people.

6. Make up a story about the character

Once the new groups are settled, each person works alone, making succinct notes on paper, to create a brief story about their individual character (see Introduction, this volume).[14] This fictional story should (1) present the character in their environment, (2) give the character a specific need, aspiration or desire to pursue, (3) throw up an obstacle to the fulfilment of that desire, (4) offer some way to overcome this obstacle, and (5) reach a resolution in which the character at least partly achieves their desire. Each participant now takes a turn to tell their story, in present tense, to their small group. Each story should last 7–10 minutes.

Here's an excerpt from one such story:

It's 2030, and Alex is a ten-year-old boy. He and his mother have moved to the village after they lost their flat in the London floods. They've moved in with relatives, and with help from neighbours they're building an extension into the garden, made of local materials and cob. Alex's mother runs global healthcare seminars through a virtual conference centre in the village. Alex misses his old friends; he'd really like to visit his best mate, who had to leave London too, but he lives a hundred miles away, so Alex has to save travel credits for a long time. He's starting to make new friends, though. He meets other kids while taking his turn to help grow food in the allotment.

Whereas stories that are designed to entertain, whether fiction or folktale, usually involve an interruption of routine life which plunges the protagonist into some extraordinary experience (see Introduction, this volume), the 'vignettes' this exercise generates are about routine life, albeit in an imagined future. They don't need to be dramatically compelling. Their very ordinariness makes them easy for others to relate to; it gives them a credibility that makes the changes they depict seem possible.

Implicit within each of these vignettes is another narrative: the 'back story' of developments between now and the imagined future which have enabled the way of life described in the vignette to come into being. Futures practitioners speak of 'backcasting' from a future scenario to work out, in reverse order – 'What happened before that? ... And before that?' – the stepladder of change needed to get from the situation today to the one imagined for the future. The next stage of this process seeks to tease out some of the back story of change behind each vignette.

7. Describe what actions created positive change
After each story the listeners note down something that mattered to them in this story (see Introduction, this volume).[15] In role as their fictional character, the teller then answers the following questions:

1. What main changes have happened since 2012?

2. What really important trends were recognised and acted on?

3. What wise decisions and actions were taken?

4. What is my character most grateful for?

One listener in each small group records the character's responses on post-its, one point per note, indicating the number of the question. The group then goes on to hear the next tale.

People can become very involved with their characters. Sometimes there's laughter; sometimes there are tears. As Alex's story illustrates, and exploration of the back story may unpack, these vignettes of the future are likely to imply loss as well as resilience. They describe people coping as best they can with great challenges and change; adjusting, sometimes painfully, to an emerging new paradigm.

8. Reflect on the process

When everyone has told their tale, they reflect together on the making and hearing of the stories, any insights that arose, and how it was to speak in the role of their imagined character. Here are some examples of the sorts of things they may say:

> It was so obvious we need to be giving kids – and ourselves – skills we've forgotten about that they're going to need – like growing food. In my story, people were growing food every-where, on roofs and in places where car parks used to be.

> The idea of everyone owning their own car hasn't changed much in 20 years, but it's got to change now, and quickly. I want to make car-share schemes an attractive win for people now.

> In this future the media are not pumping messages at people to buy more stuff. I've worked in the media for years, and we just assume this is the way. I'm going to work to make another way.

9. Thematise ideas and look for resonance

The whole group now puts together the insights from the stories to seek points of resonance between them. They cluster the post-it notes from stage 7 on four sheets or flip charts titled (1) 'Main changes made', (2) 'Key trends acted on', (3) 'Wise decisions, and (4) 'Actions taken'. Everyone surveys them to identify two or three main themes that stand out. These are shared with the group and reflected upon. Patterns can emerge that transform individual concerns into a collective conviction about specific needs for action. Action researcher Danny Burns says of stories that

'On their own they can easily be dismissed as (separate) anecdotes; if we put them together so that people can connect stories and see if there is a resonance with their own experience, people would see the world differently and different sources of action would emerge.'[16] I've found that certain recurring themes emerge from this process: needs, for example, to shift towards renewable energy and greener technologies; to grow more local food; to re-engage with local communities and build supportive social networks; to develop new forms of finance.

Participants in this process have said they came away with a strong sense of what change they felt committed to creating. Burns says, 'Sustained action can only be maintained where people can act in the service of what they believe in and are passionate about.'[17] In contrast to the overwhelmed feeling that follows the listing of challenges in stage 1, at the end of the process I've observed a focused energy as people discuss with openness and purpose what they individually feel inspired to do, and where they could collaborate.

Application of the process in a community project

A group of residents in my home community, a large village in southern England, wanted to develop a vision for a sustainable future 25 years ahead as well as a plan with a timeline about how to get there.[18] Seven subgroups focused on different sectors of the village's life – transport, health, food, energy, local economy, housing, education – and each identified a number of sustainability priorities for their sector. Systems theory tells us that making a change in one sector alone is unlikely to create significant positive change; there has to be awareness of the web of connections between different sectors, and how changes in each sector may interact.[19] So we decided to create a narrative to link together our vision-building for the seven sectors: transport with food; health with energy and education; food and energy with transport; and so on. To do this I adapted the process described above for a steering group of a dozen or so people who represented the priorities identified by their sector groups. We wanted to explore how living creatively with fewer resources could be compatible with meaningful and happy lifestyles.

The group, being already familiar with the challenges to sustainability as well as trends that could support it, began by imagining some scenes in our village in 2025. Together we described the high street, the village green, a business park, a family home. Once we had vivid images of these scenes in mind, we developed some characters: a man and woman, their two children, plus a relative and her teenage son they shared their house with. We had fun deepening the characters as we walked them through different activities. We also explored our future village through the eyes of an imagined elderly man and of a child, among others, to get perspectives on the whole fabric of village life. Through this, lots of creative ideas emerged about how these characters might meet their needs and overcome obstacles. How did they get their clothes? Local producers were downloading the latest designer patterns to sew. How did they cope with the high price of medicines? A medicinal garden was planted beside the medical centre. What became of people whose homes had been ruined by floods? They moved in with relatives and helped out with tasks like growing food. How did people preserve the large quantities of locally grown food? Cafés opened a service where people could drop off their produce for preserving. Thinking about the everyday tasks of people's lives enabled us to join up developments in the different sectors, to spot gaps that needed addressing, and to innovate potential solutions together.

We worked backwards from our vision of 2025 to backcast a timeline for key steps towards sustainability from the present day. We asked what our characters were most grateful for; what they would thank us for having done in our time. The answers came readily: that we'd pushed for renewable energy, supported local farms, built up a sense of community and a culture of helping each other, to name a few. These insights helped us in turn to renew our own commitment to working for sustainability.

The steering group involved as many other people as possible in exploring the possibilities, and the linkages between the different sectors. Some people got very attached to one or other aspect of the vision, or their version of a character or events. It occasionally needed a firm but tactful hand from the steering group to make the final decisions.

The narrative we developed comprises a sequence of vignettes following our main characters through a typical day. They wake up in a house heated by solar energy and a wood-burning stove and eat a locally sourced breakfast. They walk to school or travel to work by bicycle, light rail, or electric vehicle. They grow vegetables in allotments, shop in a local market, drop off appliances for repair, and visit the doctor. The day closes with a festival. Their lifestyles combine high-tech solutions with low-impact practices and strong community support structures.

The work of this project was captured in a booklet that tells the story of the characters' day, including explanations of the technologies and practices involved, plus a timeline of change.[20] Local children provided lively illustrations. The booklet was distributed to every household in the village. Parts of the story were told aloud at local gatherings as a basis for discussion. However, the narrative was not intended to be a performance piece. It describes routine activities that local people should be able to relate to, though various habits and assumptions have changed.

Systems, sustainability, and struggle

From a systems theory perspective, those changes in assumptions are fundamental. The significance of the project I've described lies less in the narrative that emerged than in the process through which it was created and in which the changes in assumptions were negotiated. By accompanying our imagined characters through their daily activities we built a vivid picture of how the various elements that support village life might come together and interact. There was a transformative linkage between our imagining of our community's future and our own real-life participation in the community's life today. Through our storymaking we found a vision of something real that we are now working towards. Some of the things we envisioned have now happened in reality (a crafts cooperative, a car-share scheme); others are in process. Many may not happen in the way we imagined, or at all.

Grassroots community initiatives can only accomplish so much before they encounter the constraints of multiple larger systems – of government, civil society, and economy, at both national and international levels. These tend to operate to reinforce the way things are currently done, i.e. to resist radical change towards sustainability. As the critic Fredric Jameson points out, the globalised economy has closed the loopholes in which utopian enclaves might aspire to act unilaterally.[21] How then can community sustainability initiatives make an impact at this 'systemic' level? One way is by showcasing niche innovations – a local transport plan, a food-preserving scheme – which if they succeed in penetrating the mainstream may then contribute to system-level change.[22]

For there to be major progress towards sustainability, I believe, initiative must be taken at the systemic level; but this brings us back to the problem that a vision imposed from on high is likely to be resisted if it's not owned by ordinary people. Also, only some initiatives are likely to succeed. To create significant and lasting change we will need to engage in ongoing cycles of experimentation and learning. 'The purpose of any futures exercise is to create a guiding vision, not a final solution or limiting blueprint.'[23] All of this implies an *ongoing* need for community visioning in which people repeatedly negotiate a desirable future and a tolerable pathway there, and which maintains channels of engagement with government and other systems. There's no ultimate destination; only the journey of people's lives.

Creating narratives together about what might be is a form of enquiry into the unknown, where people wrestle with hopes, fears, and the burden of knowledge about what is already happening. Can you engage in this struggle and develop a helpful perspective on the future without making up stories? Perhaps, but I think your perceptions will be less rich in detail and connections. In facilitating the creation of stories about the future, I've seen that people can find possibilities for action that they haven't considered before, and a catalyst for collaborating to imagine wiser ways of managing our world and our lives together.

Acknowledgement

The author would like to thank the editors, and Anthony Nanson in particular, for sharing insights that have contributed to this chapter.

Notes

1. Porritt, *Capitalism as if the World Matters*.
2. Mead, *Coming Home to Story*, p. 178.
3. Beddington, 'Food, Energy, Water and the Climate'.
4. See de Vries, 'Introduction'.
5. Nanson, *Words of Re-enchantment*, p. 163.
6. See Senge et al., *Presence*.
7. Boulding, 'Turning Walls into Doorways'.
8. Van der Heijden, *Scenarios*.
9. Berneri, *Journey through Utopia*, p. 259.
10. Dator, 'What Future Studies Is and Is Not'.
11. Boulding, 'Turning Walls into Doorways'.
12. Wheatley, *Turning to One Another*, p. 24.
13. Macy & Brown, *Coming Back to Life*.
14. On creating stories by means of answers to a series of carefully formulated questions, see Gersie, *Reflections on Therapeutic Storytelling*, pp. 65–70.
15. On the uses of a response-task such as this one, see Gersie, *Reflections on Therapeutic Storymaking*, pp. 134–140.
16. Burns, *Systemic Action Research*, p. 54.
17. Ibid.
18. Grateful acknowledgements to the village of Forest Row, East Sussex, for the use of this example. See Collison & Lewin, *Forest Row in Transition*.
19. Meadows, *Thinking in Systems*.
20. Collison & Lewin, *Forest Row in Transition*.
21. Jameson, *Archaeologies of the Future*.
22. Geels et al., *System Innovation*.
23. Dator, 'What Future Studies Is and Is Not'.

Acknowledgements

This book has its roots in five gatherings of environmentalist storytellers, held under the banner of 'Tales to Sustain' at various locations in the UK since 2005. These symposia addressed key issues around the question: How can storytelling best be used to promote pro-environmental mindfulness and more sustainable behaviour? Much is owed to the tireless energy of Eric Maddern, Malcolm Green, Alida Gersie, and Jon Cree, who planned and evaluated these events, and to the other participants who contributed in many different ways. Special thanks are due to Eric for hosting two of these symposia in his wonderful eco-retreat centre Cae Mabon; to Jane Flood, who hosted one in her home community at Rookery Farm; and to David Ambrose, Director of Beyond the Border: Wales International Storytelling Festival, for his keen inclusion of 'Tales to Sustain' events in the programme.

Many individuals and organisations over the years have expressed their support for the production of a book of this kind. Their eager anticipation of the finished product encouraged out work. We are grateful to Martin Large at Hawthorn Press, whose unflagging expression of interest in our book mattered more than he'll ever know.

We particularly wish to thank: Charlene Collison and Jon Cree for their contribution to the early stages of creating this book, including the peer-review process; Sir Jonathon Porritt for his enthusiastic foreword; and Kirsty Hartsiotis for offering her constant support in ways we cannot begin to enumerate.

Finally, we thank the many participants in workshops and events that made the book's creation possible, the often anonymous tellers of the stories we've been privileged to pass on, as well as the creatures and places that inspire and sustain us. We hope this book will help to bring about benign change in the ways we treat the natural world, if only for their beloved sake.

A.G., A.N., E.S.

List of Stories and Story Fragments

MALCOLM GREEN AND NICK HENNESSEY

The Birch Tree	Personal
The Nest	Personal
The Awarded Ways	Fictional history
The Duergar	Traditional

KELVIN HALL

Marya Morevna	Traditional
Theseus and Hyppolyta	Reworked traditional

CHRIS HOLLAND

The Elf and the Farmers	Traditional
The Little House by the Sea	Fiction

SARA HURLEY AND ALIDA GERSIE

The Mariner's Way	Story-starter
The Wreck of the *London*	Story-starter
Tom Faggus	Story-starter
Princess Caraboo	Story-starter
King of the Gypsies	Story-starter

HUGH LUPTON

The Judgment of King Midas	Traditional
The Judgment of King Midas II	Reworked traditional

GORDON MACLELLAN

The Giant Stone	Group composition
The Counting Ghost	Group composition

ERIC MADDERN

The Tree with Three Fruits	Traditional
Erysichthon and the Curse of Insatiable Hunger	Traditional
The Most Beautiful Thing in the World	Traditional
Bird in the Hand	Traditional

KEVAN MANWARING
The Gate   Fiction

MARY MEDLICOTT
The Legend of Skomar Oddy   Local legend
Skomer and Gog   Fiction

DAVID METCALFE
The Yew of the Disputing Sons   Traditional
Stone Soup   Traditional
The Golden Toad   Natural history
The Ghost Shirt   History

ANTHONY NANSON
The Passenger Pigeon   Natural history
The Coming of the Wildwood   Natural history
Why Owls Stare   Traditional

ASHLEY RAMSDEN
Señor Lobo   Traditional
Indra's Net   Traditional
The Arrow and the Target   Traditional
The Golden Key   Traditional

CHRIS SALISBURY
The Golden Feather   Traditional

EDWARD SCHIEFFELIN
When Things Went Their Separate Ways   Traditional
The Mother of the Animals   Traditional

MARTIN SHAW
Valemon and the Wild Third Daughter   Traditional

Recommended Resources

Organisations

We strongly recommend affiliation to one or more organisations dedicated to storytelling in all its forms. These include:

American Folklore Society (USA)
Centre for Digital Storytelling (UK)
Folklore Society (UK)
George Ewart Evans Centre for Storytelling (UK)
International Storytelling Centre (USA)
National Storytelling Guild of Australia (Australia)
National Storytelling Network (USA)
Scottish Storytelling centre (UK)
Story Museum (UK)
Storytellers of Canada – Conteurs du Canada (Canada)
Society for Storytelling (UK)
Sussex Centre for Folklore, Fairy Tales and Fantasy (UK)

We also strongly recommend affiliation to one or more environmental organisations, such as:

Association for Literature, Environment, and Culture in Canada
Association for the Study of Literature and the Environment
Birdlife Australia
Botanic Gardens Conservation International
Centre for Ecoliteracy (USA)
Conservation International
European Association for the Study of Literature, Culture and Environment
Fauna and Flora International
Forest & Bird (New Zealand)
Friends of the Earth
Greenpeace
Mammal Society (UK)
Marine Conservation Society
National Audubon Society (USA)
The National Trust (UK)
Nature Canada (Canada)
Oceanic Society

Royal Society for the Protection of Birds (UK)
The Sierra Club (USA)
Wildfowl and Wetland Trust (UK)
Wildlife Conservation Society (USA)
The Wildlife Trusts (UK)
The Woodland Trust (UK)
WWF

Periodicals (additional to those of organisations listed above)

EarthLines (UK)
Facts & Fiction (UK)
Marvels & Tales (USA)
Orion (USA)
Parabola (USA)
Resurgence & Ecologist (UK)

Story collections online (in English)

www.forgottenbooks.org
www.gutenberg.org
www.healingstory.com
www.journal.oraltradition.org
www.livingmyths.com
www.mythstories.com
www.openstorytellers.org.uk
www.pitt.edu/~dash/folktexts
www.oraltradition.org
www.sacred-texts.com
www.spiritoftrees.org
www.storynet.com
www.story-lovers.com
www.surlalunefairytales.com
www.theoi.com
www.timsheppard.co.uk
www.worldoftales.com

Books

Abram, David. *Spell of the Sensuous.* New York: Vintage, 1996
Explains the relationship between oral language and storytelling and various cultures' relationship to their physical environment, and what this means for modern culture's dislocation from the environment.

Birch, Carol & Melissa A. Heckler (eds). *Who Says? Essays on Pivotal Issues in Contemporary Storytelling.* Little Rock: August House, 1996
Thoughtful essays on questions of storytelling and story-listening in several different cultural traditions.

Briggs, Katharine M. *A Dictionary of British Folk-Tales in the English Language.* 4 vols. London: Routledge, 1970–71
One of the best sources for British folktales, which our contributors use a lot.

Gersie, Alida. *Earthtales: Storytelling in Times of Change.* London: Merlin Press, 1992
A collection of 42 great environmental stories with many helpful ideas (including session plans) on how to use them to nurture a balanced relationship with the earth.

Gersie, Alida & Nancy King. *Storymaking in Education and Therapy.* London: Jessica Kingsley, 1990
An excellent book if you work with emotional literacy and emotional intelligence in relation to environmental issues. It has many creative techniques for storymaking and responding to stories, contains 42 carefully chosen stories and over 130 session plans, and describes the thinking behind this work.

Johnstone, Keith. *Impro: Improvisation and the Theatre.* London: Eyre Methuen, 1981
Johnstone, Keith. *Impro for Storytellers: Theatre Sports and the Art of Making Things Happen.* London: Routledge, 1999
These books offer ideas and exercises from theatre education which can be applied to environmental story-based learning. They emphasise people's innate sense of what works and what doesn't and explore the vagaries of spontaneous thinking.

Lopez, Barry. *Arctic Dreams: Imagination and Desire in a Northern Landscape.* London: Harvill Press, 1999
An exploration of human beings' changing relationship with the Arctic, written with beautiful insight and sensitivity towards the different motivations people bring and the different sense they make of what they find.

Ludwig, L.K. *Mixed-Media Nature Journals.* Beverly, MA: Quarry, 2007

This book is not about writing so much as about handling and being creative with materials to help inspire words and observation.

Macy, Joanna. *World as Lover, World as Self: Courage for Global Justice and Ecological Renewal.* Berkeley: Parallax Press, 2007

A loving tribute to the earth and a road map for change, integrating past, present, and future.

Macdonald, Margaret Read. *Earth Care: World Folktales to Talk About.* North Haven, CT: Linnet Books, 1999

This fine book has 41 tales, some told in prose, some as poems, plus lots of proverbs, all touching on crucial human and ecological themes. It also includes illuminating notes on the tales plus other useful resources.

Martin, Paul S. & Richard G. Klein (eds). *Quaternary Extinctions: A Prehistoric Revolution.* Tucson: Arizona University Press, 1984

Authoritative multi-author textbook providing detailed evidence to back up the shaping of stories about humankind's extermination of many species of large animals.

Nabhan, Gary Paul. *Cultures of Habitat: On Nature, Culture, and Story.* Washington: Counterpoint, 1997

Collection of elegant, insightful essays that illuminate the interdependence of local culture and local ecology. Many pertinent anecdotal stories are embedded in the discussion.

Nanson, Anthony. *Storytelling and Ecology: Reconnecting Nature and People through Oral Narrative.* Reading: Society for Storytelling, 2005

Creative ideas and deep thinking about the application of stories and storytelling in the environmentalist movement.

Penn, W.S. (ed.). *The Telling of the World: Native American Stories and Art.* New York: Stewart, Tabori & Chang, 1996

Stories and understanding of the natural world and our relationship with it, arising out of generations of living in interdependent harmony with the land beneath your feet.

Ramsden, Ashley & Sue Hollingsworth. *The Storyteller's Way: Sourcebook for Inspired Storytelling.* Stroud: Hawthorn Press, 2013

This book presents a thorough course of practical exercises, backed up by the counsel of long experience, for learning the fundamental skills of storytelling. It links the process of developing as a storyteller to one's lifelong journey into authentic being and relating.

Wheatley, Margaret. *Turning to One Another: Simple Conversations to Restore Hope to the Future*. San Francisco: Berrett-Koehler, 2002

An insightful handbook on how to generate transformative conversations about what really matters.

Whybrow, H. *The Story Handbook. Language and Storytelling for Land Conservationists*. San Francisco: The Trust for Public Land, 2002

A succinct anthology with wonderful contributions by leading environmentalist thinkers such as Barry Lopez and John Elder. It offers some great ideas about storied ways to advance the relationships between people and land and to make thinking about land conservation an integral part of everyday life.

Williamson, Duncan. *The Horsieman: Memories of a Traveller 1928–58*. Edinburgh: Canongate Press, 1994

Recorded reminiscences of the great storyteller Duncan Williamson's life as a Scottish Traveller. His words give a sense of the umbilical link between true tales of life lived and the inner truth of oral folktales.

Williams, Raymond. *People of the Black Mountains*. 2 vols. London: Chatto & Windus, 1989

A recreation, through a chronological sequence of fictional episodes, of the prehistory and more recent history of the Black Mountains in Wales. It is an extraordinary evocation of the changing relationship between people and the land.

Zipes, Jack. *Creative Storytelling: Building Community, Changing Lives*. New York: Routledge, 1995

Offers practical ideas for storywork informed by an astute critical awareness of the political dynamics at play within stories and the storywork situation, especially those pertaining to children and the non-human.

Bibliography

Abram, David. *The Spell of the Sensuous*. New York: Vintage, 1996.

Adams, W.M. & S.J. Jeanrenaud. *Transition to Sustainability: Towards a Humane and Diverse World*. Gland: IUCN, 2008.

Aesop. *The Complete Fables*, trans. Olivia Temple & Robert Temple. London: Penguin Books, 1998.

Afanas'ev, Aleksandr. *Russian Fairy Tales*, trans. Norbert Guterman. New York: Pantheon, 1945.

Afanas'ev, Alexander. *Russian Fairy Tales*, trans. Post Wheeler. New York: Dutton, 1916.

Armitage, D. & R. Plummer. *Adaptive Capacity and Environmental Governance*. New York: Springer-Verlag, 2010.

Bachelard, Gaston. *The Poetics of Space*, trans. Maria Jolas. Boston: Beacon Press, 1994.

Barabási, Albert-László. *Linked: How Everything Is Connected to Everything Else and What It Means for Business, Science, and Everyday Life*. New York: Plume Books, 2003.

Barnett, Mary, *Gods and Myths of Ancient Egypt*. Leicester: Silverdale Books, 2006.

Bateson, Gregory. *Mind and Nature: A Necessary Unity*. London: Wildwood House, 1979.

Bauman, Richard. *Story, Performance and Event: Contextual Studies of Oral Narrative*. Cambridge: Cambridge University Press, 1986.

Beddington, J.C. (2008) 'Food, Energy, Water and the Climate: A Perfect Storm of Global Events?' 2008, <http://www.bis.gov.uk/assets/goscience/docs/p/perfect-storm-paper.pdf>.

Bell, S., V. Hamilton, A. Montarzino, H. Rothnie, P. Travlou & S. Alves. 'Greenspace and Quality of Life: A Critical Literature Review'. Greenspace Scotland, 2008, <http://www.greenspacescotland.org.uk>.

Benjamin, Walter. *Selected Writings 1931–1934*, ed. M.W. Jennings. Boston: Harvard University Press, 2005.

Berneri, Marie Louise. *Journey through Utopia*. London: Routledge & Kegan Paul, 1950.

Bernstein, Jerome. *Living in the Borderland*. Hove: Routledge, 2005.

Berry, Wendell. *Jayber Crow*. Washington: Counterpoint, 2000.

Birch, Carol L. *The Whole Story Handbook*. Little Rock: August House, 2000.

Birch, Carol L. 'Who Says? The Storyteller as Narrator'. In *Who Says? Essays on Pivotal Issues in Contemporary Storytelling*, ed. Carol L. Birch & Melissa A. Heckler. Little Rock: August House, 1996.

Bird, William. 'Natural Thinking'. Royal Society for the Protection of Birds, 2007, <http://www.rspb.org.uk/Images/naturalthinking_tcm9-161856.pdf>.

Birge Vitz, E., N. Freeman Regaldo & M. Lawrence. *Performing Medieval Narrative*. Woodbridge: Brewer, 2005.

Blackburn, W.R. *The Sustainability Handbook*. London: Earthscan, 2007.

Blathwayt, Benedict. *The Little House by the Sea*. London: Random House, 1994.

Blewitt, J. *Understanding Sustainable Development*. London: Earthscan, 2008.

Blyton, Enid. *The Magic Faraway Tree*. London: George Newnes, 1943.

Boal, A. *Games for Actors and Non-actors*. London: Routledge, 1992.

Bordin, Edward S. 'The Generalizability of the Psychoanalytic Concepts of the Working Alliance'. *Psychotherapy*, Vol. 16, 1979, pp. 252–266.

Boshyk, Yury & Robert L. Dilworth. *Action Learning: History and Evolution*. Basingstoke: Macmillan, 2010.

Botkin, Daniel B. *Discordant Harmonies: A New Ecology for the Twenty-First Century*. Oxford: Oxford University Press, 1992.

Boulding, Elise. 'Turning Walls into Doorways'. *Inward Light*, Spring 1986, <http://fcrp. quaker.org/InwardLight101/101Index.html>.

Brandler, S. & C. Roman. *Group Work: Skills and Strategies for Effective Interventions*. London: Routledge, 1999.

Briggs, Katharine M. *A Dictionary of British Folk-Tales in the English Language*. London: Routledge, 1970–71.

Brody, E., S. Goldspinner, K. Green, R. Leventhal & J. Porcino. *Spinning Tales Weaving Hope*. Gabriola Island, BC: New Society, 1999.

Brooks, Peter. *Reading for the Plot: Design and Intention in Narrative*. New York: A.A. Knopf, 1984.

Brown, J.E. *The Sacred Pipe. Black Elk's Account of the Seven Rites of the Oglala Sioux*. Norman: University of Oklahoma Press, 1953.

Bruner, J. *Acts of Meaning*. Cambridge, MA: Harvard University Press, 1990.

Buber, M. *I and Thou*. New York: Charles Scribner's Sons, 1937

Burnett, Frances Hodgson. *The Secret Garden*. London: Heinemann, 1911.

Burns, Danny. *Systemic Action Research: A Strategy for Whole System Change*. Bristol: Policy Press, 2007.

Caballero, C. *Mixed Families: Assumptions and New Approaches. In Mixed Heritage: Identity, Policy and Practice*, ed. J. Smith. London: Runnymede Trust, 2007.

Caduto, Michael J. & Joseph Bruchac. *Keepers of the Night: Native American Stories and Nocturnal Activities for Children*. Golden, CO: Fulcrum, 1994.

Callimachus. *Hymn to Demeter*, ed. Neil Hopkinson. Cambridge: Cambridge University Press, 2004.

Campbell, Joseph. *Primitive Mythology*. London: Secker & Warburg, 1960.

Carroll, Lewis. *Alice's Adventure's in Wonderland*. London: Macmillan, 1865.

Capra, Fritjof & Michael Stone. 'Smart by Nature: Schooling for Sustainability'. *Journal of Sustainability Education*, 25 May 2010.

Carson, Don. 'Environmental Storytelling: Creating Immersive 3D Worlds Using Lessons Learned from the Theme Park Industry'. Gamasutra, <http://www.gamasutra.com/view/feature/3186/environmental_storytelling_.php>.

Carter, Angela (ed.). *The Second Virago Book of Fairy Tales*. London: Virago Press, 1993.

Catterell, James, S. 'A Neuroscience of Art and Human Empathy: Aligning Behavioural and Brain Imagining Evidence'. 2011, <http://www.croc-lab.org>.

Cohen, Jack & Stewart, Ian. *The Collapse of Chaos*. London: Penguin 2000.

Collison, Charlene & Tony Lewin (eds). *Forest Row in Transition: A Community Work in Progress*. Forest Row: Brambletye, 2009, <http://there.is/TransitionForestRow-EDAP/ForestRow_In_Transition-EDAP.pdf>.

Cook, Francis H., *Hua-Yen Buddhism: The Jewel Net of Indra*. University Park: Pennsylvania State University Press, 1977.

Corbett, P. *Jumpstart Storymaking*. London: Routledge, 2009

Cornell, Joseph. *Sharing Nature with Children*. Nevada City: DAWN, 1998.

Cowell, E.B. (ed.). *The Jataka; or, Stories of the Buddha's Former Births*. Cambridge: Cambridge University Press, 1895.

Curtin, Jeremiah & J.N.B Hewitt. *Seneca Fiction, Legends, and Myths*. Washington: Government Printing Office, 1918.

Dator, Jim. 'What Future Studies Is and Is Not'. University of Hawaii, 1995, <http://www.futures.hawaii.edu/publications/futures-studies/WhatFSis1995.pdf>.

Day, David. *The Doomsday Book of Animals*. London: Ebury Press, 1981.

De Blécourt, Willem, Ruben A. Koman, Jurjen van der Kooi & Theo Meder. *Verhalen van Stad en Streek: Sagen en Legenden in Nederland*. Amsterdam: Bert Bakker, 2010.

De Quincey, Christian. *Radical Knowing*. Rochester, VT: Park Street Press, 2005.

Devall, W. & G. Sessions. *Deep Ecology: Living as if Nature Mattered*. Layton, UT: Gibbs Smith, 1985.

De Vries, Jetse. 'Introduction'. In *Shine: An Anthology of Near-Future Optimistic Science Fiction*, ed. Jetse de Vries. Oxford: Solaris, 2010.

Dewart, Hazel & Susie Summers. 'The Pragmatics Profile of Everyday Communication Skills in Adults'. <http://www.edit.wmin.ac.u/psychology/pp./>.

Diamond, Jared. *Collapse: How Societies Choose to Fail or Survive*. London: Penguin, 2006.

East, Helen & Eric Maddern. *Spirit of the Forest: Tree Tales from Around the World*. London: Frances Lincoln, 2002.

Eckhart, Meister Johann. *Die Deutschen und Lateinischen Werke*. Stuttgart: Verlag W. Kohlhemmer, 1936.

Ede, Piers Moore. *All Kinds of Magic*. London: Bloomsbury, 2010.

Edgerton, David. *The Shock of the Old: Technology and Global History since 1900*. London: Profile, 2006.

Ellis, Shaun. *Wolf Within: How I Learned to Talk Dog*. London: Harper, 2011.

Ellwood, Wayne. *The No-Nonsense Guide to Globalization*. Oxford: New Internationalist, 2001.

Feld, Steven. *Sound and Sentiment: Birds, Weeping, Poetics, and Song in Kaluli Expression*, 2nd edn. Philadelphia: University of Pennsylvania Press, 1990.

Finnegan, R. *Oral Tradition and the Verbal Arts*. London: Routledge, 1992.

Fire Springs. *An Ecobardic Manifesto: A Vision for the Arts in a Time of Environmental Crisis*. Bath: Awen, 2008.

Flannery, Tim. *The Weather Makers: The History and Future Impact of Climate Change.* London: Allen Lane, 2006.

Foster, Steven & Meredith Little. *The Book of the Vision Quest: Personal Transformation in the Wilderness.* New York: Prentice Hall Press, 1988.

Freire, Paolo. *Pedagogy of the Oppressed,* trans. M. Bergman Ramos. Harmondsworth: Penguin, 1972.

Fromm, Eric. *The Heart of Man: Its Genius for Good and Evil.* New York: Harper, 1964.

Garner, Alan. *Book of British Fairy Tales.* London: Collins, 1984.

Garner, Alan. *The Voice that Thunders.* London: Harvill Press, 2000.

Geels, F.W., B. Elzen & K. Green. *System Innovation and the Transition to Sustainability: Theory, Evidence and Policy.* Cheltenham: Edward Elgar, 2004.

Genette, G. *Narrative Discourse: An Essay in Method,* trans. J.E. Lewin. Ithaca, NY: Cornell University Press, 1980.

Gersie, Alida. 'Arts Therapies Practice in Inner City Slums: Beyond the Installation of Hope'. *Arts in Psychotherapy,* Vol. 22, No. 3, 1995, pp. 207–215.

Gersie, Alida (ed.). *Dramatic Approaches to Brief Therapy.* London: Jessica Kingsley, 1996.

Gersie, Alida. *Earthtales: Storytelling in Times of Change.* London: Merlin Press, 1992.

Gersie, Alida. *Reflections on Therapeutic Storymaking: The Use of Stories in Groups.* London: Jessica Kingsley, 1997.

Gersie, Alida. *Storymaking in Bereavement: Dragons Fight in the Meadow.* London: Jessica Kingsley, 1991.

Gersie, Alida. *Storytelling, Stories and Place.* Reading: Society for Storytelling, 2011.

Gersie, Alida & Nancy King. *Storymaking in Education and Therapy.* London: Jessica Kingsley, 1990.

Gifford, Terry. *Pastoral.* London: Routledge, 1999.

Gladwell, M. *The Tipping Point: How Little Things Can Make a Big Difference.* London: Abacus, 2000.

Global Footprint Network. 'Ecological Footprint Standards 2009'. <http://www.footprintnetwork.org/images/uploads/Ecological_Footprint_Standards_2009.pdf>

Goethe, J.W. *Goethe Werke, Hamburger Ausgabe.* Munich: C.H. Beck, 2012.

Goodchild, Philip. *Capitalism and Religion: The Price of Piety.* London: Routledge, 2002.

Gottschall, J. *The Storytelling Animal: How Stories Make Us Human.* Boston: Houghton Mifflin Harcourt, 2012.

Graham, B. & S. Bird. 'Down the Garden Path: The Use of Stories and Storytelling to Raise Environmental Awareness'. Botanic Gardens Conservation International, <http://www.bgci.org/education/1716/>.

Graves, Robert. *The White Goddess.* London: Faber & Faber, 1961.

Gray, T. *Black History Report.* Exeter: Friends of Devon Archives, 1999.

Green, Melanie C., Jeffrey J. Strange & Timothy C. Brock. *Narrative Impact: Social and Cognitive Foundations.* London: Taylor & Francis, 2002.

Green, Roger Lancelyn, *Tales of Ancient Egypt,* London: Penguin, 1995.

Grice, Frederick. *Folktales of the North Country*. Edinburgh, T. Nelson, 1947.

Grimm, Jacob & Wilhelm Grimm. *Complete Fairy Tales*, trans. Margaret Hunt. London: Routledge & Kegan Paul, 2002.

Grumbine, Edward. 'Wilderness, Wise Use, and Sustainable Development'. In *Deep Ecology for the Twenty-First Century: Readings on the Philosophy and Practice of the New Environmentalism*, ed. George Sessions. Boston: Shambhala, 1995.

Hafiz. 'Because of Our Wisdom'. In *The Subject Tonight Is Love*, trans. D.J. Ladinsky, New York: Penguin, 1996, p. 9.

Hafiz. 'It Felt love'. In *The Gift: Poems by Hafiz*, trans. Daniel Ladinsky, New York: Penguin, 1999.

Haggarty, Ben. *Seek Out the Voice of the Critic*. London: Society for Storytelling, 1996.

Hartigan, Pamela. 'Beyond the Humpty Dumpty Economy'. Breakthrough Capitalism, <www.breakthroughcapitalism.com/video02.html>.

Harvey, M. 'Staging the Story'. George Ewart Evans Centre for Storytelling, <http://storytelling.research.southwales.ac.uk/media/files/documents/2010-03-01/Staging_the_Story_Final_version.pdf>.

Haven, K. *Storyproof: The Science Behind the Startling Power of Story*. Westport, CT: Libraries Unlimited, 2007.

Heinrich, Paul. 'The Artist as Bard'. *The Cut*, Winter 1992, pp. 12–15.

Hillman, James & Wilhelm Heinrich Roscher. *Pan and the Nightmare*. New York: Spring, 2000

Hopkins, Rob. 'A Natural Way of Building'. *Transition Culture*, 2002, <http://transition-culture.org/essential-info/articles/a-natural-way-of-building-2002/>.

Hopkins, Rob. 'Resilience Thinking'. *Resurgence*, No. 257, 2009, pp. 12–15.

Hopkins, Rob. *The Transition Handbook: From Oil Dependency to Local Resilience*. Totnes: Green Books, 2008.

Hughes, Ted. *Tales from Ovid*. London: Faber & Faber, 1997.

Hurley, Sara. *Blazing Tales: The River Exe-pedition*. Exeter: Insider Art, 2012.

Hyde, Lewis. *The Gift: How the Creative Spirit Transforms the World*. Edinburgh: Canongate, 2006.

Jaffe, Nina & Steve Zeitlin. *While Standing on One Foot: Puzzle Stories and Wisdom Stories from the Jewish Tradition*. New York: Henry Holt, 1996.

Jameson, Fredric. *Archaeologies of the Future: The Desire Called Utopia and Other Science Fictions*. London: Verso, 2007.

Jenkins, Henry. 'Game Design as Narrative Architecture'. Massachusetts Institute of Technology, <http://web.mit.edu/cms/People/henry3/games&narrative.html>.

Jensen, Derrick. *A Language Older than Words*. London: Souvenir Press, 2000.

John, Brian. *Fireside Tales from Pembrokeshire*. Newport, Pembrokeshire: Greencroft Books, 1993.

John, Brian *The Last Dragon: A Book of Pembrokeshire Folk Tales*. Newport, Pembrokeshire: Greencroft Books, 1992.

Jones, Brenda Wyn. *Giant Tales from Wales*. Llandysul: Pont Books, 1998.

Jordan, M. 'Nature and Self: An Ambivalent Attachment'. *Ecopsychology*, Vol. 1, No. 1, 2009, pp. 26–31.

Kahn, Lloyd & B. Easton. *Shelter*. Bolinas, CA: Shelter, 1973.

Kaplan, R. & S. Kaplan. 'Preference, Restoration, and Meaningful Action in the Context of Nearby Nature'. In *Urban Place: Reconnecting with the Natural World*, ed. P.F. Barlett. Cambridge, MA: MIT Press, 2005.

Keysers, Christian. *The Empathic Brain: How the Discovery of Mirror Neurons Changes Our Understanding of Human Nature*. Createspace, 2011.

Kingdon, Jonathan. *Lowly Origin: Where, When, and Why Our Ancestors First Stood up*. Princeton: Princeton University Press, 2003.

Kornfield, Jack & Christina Feldman. *Soul Food: Stories to Nourish the Spirit and Heart*. San Francisco: HarperSanFrancisco, 1996.

Krause, Bernie. *The Great Animal Orchestra: Finding the Origins of Music in the World's Wild Places*. New York: Little, Brown, 2012.

Lakoff, George & Mark Johnson. *Metaphors We Live by*. Chicago: Chicago University Press, 1980.

Lambert, Craig. 'The Horror and the Beauty: Maria Tatar Explores the Dazzle and the 'Dark Side' of Fairy Tales – and Why We Read Them'. *Harvard Magazine*, November–December 2012, pp. 37–41.

Lang, Andrew. *The Red Fairy Book*. Harmondsworth: Penguin, 1976.

Langer, Ellen. *Counter-clockwise. Mindful Health and the Power of Possibility*. London: Ballantine Books, 2009.

Lewis, C.S. *The Lion, the Witch and the Wardrobe*. London: Geoffrey Bless, 1950.

Lipman, Doug. *Improving Your Storytelling: Beyond the Basics for All Who Tell Stories in Work or Play*. Little Rock: Arkansas, 1999.

Lipman, Doug. *The Storytelling Coach: How to Listen, Praise, and Bring out People's Best*. Little Rock: August House, 2005.

Livo, Norma & Sandra Rietz. *Storytelling: Process and Practice*. Englewood, CO: Libraries Unlimited, 1986.

Lopez, Barry. *About This Life: Journeys on the Threshold of Memory*. London: Harvill Press, 1999.

Lopez, Barry. *Arctic Dreams: Imagination and Desire in a Northern Landscape*. London: Harvill Press, 1999.

Lord, Albert. *The Singer of Tales*. Cambridge, MA: Harvard University Press, 1960.

Louv, Richard. *Last Child in the Woods: Saving Our Children from Nature-Deficit Disorder*. New York: Workman, 2005.

Lupton, Hugh. *The Dreaming of Place: Storytelling and Landscape*. Reading: Society for Storytelling, 2001.

MacDonald, M. (ed.). *Traditional Storytelling Today: An International Sourcebook*. Chicago: Fitzroy Dearborn, 1999.

Macy, Joanna. *World as Lover, World as Self: Courage for Global Justice and Ecological Renewal*. Berkeley: Parallax Press, 2007.

Macy, Joanna & Molly Young Brown. *Coming Back to Life: Practices to Reconnect Our Lives, Our World.* Gabriola Island, BC: New Society, 1998.

Maddern, Eric. *A Teacher's Guide to Storytelling at Historic Sites.* London: English Heritage, 1992.

Maguire, G. *The Power of Personal Storytelling: Spinning Tales to Connect with Others.* New York: Penguin Putnam. 2007.

Manwaring, Kevan. *The Bardic Handbook: The Complete Manual for the Twenty-First Century Bard.* Glastonbury: Gothic Image, 2006.

Martin, Andrew & Bill Krouwel. 'Rejuvenating Outward Bound Programme Design'. Paper presented at 8th International Conference on Experiential Learning, Ljubljana, 1–5 July 2002.

Martin, Paul S. 'Prehistoric Overkill: The Global Model'. In *Quaternary Extinctions: A rehistoric Revolution*, ed. Paul S. Martin & Richard G. Klein. Tucson: University of Arizona Press, 1984.

Martin, Rafe. 'Between Teller and Listener: The Reciprocity of Storytelling'. In *Who Says? Essays on Pivotal Issues in Contemporary Storytelling*, ed. Carol L. Birch & Melissa A. Heckler. Little Rock: August House, 1996.

McAslan, R.R. 'Community Resilience: Understanding the Concept and Its Application'. Sustainable Communities SA, <http://sustainablecommunitiessa.files.wordpress.com/2011/06/community-resilience-from-torrens-institute.pdf>.

McIntosh, Alistair. *Rekindling Community: Connecting People, Environment and Spirituality.* Totnes: Green Books. 2008.

McKeith, L. *Local Black History: A Beginning in Devon.* London: Archives and Museum of Black Heritage, 2005.

Mead, Geoff. *Coming Home to Story: Storytelling Beyond Happily Ever After.* Bristol: Vala, 2011.

Meadows, Donella H. *Thinking in Systems: A Primer.* Abingdon: Routledge, 2009.

Meier, Dave. *The Accelerated Learning Handbook.* New York: McGraw-Hill, 2000.

Moore, C. & P. Dunham. *Joint Attention: Its Origins and Role in Development.* Hillsdale, NJ: Lawrence Erlbaum, 1995.

Morris, William. *News from Nowhere.* London: Longmans, Green, 1891.

Nabhan, Gary Paul. *Cultures of Habitat: On Nature, Culture, and Story.* Washington: Counterpoint, 1997.

Naess, Arne. 'The Deep Ecological Movement: Some Philosophical Aspects'. In *Deep Ecology for the Twenty-First Century: Readings on the Philosophy and Practice of the New Environmentalism*, ed. George Sessions. Boston: Shambhala, 1995.

Naess, Arne. 'Self-Realization: An Ecological Approach to Being in the World'. In *Deep Ecology for the Twenty-First Century: Readings on the Philosophy and Practice of the New Environmentalism*, ed. George Sessions. Boston: Shambhala, 1995.

Nanson, Anthony. 'Composting Dragons: Recovery and Eco-radicalisation of Oral Folklore in a Gloucestershire Landscape'. *Green Letters*, Vol. 18, No.1, 2014.

Nanson, Anthony. *Storytelling and Ecology: Reconnecting Nature and People through Oral*

Narrative. Reading: Society for Storytelling, 2005.

Nanson, Anthony. *Words of Re-enchantment: Writings on Storytelling, Myth, and Ecological Desire*. Stroud: Awen, 2011.

Ong, W.D. *Orality and Literacy: The Technologizing of the Word*. London: Routledge, 1982.

OPENspace. 'Wild Adventure Space: Its Role in Teenagers' Lives'. Report commissioned by Natural England, 2010, <www.openspace.eca.ac.uk/researchprojects_wildadventures-paces.php>.

Orr, David. *Earth in Mind: On Education, Environment and the Human Prospect*. Washington: Island Press, 1994.

Ovid. *Metamorphoses*, trans. Mary M. Innes. London: Penguin, 1955.

Parker, L.A. *Salt, Sweat and Tears*. Blaenau Ffestiniog: Cinnamon Press, 2007.

Paul, Gregory S. *Dinosaurs of the Air: The Evolution and Loss of Flight in Dinosaurs and Birds*. Baltimore: Johns Hopkins University Press, 2002.

Pellowski, Anne. *The World of Storytelling: A Practical Guide to the Origins, Development, and Applications of Storytelling*. New York: Bowker, 1977.

Pert, Candace. *Molecules of Emotion: Why You Feel the Way You Feel*. New York: Simon & Schuster, 1997.

Plumwood, Val. *Feminism and the Mastery of Nature*. London: Routledge, 1993.

Plutarch. *The Rise and Fall of Athens: Nine Greek Lives*, trans. Ian Scott-Kilvert. Harmondsworth: Penguin, 1973.

Porritt, Jonathan. *Capitalism as if the World Matters*. London: Earthscan, 2007.

Prendergast, M. & J. Saxton (eds). *Applied Theatre: International Case Studies and Challenges for Practice*. Bristol: Intellect. 2009.

Pressfield, Steven. *Last of the Amazons*. London: Bantam, 2003.

Propp, Vladimir. *Morphology of the Folktale*, trans. Laurence Scott. Austin: University of Texas Press, 1968.

Radin, Paul. *Primitive Man as a Philosopher*. Madison: University of Wisconsin Press, 1957.

Radin, Paul. *The Trickster: A Study in Native American Mythology*. New York: Schocken Books, 1956.

Ramsden, Ashley & Sue Hollingsworth. *The Storyteller's Way: Sourcebook for Inspired Storytelling*. Stroud: Hawthorn Press, 2013.

Ranelagh, E.L. *The Past We Share: The Near Eastern Ancestry of Western Folk Tradition*. London: Quartet Books, 1979.

Ransome, Arthur. *Old Peter's Russian Tales*. London: Thomas Nelson, 1916.

Renault, Mary. *The Bull from the Sea*. Harmondsworth: Penguin, 1973.

Rideout, V.J., U.G. Foehrs & D.F. Roberts. *Generation M2: Media in the Lives of 8–18 Year Olds*. Menlo Park, CA: Kaiser Family Foundation, 2010.

Robinson, Kim Stanley (ed.). *Future Primitive: The New Ecotopias*. New York: Tom Doherty, 1994.

Rocas, S. & M.B. Brewer. 'Social Identity Complexity'. *Journal of Personality and Social*

Psychology Review, No. 6, 2012, pp. 88–106.

Rolle, Renate. *The World of the Scythians*. Bath: Batsford, 1989.

Roszak, T., M. Gomes & A. Kanner. *Ecopsychology: Restoring the Earth, Healing the Mind*. San Francisco: Sierra Club Books. 1996.

Rueckert, William. 'Literature and Ecology: An Experiment in Ecocriticism'. In *The Ecocriticism Reader: Landmarks in Literary Ecology*, ed. Cheryll Glotfelty & Harold Fromm. Athens, GA: University of Georgia Press, 1996.

Rumi. 'Storywater'. In *The Essential Rumi*, trans. Coleman Barks & John Moyne. Athens, GA: Maypop Press, 1992.

Russell, Peter. *The Awakening Earth: Our Next Evolutionary Leap*. London: Routledge & Kegan Paul, 1982.

Rust, M.J. & N. Totton. *Vital Signs: Psychological Responses to Ecological Crisis*. London: Karnac Books, 2012.

Ryan, Patrick. 'The Contemporary Storyteller in Context: A Study of Storytelling in Modern Society'. PhD thesis, University of Glamorgan.

Sawyer, Ruth. *The Way of the Storyteller*. New York: Viking Press, 1942.

Schapiro, Meyer. *Late Antique, Early Christian and Mediaeval Art: Selected Papers*. London: Chatto & Windus, 1980.

Schieffelin, Edward L. 'The Retaliation of the Animals: On the Cultural Construction of Time and Events in a New Guinea Culture'. In *History and Ethnohistory in Papua New Guinea*, ed. Edward L. Schieffelin & Deborah Gewertz. Sydney: University of Sydney Press, 1985.

Schieffelin, Edward L. *The Sorrow of the Lonely and the Burning of the Dancers*, 2nd edn. New York: Palgrave Macmillan, 2005.

Segal, Robert A. *Joseph Campbell: An Introduction*. New York: Garland, 1987.

Senge, P., C.O. Scharmer, J. Jaworski & B.S. Flowers. *Presence: Exploring Profound Change in People, Organizations and Society*. London: Nicholas Brealey, 2005.

Shaw, P. *Changing Conversation in Organisations: A Complexity Approach to Change*. London: Routledge, 2002.

Silverberg, Robert. *The Dodo, the Auk and the Oryx: Vanished and Vanishing Creatures*. Harmondsworth: Penguin, 1993.

Simpson, S.P. & M.C. Strauss (eds). *Horticulture as Therapy*. Binghamton, NY: Haworth Press, 1998.

Skinner, Charles. *Myths and Legends of Flowers, Trees, Fruits and Plants*. Philadelphia: J.B. Lippincott, 1911.

Sleigh, Barbara. *Winged Magic*. London: Hodder & Stoughton, 1979.

Snyder, Gary. *The Gary Snyder Reader: Prose, Poetry and Translations 1952–1998*. Washington: Counterpoint, 1999.

Sobol, Joseph D. *The Storytellers' Journey: An American Revival*. Urbana: University of Illinois Press, 1999.

Speth, J.G. *Red Sky at Morning: America and the Crisis of the Global Environment*. New Haven: Yale University Press, 2004.

Sproul, Barbara C. *Primal Myths: Creating the World*. New York:, HarperCollins, 1992.

Stallings, Fran. 'The Web of Silence: Storytelling's Power to Hypnotize'. *National Storytelling Journal*, Spring/Summer 1988, pp. 6–19.

Stearns, Peter N. *Global Outrage: The Impact of World Opinion on Contemporary History*. Oxford: Oneworld, 2005.

Stibbe, Arran (ed.). *The Handbook of Sustainability Literacy: Skills for a Changing World*. Totnes: Green Books, 2009.

Stone, Michael K. *Ecological Literacy: Educating Our Children for a Sustainable World*. San Francisco: Sierra Club Books, 2005.

Strauss, Kevin. *Pecos Bill Invents the Ten-Gallon Hat: A Guidebook for Environmental Storytelling*. New Orleans: Pelican, 2013.

Strauss, Kevin. *Tales with Tails: Storytelling the Wonders of the Natural World*. Westport, CT: Libraries Unlimited, 2006.

Strauss, Susan. *The Passionate Fact: Storytelling in Natural History and Cultural Interpretation*. Golden, CO: Fulcrum, 1996.

Sunderland, Chris. *In a Glass Darkly: Seeking Vision for Public Life*. Carlisle: Paternoster Press, 2001.

Taylor, Peter. *Beyond Conservation: A Wildland Strategy*. London: Earthscan, 2005.

Thiele, J.M. *Danmarks Folkesagn*. Copenhagen: Universitetsboghandler C.A. Reitzels Forlag, 1843.

Thomas, Taffy & Steve Killick. *Telling Tales: Storytelling as Emotional Literacy*. Blackburn: Educational Printing Services, 2007.

Thompson, Stith. *The Folktale*. Berkeley: University of California Press, 1977.

Thoreau, Henry D. *Walden; or, Life in the Woods*. Boston: Ticknor & Fields, 1854.

Tolkien, J.R.R. 'On Fairy Stories'. In *The Monsters and the Critics and Other Essays*, ed. Christopher Tolkien. London: HarperCollins, 2006.

Tolkien, J.R.R. *Tree and Leaf*. George Allen & Unwin, London, 1964.

Turner, G.M. 'A Comparison of *The Limits to Growth* with 30 Years of Reality'. *Global Environmental Change*, Vol. 18, 2008, pp. 397–411.

Van der Heijden, Kees. *Scenarios: The Art of Strategic Conversation*. New York: John Wiley, 1996.

Van Gennep, Arnold. *The Rites of Passage*, trans. N.B. Vizedom & G.L. Caffee. London: Routledge & Kegan Paul, 1960.

Vare, Paul & John Blewitt. 'Sustainability Literacy: Two Perspectives'. University of Brighton, Faculty of Arts, <http://arts.brighton.ac.uk/__data/assets/pdf_file/0010/6202/Sustainability-Literacy-Blewitt-and-Vare.pdf>.

Vice, Sue. *Introducing Bakhtin*. Manchester: Manchester University Press, 1997.

Von Sydow, Carl Wilhelm. 'Geography and Folk-Tale Oicotypes'. In *International Folkloristics: Classic Contributions by the Founders of Folklore*, ed. Alan Dundes. Lanham, MD: Rowman & Littlefield, 1999.

Wackernagel, M. & W. Reed. *Our Ecological Footprint*. Gabriola Island, BC: New Society Press, 1996.

Walker, Barbara K. *The Most Beautiful Thing in the World: A Folktale From China*. New York: Scholastic, 1993.

Walton, Evangeline. *The Sword Is Forged*. New York: Pocket Books, 1983.

Walsh, Caspar. 'A Mythology for Our Time'. *Resurgence*, No. 261, 2010, pp. 44–46.

Westwood, Jennifer & Sophia Kingshill. *The Lore of Scotland: A Guide to Scottish Legends*. London: Random House, 2009.

Westwood, Jennifer & Jacqueline Simpson. *The Lore of the Land: A Guide to England's Legends from Spring-Heeled Jack to the Witches of Warboys*. London: Penguin, 2006.

Wheatley, Margaret. *Turning to One Another: Simple Conversations to Restore Hope to the Future*. San Francisco: Berrett-Koehler, 2002.

Wheeler, Wendy. *The Whole Creature: Complexity, Biosemiotics and the Evolution of Culture*. London: Lawrence & Wishart, 2006.

Whybrow, H. *The Story Handbook*. San Francisco: Trust for Public Land, 2002.

Williams, Michael. *Deforesting the Earth: From Prehistory to Global Crisis*. Chicago: University of Chicago Press, 2006.

Williamson, Duncan. *The Broonie, Silkies and Fairies: Travellers' Tales*, ed. Linda Williamson. Edinburgh: Canongate, 1985.

Williamson, Duncan. *Land of the Seal People*, ed. Linda Williamson. Edinburgh: Birlinn, 2010.

Wilson, Edward O. *Biophilia*. Boston: Harvard University Press, 1984.

Wilson, Edward O. *The Diversity of Life*. Cambridge, MA: Belknap Press, 1992.

Wilson, Edward O. *The Future of Life*. London: Little, Brown, 2002.

World Economic Forum. *Global Risks 2010: A Global Risk Report*. Geneva, 2010.

Young, E. *Lon Po Po*. New York: Philomel Books, 1989.

Zipes, Jack. *Creative Storytelling: Building Community, Changing Lives*. New York: Routledge, 1995.

Zolli, A. & A.M. Healy. *Resilience: Why Things Bounce Back*. New York: Simon & Schuster, 2012.

Notes on Contributors

Fiona Collins (PhD) supports innovative story-based community projects that reconnect adults and children with the places they inhabit, with the aim of facilitating more sustainable ways of living. Fiona has contributed to the development of young and emerging voices in, for example, the Young Storytellers' Festival of Wales / Gwyl Storiwyr Ifainc Cymru and the Gwobr Esyllt Prize. Her writing includes five books of Welsh folktales, written in English and published by the History Press, and a collection in the Welsh language, published by Gwasg Carreg Gwalch and written for adult Welsh learners.

Charlene Collison (PhD) is Associate Director at the international NGO Forum for the Future, which works to address complex global sustainability challenges. The collaborative initiatives she leads seek to create global value chains that are regenerative, just, and resilient in an increasingly disrupted world. She works with leaders in business, civil society, and foundations to change the way that value chains work, helping them use systems thinking and futures techniques to look beyond today's issues into tomorrow's world. She describes herself as a 'storyteller of the future', using evidence of what's happening now to construct narratives about the future that enable people to imagine it as a lived experience.

Jon Cree (BSc, DipEd) is a long-time ecological educator and trainer. He has worked in local authorities throughout his career, with teachers and children of all ages, and in particular with adolescents who are challenged by the education system. He was the founding chair of the Forest School Association and is co-author of the highly acclaimed *The Essential Guide to Forest School and Nature Pedagogy* (Routledge, 2021). Jon has been an international trainer for the Institute for Earth Education for 35 years and a passionate advocate for integrating ecological understanding and sensory connection to the earth into the education system. Storytelling has long been an ally in this work.

Helen East (BEd) has told, heard, and taught sustaining stories all over the world, and has directed innovative 'story and place' programmes. These include Shropshire's pride of place project 'Breaking the Silence'; Kent Countryside's award-winning 'Charting the Changes'; and, recently, 'After Offa: Living Life along the Border', a major English/Welsh heritage project. Helen's publications include *The Singing Sack*, a bestselling collection of world tales; 'new folktales' for BBC World Service's IT series *Everyday Science*; WWF's *Green Umbrella Assembly Book* (as story consultant); *Spirit of the Forest*, with Eric Maddern; *How the Olympics Came to Be*; and *London Folk Tales*.

Alida Gersie (PhD) consults with national and global organisations on creative means to improve outcomes in health, education, sustainable development, and the arts. A lifelong environmentalist, she has developed innovative community intervention and training programmes, instigated an MA in Dramatherapy, and directed the Postgraduate Arts Therapies Department at the University of Hertfordshire, UK. During the 1970s she pioneered storymaking techniques that strengthen people's empathy and resilience. Presently these are used by change agents in over 40 countries. Her (much translated) books include *Storymaking in Education and Therapy* (with Nancy King), *Dramatic Approaches to Brief Therapy*, *Storymaking in Bereavement*, *Reflections on Therapeutic Storymaking: The Use of Stories in Groups*, and *Earthtales: Storytelling in Times of Change*.

Malcolm Green (BSc, CertEd) is a naturalist and professional storyteller. He has taught storytelling at Newcastle University and elsewhere for over 20 years. As manager of the Rising Sun Country Park (a 400-acre reclaimed coal mine), he made storytelling central to the interpretation. In performances such as *Shearwater* and *Gone Cuckoo*, he endeavours to view the world from an other-than-human perspective, collaborating with scientists and musicians to create a tapestry of ecology, myth, and personal experience that conveys the wonder and fragility of life. As a founder member of A Bit Crack Storytellers, he organised the collaborative 'Dreaming the Land' walking project. He is the author of *Northumberland Folktales*.

Kelvin Hall (MA HIP) was storyteller-in-residence at the Ruskin Mill Centre in Gloucestershire throughout the 1990s and has been a devoted horseman since childhood. He also practised psychotherapy for over 30 years. Since 2008 he has frequently written, presented, and tutored on the human dialogue with nature, after undertaking PQMA research into 'Conversation with Nature and Its Significance in Therapy'. His most recent writing on this theme is featured on the website of the Climate Psychology Alliance and he is about to launch a new live programme: 'How to Be on Earth: Tales from the Zone'.

Nick Hennessey (BSc Hons) is an internationally acclaimed storyteller, singer, songwriter, and musician. Inspired by North European cultural traditions, he has been awarded high honours in Finland for his work on the Finnish national epic, *Kalevala*. The relationship between story and place lies at the back of his creative work; he grew up in Alderley Edge, an ordinary and extraordinary place, deeply embedded in the myth of the Sleeping King. He is a sought-after artistic collaborator, working with top-of-the-field musicians and storytellers. He has broadcast documentaries for BBC Radio 4 and the World Service and his musical work has featured on BBC Radio 3's *Late Junction*.

Sara Hurley (BA Hons) is a storyteller, participatory artist, and producer based in Devon. She has 30 years' experience of engaging people of all ages with storytelling and the arts, and works across various sectors, including education, community, environment, heritage, and health. She facilitates creative workshops that help connect people to place and to each other, using the inspiration of the environment and both true and traditional stories. Dartmoor National Park and heritage sites have commissioned her to write films and audio tours inspired by their history. Sara also uses storytelling in healthcare settings and teaches at Plymouth and Exeter Medical Schools.

Chris Holland (BSc) is the author of the bestselling playful nature connection guidebook *I Love My World* and a leading inspiration in the field of nature connection and environmental education for families and schools in the UK and increasingly worldwide. His teaching bundle includes a degree in environmental science and a talent for working with groups of people, telling stories, sharing bushcraft skills, foraging, creating environmental art, and playing the didgeridoo. He has created 'absolutely incredible' CPD and nature connection courses online, including the 'Storytelling for Outdoor Learning' yearlong course available on his website. He's a dad, lives in Devon, and loves swimming, surfing, and climbing trees barefoot.

Hugh Lupton has been a professional storyteller since 1981. He tells stories from all over the world, but his particular passion is for the hidden layers of the British landscape and the stories and ballads that give voice to them. He has written many collections of folktales for children (published by Barefoot Books). His published work for adults includes *Norfolk Folk Tales* and two novels: *The Ballad of John Clare* (2010) and *The Assembly of the Severed Head* (2018). He is also a poet and lyricist.

Gordon MacLellan (BSc), aka environmental artist and storyteller 'Creeping Toad', works with groups to celebrate the relationships between people and the places where they live, work, and play. Local landscapes, museum artefacts, the value of storytelling across generations, and bumblebee lanterns have all featured in recent projects. With an international reputation as a trainer, writer, and project leader, Gordon creates dynamic and innovative projects. Since 2019, he has been the arts advisor on several Faith, Arts, and Nature projects, including 'CelebrationEarth!' and '8 Billion'. His acclaimed books include *Old Stones and Ancient Bones*, *The Wanton Green*, *Celebrating Nature*, and *Sacred Animals*.

Eric Maddern (BA Psychology) is an Australian-born teacher, author, storyteller, and songwriter who specialises in telling stories in historic sites and natural places. For 25 years he and Hugh Lupton ran retreats for storytellers on 'storytelling and the mythological landscape'. His books include *The Human Story* (Commonwealth Institute), *Storytelling at Historic Sites* (English Heritage), *Snowdonia Folk Tales* (History Press), and 11 children's picture books (Frances Lincoln). He has also recorded two albums of his own songs: *Full of Life* and *Rare and Precious Earth*. He lives in Gwynedd, where he has co-created Cae Mabon, a renowned eco-retreat centre at the foot of Snowdon, once described as 'a Welsh Shangri-La'.

Kevan Manwaring (PhD) is Senior Lecturer in Creative Writing at the Arts University Bournemouth. His research is in the field of ethics, ecology, and the imagination. He is the founder of the small press Awen Publications and a member of the storytelling group Fire Springs. His published works include *Heavy Weather* (British Library) and collections of folktales for the History Press. He has adapted his prizewinning eco-science-fiction novel *Black Box* into an audio drama for Alternative Stories and Fake Realities. He lives on the Wiltshire Downs, where brown hares and red kites keep him company on his runs, rides, and rambles. He blogs and tweets as 'The Bardic Academic'.

Mary Medlicott (MA) is a leading UK storyteller whose performances and courses have attracted national and international attention. She has often worked abroad and has frequently been a keynote speaker at educational events. In 1990 Mary devised *By Word of Mouth*, an acclaimed Channel 4 TV series about the storytelling revival. She has been chair of the Society for Storytelling and editor of its publications. Her work emphasises the importance of personal storytelling and of local legends and environment. Publications include *Time for Telling, Tales from Africa, Story-Reading in Early Years*, and *Shemi's Tall Tales*, about a famed nineteenth-century Welsh storyteller.

David Metcalfe (MPhil) is an organisational development consultant, storyteller, and lifelong history student. After working as an archaeologist, David turned his investigative skills to examining public bodies' use of resources with the National Audit Office and the Wales Audit Office. His company Applied Cognition today supports enterprises in evolving, adapting, and becoming more resilient. Under the banner of Future Folklore and with his Fire Springs colleagues, he co-produces storytelling shows and conducts story-based workshops. David has authored and contributed to many varied publications, including *An Ecobardic Manifesto, Sustainable Development and Business Decision Making in the Welsh Assembly Government*, and items in *The Guardian*.

Anthony Nanson (MA) works widely as a storyteller and creative coach in Britain and internationally. His clients have included the Forestry Commission, National Trust, Wildfowl & Wetland Trust, and WWF. With Fire Springs he co-produced the storytelling epics *Arthur's Dream, Robin of the Wildwood, Return to Arcadia*, and *Dark Age Deeds of the Celtic Saints*. His books include *Exotic Excursions, Deep Time*, award-winning *Words of Re-enchantment* and *Gloucestershire Folk Tales* – and a major monograph, *Storytelling and Ecology*, published by Bloomsbury in 2021. Anthony lectured in creative writing for 18 years at Bath Spa University and also runs the ecobardic press Awen Publications and writes on folklore for *Cotswold Life*.

Ashley Ramsden is the founding director of the International School of Storytelling, the longest-established centre of its kind in the UK. In 2008 his collaboration with Nancy Mellon resulted in *Body Eloquence: The Power of Myth and Story to Awaken the Body's Energies*, which won the National Book Award in the field of Alternative Medicine in the USA. In 2012 he published with Sue Hollingsworth *The Storyteller's Way: Sourcebook for Inspired Storytelling*. Ashley has toured as a storyteller on all five continents and appeared at major storytelling festivals in many countries. His concern with environmental issues has informed his work since its beginnings.

Chris Salisbury founded WildWise in 1999 after many years as education officer for Devon Wildlife Trust. He directs the acclaimed 'Call of the Wild' leaders' course and 'Where the Wild Things Are', a rewilding adventure based at Embercombe. His theatre background, therapy training, and work as an environmental educator equip him to work creatively to help people enjoy and value the natural world. Chris is also a professional storyteller and co-founded the Westcountry and Oxford Storytelling Festivals. His book *Wild Nights Out: The Magic of Exploring the Outdoors at Night* (2021) has received rave reviews. He is married with four children and lives in enchantment on the edge of a forest.

Edward Schieffelin (PhD), author of the acclaimed *The Sorrow of the Lonely and the Burning of the Dancers* and *Like People You See in a Dream*, is Emeritus Reader in Anthropology at University College London. He has published extensively on performance, social reciprocity, ethnohistory, and the social construction of emotional life. In the 1990s multinational timber companies began to move into the tropical forest region of Papua New Guinea where he did his fieldwork. Since then, in collaboration with conservation NGOs, Edward has been helping the local tribal people to understand the threat of logging to their livelihoods to enable them to make informed decisions about creating a sustainable future for themselves and their forest.

Martin Shaw(PhD) is currently Reader in Poetics at Dartington Arts School and founded both the 'Oral Tradition' and 'Mythic Life' courses at Stanford University. His collection of Celtic stories and poems with Tony Hoagland – *Cinderbiter: Celtic Poems* – was published in 2020 by Graywolf Press. Martin's other recent books include *Smoke Hole: Looking to the Wild in the Time of the Spyglass* (2021), *Courting the Wild Twin* (2020), *The Night Wages* (2019), and *Wolf Milk* (2019). He lived in a tent for four years on a succession of British hills and often draws from that experience in his writing

Index

Other Books from Hawthorn Press

The Natural Storyteller
Wildlife Tales for Telling
Georgiana Keable
272 pages; 228 x 186mm; paperback;
978-1-907359-80-4

Small Steps to Less Waste
Stories to Inspire Change
Claudi Williams
96 pages; 186 x 256mm; paperback;
978-1-912480-29-6

An Enchanted Place
Jonathan Stedall
112 pages; 234 x 156mm; hardback;
978-1-912480-46-3

The Children's Forest
Dawn Casey, Anna Richardson,
and Helen d'Ascoli
336 pages; 250 x 200mm;
paperback; 978-1-907359-91-0

Ordering Books
If you have difficulties ordering Hawthorn Press books
from a bookshop, you can order direct from our website
www.hawthornpress.com, or from our UK distributor
BookSource: 50 Cambuslang Road, Glasgow, G32 8NB
Tel: (0845) 370 0067, Email: orders@booksource.net.
Details of our overseas distributors can be found
on our website.

Hawthorn Press
www.hawthornpress.com